ROUTLEDGE LIBRARY EDITIONS: FREE WILL AND DETERMINISM

I0131166

Volume 5

FREEDOM

FREEDOM

Negative and Positive Conceptions

YILDIZ SİLİER

Routledge
Taylor & Francis Group

LONDON AND NEW YORK

First published in 2005 by Ashgate

This edition first published in 2017
by Routledge
2 Park Square, Milton Park, Abingdon, Oxon OX14 4RN

and by Routledge
711 Third Avenue, New York, NY 10017

Routledge is an imprint of the Taylor & Francis Group, an informa business

British Library Cataloguing in Publication Data
A catalogue record for this book is available from the British Library

ISBN: 978-1-138-63228-8 (Set)
ISBN: 978-1-315-20086-6 (Set) (ebk)
ISBN: 978-1-138-70348-3 (Volume 5) (hbk)
ISBN: 978-1-138-70364-3 (Volume 5) (pbk)
ISBN: 978-1-315-20307-2 (Volume 5) (ebk)

Publisher's Note
The publisher has gone to great lengths to ensure the quality of this reprint but points out that some imperfections in the original copies may be apparent.

Disclaimer
The publisher has made every effort to trace copyright holders and would welcome correspondence from those they have been unable to trace.

Freedom: Negative and Positive Conceptions

YILDIZ SİLİER

ASHGATE

Published by
Ashgate Publishing Limited
Gower House
Croft Road
Aldershot
Hants GU11 3HR
England

Ashgate Publishing Company
Suite 420
101 Cherry Street
Burlington, VT 05401-4405
USA

Ashgate website: http://www.ashgate.com

British Library Cataloguing in Publication Data
Silier, Yıldız
    Freedom : political, metaphysical, negative, and positive. – (Ashgate new critical thinking in philosophy)
    1.Free will and determinism
    I.Title
    123.5

Library of Congress Cataloging-in-Publication Data
Silier, Yıldız, 1975-
    Freedom : political, metaphysical, negative, and positive / Yıldız Silier.
        p. cm. – (Ashgate new critical thinking in philosophy)
    Includes bibliographical references and index.
    ISBN 0-7546-5267-X (hardcover : alk. paper)
    1. Liberty – Philosophy. I. Title. II. Series.

    B105.L45S55 2005
    123'.5–dc22

                                                                    2005002552

ISBN 0 7546 5267 X

Printed and bound in Great Britain by MPG Books Ltd, Bodmin, Cornwall

Contents

Acknowledgements

This book is largely based on my PhD thesis, completed in 2003. A few years ago when I read Prof Sean Sayers' *Marxism and Human Nature*, I was about to finish my Master's dissertation. I was so much inspired and illuminated by this book that I knew I had to be supervised by its author, when writing my PhD thesis. My dreams came true when I was accepted to the University of Kent at Canterbury, under his supervision. He has been an excellent supervisor, both setting me free to find my own voice and patiently inviting me to flourish, guiding me with valuable comments and suggestions. I am especially grateful for his insistence that I should incorporate Hegel in my thesis, in so far as he provides fundamental insights on the positive conception of freedom, even though I showed resistance for a long time because Hegel's language seemed so impenetrable when compared with the language of analytical philosophy that was my background context.

I am more than grateful to my mother Prof Oya Koymen, who has supported me in every way and has enabled me to continue without diverting my path. I would like to thank my father Orhan Silier for encouraging me to achieve self-mastery by continuously setting up higher expectations and standards.

I owe many thanks to my jury members Prof Ellen Meiksins Wood and Prof Richard Norman for their valuable suggestions and inspiring questions in the viva exam.

Being in Britain, first time away from my family and country has been a great and challenging experience, helping me to discover a lot about myself. I would like to thank the University of Kent at Canterbury for providing a cosy atmosphere and to Britain for showing me a glimpse of what it means to be living in a free country with a welfare state.

This first book is dedicated to my dearest mother Oya Koymen.

Introduction

'What is freedom?' For a long time this has been the question I was most curious about. I thought that in order to be free, I first needed to know what freedom meant. Is it merely satisfaction of desires without being interfered with by others? Being a single child, brought up by a devoted mother who fulfilled all my wishes I should have been free with respect to that 'common sense' definition. But still I did not feel free; I always felt something was missing which was beyond my individual control. Then, another possibility occurred to me: maybe I was free, but mistakenly thought I wasn't. Another question was added to my list: is a person always the best judge of her own freedom, or can she sometimes be mistaken? If she is mistaken, then can somebody else know better whether she is free or not, and help her become more free? What is the relation between the objective and the subjective aspects of freedom? These questions were my starting point when I started writing my PhD thesis in philosophy, which laid the basis of this book.

I should confess this wasn't my first attempt at this broad project. In my Master's dissertation, I had approached freedom from another aspect, by comparing the relationship between needs and freedom. I thought, if freedom is not doing what one desires, then probably it is related to doing what one needs. But what do we really need? Is there a universal set of needs, or do needs change through history and vary across different cultures? Can we be mistaken about our needs? There, I focused on the debate between Rousseau and Marx, the former defending the view that the historical evolution of needs enslave us, whereas the latter claimed the same process to be liberating. When I finished my Master's dissertation, I thought both of them were right in a sense. But now I realize that it was Marx who had won the debate; he has much more to offer us about the meaning and the social conditions of freedom, as we shall see in the last chapter of this book, from a different perspective.

My analysis of the meaning and the conditions of freedom is based mainly on Isaiah Berlin's influential distinction between negative and positive conceptions of freedom. Although his distinction introduces a useful theoretical tool, the way he defines positive freedom is far from rigorous. His clear definition of negative freedom (as the absence of state coercion and interference by others) is in sharp contrast with his vague characterisation of positive freedom, which seems like an aggregate of all that Berlin loathes.[1]

---

[1] Berlin, I. (1969), "Two Concepts of Liberty", *Four Essays on Liberty*, Oxford University Press. Some of the major articles that challenge Berlin's distinction, or his definition of positive freedom are the following. MacCallum, G. (1991), "Negative and Positive Freedom", *Liberty* (ed. Miller, D.), Oxford University Press; Taylor, C. (1991), "What's Wrong with Negative Liberty?", *Liberty* (ed. Miller, D.), Oxford University Press; Macpherson, C. B. (1973), "Berlin's Division of Liberty", *Democratic Theory: Essays in*

Throughout this book, I will replace Berlin's inadequate definition of positive freedom with my own interpretation of positive freedom and then defend it against Berlin's criticisms. We can define positive freedom as having two aspects: rational self-determination (chapter 7) and the power for self-determination (chapter 10). The former aspect contrasts with negative freedom as the arbitrary satisfaction of desires, whereas the latter aspect challenges the distinction between unfreedom and inability that lies at the basis of the negative view (chapter 2).

Are negative and positive conceptions of freedom rival theories, or does the latter include and go beyond the former? On the one hand, they are rival views because they start with different conceptions of the self and derive opposite social and political conditions of freedom. On the other hand, the positive conception of freedom includes and transcends the negative conception. The positive view provides us with a more comprehensive account of the metaphysical grounds and the essential normative aspect of freedom. Furthermore, it succeeds in combining the objective and subjective aspects of freedom.

This book demonstrates how the inadequacies of the negative conception of freedom carry us towards the 'hybrid view' and its defects opens the way towards the positive conception of freedom. The *negative view* focuses entirely on finding out the universal constraints on freedom of action; it reduces constraints to personal interventions and state coercion. The *hybrid view* investigates the goal of freedom underlying the negative view and reveals the internal constraints on freedom, as well as incorporating the notions of free agency and freedom of choice. The *positive view* explicitly discusses the goals of freedom and includes impersonal social and economic constraints. Finally, the *historical account of freedom* (the 'concrete' version of positive freedom) explores the changing conditions of freedom through history, in parallel with the changing forms of domination. My analysis will culminate with an application of the historical view to elaborate the new freedoms and unfreedoms in capitalism.

My method will significantly change in the two parts of this book because of the different methods employed by two sides of the debate. The negative view emphasizes the inter-personal aspect of freedom, and analyses various configurations of the relation between a coercer and a coerced person. This approach takes free action as the unit of analysis and considers the notions of free individual and free society as either derivative or meaningless. It claims to give a purely descriptive theory of freedom and denies that there is a specific notion of human nature, or any particular vision of the good life underlying the negative conception of freedom. In contrast, the advocates of positive freedom focus on the relationship between a free agent and a free society by explicitly defending a specific theory of human nature and good life, arguing that any conception of freedom has a normative dimension.

This is why the first part on negative freedom will basically include the debates between different versions of the negative view, as represented by contemporary 'analytical' philosophers with their distinctive micro-analysis of free action, whereas the part on positive freedom will involve a discussion of the metaphysical foundations of free agency by historical thinkers (such as Kant, Hegel and Marx) as well as some contemporary ones.

Here is a brief summary of the themes and main arguments I will explore in each chapter. I will elaborate the negative conception of freedom in the first five chapters that form Part I. Hayek's account of negative freedom that involves a tension between the subjective criteria of free action and the objective criterion of a free individual will be discussed in the first chapter.

The contemporary debate between different advocates of the negative view (Steiner, Oppenheim and Miller) about the universal constraints on free action is critically evaluated in chapter 2. They agree that freedom of action is restricted only when there is a definite person who is responsible for depriving one of his freedom. The central theme of the debate is whether to take freedom as the absence of prevention (free behaviour) or as the absence of intervention (free action), and whether causal responsibility or moral responsibility is an adequate notion to capture the source of constraints. This discussion will reveal the narrow understanding of constraints underlying the negative view, and will highlight the problems that arise in the attempts to enlarge the set of constraints to include impersonal factors, whilst remaining within the framework of negative freedom.

In chapter 3, I will analyse how the negative view considers the relation between free action, free person and free society. We will see the problems involved in deriving the overall freedom of a person by aggregating his free actions. This chapter will expose some of the pitfalls for any purely descriptive account of freedom. The negative view cannot pass from the level of free action to that of a free individual without assuming a particular hierarchy of freedoms, and thereby embracing the normative dimension of freedom. The neo-liberal followers of Hayek claim freedom of contract based on voluntary consent to be the most important freedom and the basis of a free society. This normative choice leads them to defend capitalism as the model of a free society.

Is capitalism a society where everyone has equal negative freedom? This question is the basis of chapter 4, where I will critically evaluate Cohen's internal critique of capitalism. This will include considering three pillars of capitalism (private property, wage labour and free markets) in relation to negative freedom. The chapter will also include a brief consideration of the meaning and limits of consumer freedom, as well as an argument showing that freedom of contract does not automatically yield individual freedom when it involves a relationship between individuals with unequal power.

In chapter 5, I will evaluate those thinkers who try to extend and revise the negative conception of freedom so that it will include the internal constraints on freedom. I have called this position the 'hybrid view' because it lies in the middle ground between negative and positive conceptions of freedom. I will distinguish between two versions of the hybrid view. The first version (late-Berlin, Benn, Weinstein) shifts the focus from freedom of action to freedom of choice, by defining freedom as the non-restriction of options. It challenges the implicit assumption of the negative view that takes the goal of freedom to be doing what one wants, by showing how it leads to the 'paradox of the contented slave'.

On the other hand, the second version of the hybrid view (Frankfurt, Dworkin, Watson) challenges the idea of the self as a simple unity, which is implicitly assumed by the negative view. When the self is taken as 'internally complex', it becomes possible to speak about internal constraints on freedom. Moreover, freedom can then be defined as doing what one values, rather than as doing what one desires. Although the hybrid view extends the set of constraints on freedom and introduces some central themes such as free choice and moral agency, it is still not an adequate theory of freedom in so far as it fails to conceive poverty and ignorance as restricting the effective exercise of choice. This defect leads us to move forward to the positive conception of freedom, discussed in Part II.

Chapter 6 is on Green's account of positive freedom as a social achievement, linked with self-realization and requiring the necessary abilities and social opportunities to achieve one's goals. Here, I will also answer Berlin's criticism that the positive view has 'totalitarian' tendencies in so far as it allows the possibility that we can be 'forced to be free'.

Kant's notion of rational self-determination, autonomy and their defence against Berlin's criticisms will be the main theme of chapter 7. As opposed to the negative view, Kant shows that we are free not as natural beings, but as rational and moral beings who can transcend the natural causal determination and act on self-imposed laws.

Chapter 8 focuses on Hegel's account of concrete freedom as opposed to the negative view and Kant's theory as two versions of abstract freedom. Hegel teaches us that morality and rationality are socially evolving phenomena and freedom is possible only through fulfilling social relations and identifying with one's various social roles, rather than as an isolated self-legislating agent. This introduces the vision of a socially embedded self in contrast to the atomistic self that underlies the negative view.

Recent communitarian thinkers such as Taylor and Sandel who develop some Hegelian insights will be discussed in chapter 9. I will argue that although communitarians have the merit of defending a socially embedded notion of the self and showing that autonomy is a socio-historical product rather than a universal value as the liberals suppose, their romantic portrayal of the community as based on shared values is problematic. This is partly why they cannot provide a concrete vision of a free society, which will be pursued in the following chapters.

In chapter 10, we will see why having negative freedom and having the material means to exercise negative freedom is necessary but not sufficient to be positively free. After revealing the essential normative aspect of freedom and defending it against the view that freedom should be without any concrete content, I will compare the views of Norman, Gould and Macpherson about the social conditions and the goals of positive freedom. Whereas Norman defines positive freedom in relation to effective choice, the others use self-development as the goal of positive freedom. In the end, all of these thinkers agree that a free society should be both egalitarian and democratic.

In the last chapter, I will defend the Marxist historical account of freedom as a concrete version of the positive view. Instead of trying to find universal constraints or conditions of freedom, it concentrates on the specific relations of domination and exploitation to explain the new forms of freedom and unfreedom introduced by capitalism.

The essence of freedom is self-determination and self-activity. Freedom of choice (the independence of the will from external causal determination or the freedom of the will to refuse any content) is the negative aspect of freedom, and autonomy (the ability of the will to determine itself through the self-imposition of laws) is the positive aspect of freedom. Self-determination requires the development of subjective rational abilities, which can flourish only on the basis of objective social opportunities. Freedom is not the natural starting point for all, but a social achievement. Individual freedom ultimately requires a free society—an egalitarian and social order in which the relations of domination are overcome mainly through the socialization of the means of production.

Freedom is a topic in which there is an ongoing battle between various traditions, which often takes the form of a bundle of monologues rather than a genuine dialogue. In this book, I have tried to put them in a dialogue, by incorporating the metaphysical, political, negative and positive aspects of freedom within a comprehensive account of freedom.

PART I

THE NEGATIVE CONCEPTION OF FREEDOM

Chapter 1

Hayek's Notion of Freedom

The negative conception of freedom gets its name from defining freedom in a merely negative way, as the absence of something. According to this view, freedom has no positive content; there are only various subjective uses of freedom. One is negatively free in so far as he can do what he wants without being constrained or interfered with by others. The negative view takes individual freedom as something we naturally own, and tries to specify the cases in which external agents restrict this natural freedom.

When freedom is taken as the norm then it is unfreedom that has to be explained and analysed. If there is an impairment of individual freedom then some specific agent (another person or the state) should be causally responsible for this deprivation.

The central question for this conception of freedom is where to draw the limits of the freedom of each person so that everyone can have a legally protected domain (private sphere) in which his actions will be unimpeded, and thereby free.[1] Once this protected 'private sphere' is well defined then it would be easy to charge the intruders of this sphere as responsible for depriving a person of his freedom. The private sphere is contrasted with the public sphere, based on the assumption that a distinction can be made between actions that only concern oneself and those that also concern others.[2]

The cornerstone of the negative view is the assumption of an inevitable antagonism between the individual and the society. The individual is not taken as someone who is essentially a social being, but rather as an atomistic, vulnerable being who needs to be protected from an abstract entity called 'the society'.

It is necessary for the state to have 'the monopoly of coercive power' (through the threat of legal sanctions) in order to prevent individuals constraining each other's freedom. But then how can it be assured that the state would not abuse its coercive power and interfere with the private sphere that it is supposed to protect? Drawing limits to the power of the state to protect individual freedoms is the main concern of the liberal defenders of the negative view. We should note that Hobbes is almost unique as a non-liberal proponent of the negative view. Locke, Smith and Bentham are other historical proponents of this view. Hayek is a contemporary

---

[1] Berlin expresses this key question as 'What is the area within which the subject...is or should be left to do or be what he is able to do or be, without interference by other persons?' Berlin (1969), pp. 121-2.

[2] Mill, J. S. (1985), *On Liberty*, Penguin Books, p. 71.

advocate of the negative view and is well known as a founder of neo-liberalism, besides being a stubborn critic of socialism and other projects of social reform.

Hayek defines individual freedom as 'the state in which a man is not subject to coercion by the arbitrary will of another', as the circumstance in which one 'can expect to shape his course of action in accordance with his present intentions', and as marked by the 'rule of law'.[3] Hayek's account involves three different formulations of negative freedom as the absence of deliberate coercion by others, as the possibility of acting according to one's present intentions and as the existence of a private sphere protected by the legal framework.

The first feature emphasizes that the only source of unfreedom is personal coercion. It contrasts with the positive view, which argues that there can also be internal and impersonal social constraints on freedom. The second feature (transforming intentions into action) implies that freedom is available to everybody. In contrast to the positive view, one does not need to make informed choices or achieve 'rational self-determination' in order to become free. The third feature denotes the institutional legal framework, with respect to which coercion is defined as 'arbitrary' and as 'unjustified interference'.[4] When coercion is identified with the violation of laws then it follows that that no one can restrict another's freedom in a society where everyone is law-abiding. In contrast, the positive view claims that even when everyone respects laws there can be other factors such as the lack of material resources that diminish people's freedom.

1. Freedom and Coercion

Hayek starts his exposition of freedom by clarifying what coercion means. Coercion can take two forms: whereas constraints force people to do certain things, restraints prevent people from performing certain actions. The only source of coercion is other agents; natural and social factors cannot create obstacles to personal freedom.

This establishes a distinction between incapability and unfreedom, which is central for the negative view. One's natural incapability to fly like a bird does not render him unfree because it does not deprive him of liberty. So, freedom does not mean having the ability to do whatever one wants.[5] Hayek's other example is about a rock climber who has fallen into an abyss and is unable to get out of it. Although he has a limited course of action, he is not unfree because he is not 'held captive' by another person.[6] A person becomes unfree (or his freedom is coerced) only if a specific person can be held responsible for this deprivation of liberty. Consequently, social factors such as poverty and lack of education can limit people's choices but cannot make them unfree.

---

[3] Hayek, F. A. (1991), 'Freedom and Coercion', *Liberty* (ed. Miller, D.), Oxford University Press, pp. 80, 86.
[4] Hayek, F. A. (1976), *The Constitution of Liberty*, Routledge & Kegan Paul, p. 449.
[5] Hayek (1991), p. 85.
[6] *Ibid*, p. 82.

Hayek argues that one's freedom is coerced only when another agent has deliberately attempted to change his course of action. He gives various examples to demonstrate that one cannot coerce another's freedom unintentionally. Even when a person knows that his behaviour will 'harm another person and will lead him to change his intentions...a person who has borrowed from the library the book I want, or even a person who drives me away by the unpleasant noises he produces cannot properly be said to coerce me. Coercion implies both the threat of inflicting harm and the intention thereby to bring about a certain conduct'.[7]

Violence and coercion are the basic ways in which one can harm others intentionally. Although the threat of violence is the most important form of coercion, coercion and violence should not be confused.[8] Whereas violence makes one's body 'the physical tool' of another, coercion makes his mind the tool of another person. Violence operates by violating one's mastery over his body, by transforming him from a subject into an object, and thereby leaving him with no real choice. For example, a person whose 'finger has been pressed against the trigger of a gun' has not even acted because he is not the subject of this action; it is something that is done to him rather than something that he does.[9] On the other hand, a person who has been blackmailed is subject to a threat of violence. This is an example of coercion without violence since he may still choose to disregard the threat. For Hayek, 'coercion, violence, fraud and deception' are the ways in which freedom can be constrained.[10]

Coercion cannot eliminate choice because the coerced person's action is not totally determined by an external agent; it involves the manipulation of one's alternatives to make him act in a certain way. The coerced person submits to a threat in order to avoid or minimize pain. But in the final analysis, it is the agent who decides whether the intervention constitutes a case of coercion or not. In Hayek's words, 'Although coerced, it is still I who decide which is the least evil under the circumstances'.[11] This raises the issue whether unsuccessful threats can constrain freedom, which will be discussed in the next chapter.

For Hayek, one's decision on how to interpret the coercive threat depends on two factors: his 'strength of will' and his subjective evaluation of what he would lose by submitting to the will of another, which involves a cost-benefit analysis. In Hayek's words, 'the same conditions which to some constitute coercion will be to others merely ordinary difficulties which have to be overcome, depending on the strength of the will of people involved'. An act is coercive only when the agent thinks he is thereby deprived of something that is 'crucial to his existence or the preservation of what he most values'.[12]

---

[7] *Ibid*, p. 89.

[8] *Ibid*, p. 94.

[9] *Ibid*, p. 89.

[10] Hayek (1976), p. 144.

[11] Hayek (1991), p. 89. This is similar to Sartre's claim that freedom is absolute and there are no external obstacles to freedom because it is ultimately the agent who decides which path to choose.

[12] *Ibid*, pp. 85, 91.

When the criterion of coercion is taken as being deprived of something one considers to be important, it follows that if somebody restrains another from doing an action that he never wished to do anyway, then he is not coerced.[13] It is worth noting that this subjective criterion of coercion is not widely accepted among the defenders of negative freedom in so far as they try to distinguish the meaning of freedom from the subjective value of this freedom for a specific person.[14] Elsewhere, Hayek seems to leave aside this subjectivist account by claiming 'since the value of freedom rests on the opportunities it provides for unforeseen and unpredictable actions, we will rarely know what we lose through a particular restriction of freedom'.[15]

The above discussion reveals that Hayek has two subjective criteria of freedom: not intending to constrain another's action, and not feeling a significant loss because of the interference. The latter condition can also be expressed as not being in a 'worse off' position when compared with the initial condition before the interference. The former is linked with the point of view of the coercer, whereas the latter describes freedom from the viewpoint of the coerced person. Hayek also puts forward an objective criterion of freedom (the legitimacy of the intervention with respect to laws) that we will consider in the next section.

If coercion cannot abolish choice, then in which respect does it harm a person? Coercion deprives a person of the possibility of acting according to his present intentions, by forcing him to modify his intentions. Although his course of action is still of his own choice, the coerced person cannot use his capacities and knowledge for his *own* aims. Only a free person can 'effectively use' his capacities and knowledge in the pursuit of his aims. This effective self-direction requires 'that he be able to foresee some of the conditions of his environment and adhere to a plan of action'.[16] In short, coercion harms the individual by impairing his total sovereignty in his private sphere. Coercion on personal freedom also has negative affects on the general welfare. Hayek expresses this as follows:

> Coercion thus is bad because it prevents a person from using his mental powers to the full and consequently from making the greatest contribution that he is capable of to the community. Though the coerced will still do the best he can do for himself at any given moment, the only comprehensive design that his actions fit into is that of another mind.[17]

Kley challenges Hayek's point by noting that less coercion is not always more beneficial to the society. For example, tax on environmental pollution is coercive but it is beneficial as compared to a 'less coercive regime of rules'.[18]

---

[13] This issue is related with the 'paradox of the contented slave', as we shall explore in chapter 5.

[14] Berlin (1969), p. 124.

[15] Hayek, F. A. (1979), *Law, Legislation and Liberty*, vol. 1, Routledge & Kegan Paul, p. 56.

[16] Hayek (1991), p. 89.

[17] *Ibid*, p. 90.

[18] Kley, R. (1994), *Hayek's Social and Political Thought*, Clarendon Press, p. 125.

Hayek wants to argue that all coercion is bad, even when its consequences are ultimately beneficial to the coerced person, or when it improves the social welfare. This is based on his portrayal of any society as a 'spontaneous formation' and on his epistemological scepticism, which we will briefly consider now. For him, rules that we cannot articulate govern social life. 'Constitutive traditions of social life' which are in constant evolution, can neither be grasped nor be criticised; they should be accepted as given.[19] This 'necessary or inevitable ignorance...provides the chief reason for allowing the fullest possible scope to individual freedom; it is because of this ignorance that it is better to allow society to develop by spontaneous adjustment than to control it all by some central agency'.[20]

Hayek believes that societies are made up of spontaneously evolving traditions and institutions that are subject to natural selection; the best ones survive.[21] They are self-organising and self-reproducing. Since 'tacit knowledge' is necessarily fragmented, no single body or authority (such as the state) can design a holistic social plan; 'comprehensive planning is, first and foremost, an epistemological impossibility'.[22]

Any attempt to design social order rationally (or to intervene in the 'spontaneous evolution of society') will have unpredictable consequences that would defeat its purpose. A hierarchical order of values would be imposed on the free choices of people, leading to 'totalitarianism' and a loss of individual liberty. Assuming central planning and free market society as the only alternative social organisations, Hayek claims that individuals can best utilize their fragmented knowledge in a competitive society because individual liberty is dependent upon the unimpeded existence of spontaneous orders.[23] These are the assumptions behind Hayek's defence of a limited government.

2. Social Conditions of Freedom

After considering freedom as a relation between two agents, the coercer and the coerced, let us now analyse freedom within a broader social framework and explore the kind of state and laws necessary to protect individual freedoms.

The core argument of the negative conception of freedom goes as follows. Freedom is the absence of personal constraints. But if everyone had full freedom to do whatever he wants, there would be chaos; it would be a state of war of all against all as described by Hobbes' portray of the 'state of nature'. So, unrestricted individual freedom is self-defeating. We need an external authority to draw limits to everyone's freedom through laws, so that each person would be free to do anything that does not violate a similar freedom of others.

---

[19] Gray, J. (1998), *Hayek on Liberty*, Routledge, p. 26.
[20] Acton, H. B. (1961), 'Objectives', *Agenda for a Free Society: Essays on Hayek's The Constitution of Liberty* (ed. Seldon, A.), Hutchinson of London, p. 73.
[21] Hayek (1976), p. 57.
[22] Gray, J. (1981), 'Hayek on Liberty, Rights and Justice', *Ethics*, vol. 92, p. 83.
[23] Gray (1998), pp. 75, 28.

There are two basic views about how freedom and laws are related. The first view, held by Hobbes and Bentham argues that laws are 'necessary evil'; we are 'free where laws are silent'.[24] Laws restrict some of our liberties to assure greater freedoms or other social goods. On the other hand, the second view held by Locke and Hayek claims that laws do not limit freedom. In Locke's words, 'The end of law is not to abolish or restrain, but to preserve and enlarge freedom...where there is no law there is no freedom. For liberty is to be free from restraint and violence from others, which cannot be where there is no law'.[25]

Mill synthesizes these views through his 'liberty principle' (which allows particular liberties to be limited when necessary to ensure a 'more extensive freedom') and the 'harm principle' that he explains as follows.

> The sole end for which mankind are warranted, individually or collectively, in interfering with the liberty of action of any of their number is self-protection. That the only purpose for which power can be rightfully exercised over any member of a civilised community, against his will, is to prevent harm to others.[26]

The domain where one's actions concern only himself is labelled the private sphere, which is claimed to be the realm of freedom. Hayek considers the demarcation and protection of the private sphere as the main precondition of freedom. Private sphere is the 'sphere of unimpeded action', where the individual is guaranteed that others cannot interfere.[27] This is the objective criterion of freedom; the 'rule of law' defines the scope of the private sphere, and thereby also of freedom.

Cornerstone of the private sphere is the institution of private property, which Hayek claims to be the basis of every civilization. In modern society, one's private sphere consists of his private property, the network of rights and obligations created by *voluntary contracts* between people, rights to share using public services and other rights such as privacy and secrecy. Hayek acknowledges that the scope of the private sphere changes with respect to time and society. For example, laws that prohibit slavery restrict the scope of private sphere in so far as they forbid one to own other people. Another example is the case of a socialist society in which private ownership of the means of production is restricted.

Although Hayek links freedom with the private sphere, he denies that the degree of one's freedom is directly related to the extent of his private property. He says, 'It is one of the accomplishments of modern society that freedom may be enjoyed by a person with practically no property of his own'.[28] The crucial element

---

[24] Hobbes, T. (1996), *Leviathan, Modern Political Thought: Readings from Machiavelli to Nietzsche* (ed. Wootton, D.), Hackett Publishing Company, p. 204.

[25] Locke (1996), 'The Second Treatise of Government', *Modern Political Thought: Readings form Machiavelli to Nietzsche*, (ed. Wootton, D.), Hackett Publishing Company, p. 328 (Book 2, chapter 6).

[26] Mill (1985), p. 68.

[27] Hayek (1991), p. 95.

[28] *Ibid*, p. 97.

of freedom for him is equality before the law, which he claims to be sufficient to guarantee that everyone has equal negative freedom. Laws recognize each person as self-owners, having the right to sell whatever he owns and buy whatever he wants.

The negative view starts with the assumption of a necessary conflict between individual freedoms, and argues that the only freedom-preserving social relations are those that are based on the voluntary consent of each person involved. The exchange relations based on 'freedom of contract' are the paradigm examples of free social relations.[29]

According to Hayek, competitive market economy provides a model for a free society because all economic associations between people are voluntary and non-coercive, based on free contracts. Relationships between the worker and the capitalist, the consumer and the producer are 'mutually advantageous collaboration between people based on voluntary consent rather than coercion. Each of them can determine to whom he wants to render services and on what terms'.[30]

Hayek admits that monopolies can coerce people's freedom. For example, the 'owner of a spring in oasis', being the sole controller of an 'essential commodity' has coercive power on others. Another example is about the periods of acute unemployment in which an employer may force an employee to do certain tasks other than those specified in the contract.[31] Nevertheless, Hayek discards monopolies as exceptions to the general rule in competitive capitalism. He thereby fails to acknowledge that monopolies and oligopolies are dominant in advanced market societies and their coercive affects cannot be put aside so easily.

Reducing individual freedom to freedom of action in the private sphere has direct implications on the role of the state. The function of the state is then restricted to the protection of the private sphere through well-enforced laws. As a result, the state's coercive power to punish the intruders is claimed to be necessary and sufficient to guarantee individual freedoms. If the state further takes on positive duties, such as providing welfare services and adopting redistributive policies, then it would transform from a friend to a foe of individual freedom, according to the negative view.

Hayek argues that the state does not coerce individual freedom as long as it only deals with its 'proper' function. 'The interference of the coercive power of the government with our lives is most disturbing when it is neither avoidable nor predictable'.[32]

In order to specify the proper function of the state, he makes a strange distinction between permissible and non-permissible forms of coercion, which reflects his conservative position. For example, redistribution of wealth by the state is a non-permissible coercion whereas taxation and compulsory military service are permissible forms of coercion because they are predictable just like the 'laws of nature'. It is surprising to see that Hayek considers coercion within 'voluntary

---

[29] *Ibid*, p. 97.
[30] *Ibid*, p. 91.
[31] *Ibid*, pp. 91-2.
[32] *Ibid*, p. 99.

associations' like the family to be a permissible form of coercion. He argues that the state should not do anything to regulate them because this would produce greater coercion by restricting free choice within the private sphere.[33] Hayek's argument is not valid since every legal requirement can be justified as predictable, hence as permissible including the re-distributive measures.

Hayek applies a similar method (using predictability as a sign of freedom) to justify any legal framework. Since laws are not aimed at restraining specific people, but apply 'equally to all people in similar circumstances, they are not different from natural obstacles that affect one's plans'.[34] Hayek argues that laws threaten people with coercion but they are not coercive because they can be avoided. Due to the predictability of the consequences of violating laws, people can refrain from actual coercion by obeying the laws.[35] This odd argument seems to imply that even laws that restrict freedom of speech (by punishing those who criticise the government) do not restrict freedom, since people can avoid legal sanctions by not expressing such ideas.

For Hayek, the universality of laws is sufficient to guarantee state's neutrality or impartiality with respect to people's values and aims. As the result of such considerations, equality before the laws is claimed to be sufficient for people to have equal negative freedom.

3. Critique of Hayek

Let us now make a critical assessment of Hayek's account of freedom firstly, by focusing on its internal inconsistencies about the criteria of freedom, secondly, by considering its implications about freedom of choice, and thirdly, by revealing Hayek's unrealistic understanding of a free market society.

Hayek's three criteria of freedom are not compatible; they yield opposite results when applied to concrete cases. The first subjective criterion evaluates an intervention with respect to the intentions of the coercer, whereas the second subjective criterion is related with the coerced person's evaluation of the harmful effects of the intervention, defined with respect to his assessment of its costs within the framework of his life plans. The third objective criterion (the 'rule of law') declares an action to be free unless it involves a violation of one's legal rights.

The case of an oppressed wife is an example in which a person is free with respect to the second criterion, but unfree with respect to the first one. On the other hand, when an employer fires a worker, this action is free with regards the first criterion (since the employer does not intend to harm the worker) but unfree with respect to the second criterion (since losing his job deprives the worker of something he values). For Hayek, 'the mere power of withholding a benefit will

---

[33] *Ibid*, p. 94.
[34] *Ibid*, p. 99.
[35] *Ibid*, p. 98.

not produce coercion' because the employer does not act with the intention of changing the worker's life plans.[36]

In the above examples, everything (the institution of marriage and firing of the worker) is in accordance with the laws. So, there is no unfreedom involved if we assume only the objective criterion; but whichever subjective criteria we choose these examples involve a case of unfreedom.

Let us try to resolve this inconsistency by finding out which criterion is the most crucial one for the negative view in general, and Hayek in particular. If we assume only the first criterion (intentions of the coercer) then this opens up the possibility of an 'illusion of freedom'. In the first example stated above, the wife mistakenly thinks she is free, whereas in the second example, the worker has the false belief that he is unfree. In general, somebody who is not aware of or misinterprets the intentions of the coercer would be mistaken about whether he is free or not. This seems to be in tension with the liberal view that everyone is the best judge of his freedom, in so far as freedom is doing what one wants. On the other hand, if Hayek were using only the second subjective criterion, then he would have had to accept that one may constrain another's freedom without intending it, which goes against his definition of coercion as deliberate interference.

It is even more problematic to ground a theory of freedom merely on the second subjective criterion that identifies freedom with feeling free. This leads to the 'paradox of the contented slave', which will be explored in chapter 5. As we shall see in the next chapter, all subjective criteria of coercion are rejected by Steiner and Oppenheim who want to give a purely objective and descriptive theory of freedom. Using only the objective criterion implies identification of the domain of freedom with one's legal rights. But then, the conditions of freedom would change from society to society, in parallel with different legal systems. This bothers those thinkers who want to reach universal conditions of freedom.

This problem is also related to the gap between Hayek's three formulations of freedom as the absence of deliberate coercion, as acting in accordance with one's present intentions and as the non-violation of legal rights. The first aspect of freedom is neither necessary nor sufficient for the second aspect. One might be coerced to do something he wants and one might fail to act in accordance with his present intentions due to the lack of the material means to pursue his goals, even when there is no deliberate coercion. On the other hand, legal rights cannot capture all restrictions on freedom. For example, even when a person has equal rights with others, he may suffer from racial discrimination or gender oppression that restrict his or her freedom. Hence, Hayek's notion of coercion is too narrow; it cannot account for other important cases of unfreedom. As we shall see in the next chapter, other advocates of the negative view try to extend the scope of constraints.

If one way of criticising a theory is to show its internal inconsistencies, another way is by demonstrating that it has a false implication, as I will attempt to do now. Hayek's aim is to argue that his account of freedom is the only true account of

---

[36] *Ibid*, p. 93.

freedom; the other 'so-called freedoms' do not deserve the name. He takes the most dangerous opponent to be the positive view that relates freedom to having power and the scope of alternatives one has. In order to demonstrate that freedom is related neither with the scope of choices nor with power, and material means instead of giving an argument, Hayek just reasserts his definition of freedom; since freedom only refers to a relation of men with others, the only obstacle to it is coercion by others.[37] Hayek's account of freedom seems to imply that the scope of choices is irrelevant to freedom.

However, Hayek's thoughts on this issue are inconsistent. On the one hand, he argues that the scope of choices is irrelevant to freedom. On the other hand, in his defence of freedom of contract and in his criticism of socialism due to 'the state's being the only employer' Hayek argues that the more options one has (to choose his employer) the less dependent he will be on the services of particular people and thereby the more free he would be.[38] From this perspective, the scope of choices (or at least the existence of other alternatives) is relevant to freedom.

Hayek gives two examples to demonstrate that one can be free even though one does not have much choice. A courtier who lives in luxury but submits to the prince is less free than a peasant or artisan who is his own master. A general in charge of an army has more power but he is less able to change his life than the poorest shepherd.[39] Hayek's argument is not valid because both the courtier and the general have freely chosen their life styles, they can choose to give up their wealth and power to live simpler but more independent lives. However, the poorest peasant or shepherd cannot choose to live in luxury even when he is willing to give up independence.

The above argument points out that being independent from a particular master is necessary but not sufficient for having freedom. One should also have some material means to exercise this freedom. Freedom cannot be separated from the conditions necessary to use freedom that is intimately related both with the scope of alternatives and one's consciousness of these options.[40]

As the positive view argues, the increase in one's knowledge advances his freedom in two ways. First of all, knowledge is necessary for the effective use of one's capacities in the pursuit of one's aims. Secondly, knowledge transforms one's present intentions into informed intentions and thereby enables him to generate new and more sophisticated aims that suit him better. As Norman claims, 'The acquisition of power, of wealth and of education is experienced as liberation'.[41] Such an extended theory about the conditions of freedom requires a different conception of the self, society and the function of the state. Let us take the first step by revealing and rejecting Hayek's assumptions on this issue.

---

[37] *Ibid*, p. 81.

[38] *Ibid*, p. 93.

[39] *Ibid*, p. 87.

[40] This will be our theme in chapter 10, when discussing positive freedom as the power for self-determination.

[41] Norman, R. (1982), 'Does Equality Destroy Liberty?', *Contemporary Political Philosophy* (ed. Graham, K.), Cambridge University Press, p. 96.

Hayek takes the existing socio-economic conditions as evolved to the best possible structure and thereby legitimises the *status quo*. He overlooks the effects of the 'given' distribution of income, wealth and power on individual freedom. Since he considers social institutions as 'spontaneous orders' that cannot be designed, it leaves no room for social criticism and reform.

Once this socio-economic framework is naturalised, there exists a gap between the public sphere consisting of necessities that cannot be designed and the private sphere in which one engages in voluntary relationships with others. Hayek disregards the essential link between freedom in the private and public spheres. For example, democratic and rational control of the public sphere can enhance individual freedom by increasing the domain of self-activity and by providing people with the means to exercise their freedoms.

Hayek's assumption of spontaneous social evolution does not correspond to reality. Liberals exert continuous efforts to ideologically misrepresent the market society as if it were natural and spontaneous. As Polanyi argues, free markets are established through state power and regulation, rather than being spontaneous developments.[42]

Like other defenders of the negative view, Hayek imposes an abstract and universal purpose on the state, namely making purpose-independent laws that serve everybody's interest equally. Although he emphasizes the socio-historically changing nature of institutions, he does not regard the state as a particular social institution whose goals and policies change in parallel with the changing power structures.

Hayek's expectations from laws are also not justified. Although laws are universal and impartial in the sense that they equally apply to all people, they are neither neutral, nor non-coercive. By presenting all laws as non-coercive, he makes it impossible to make a critical, comparative evaluation of different legal systems in terms of their affects on individual freedom.

Hayek's argument for the non-coerciveness of laws is based on his inadequate account of freedom, as independence from a particular will. In his words, 'the conception of freedom under the law...rests on the contention that when we obey laws, in the sense of general abstract rules laid down irrespective of their application to us, we are not subject to another man's will and are therefore free.'[43]

Although Hayek counts the strength of personality among factors that determine the degree of coercion, he fails to mention the importance of wealth for this issue. In societies where inequalities of wealth and power prevail, the universality of laws and an unregulated freedom of contract cannot guarantee an equal distribution of freedom.

Freedom is not the natural starting point of all, something that only needs protection from the threats of others. It is rather something that should be socially achieved by reforming social institutions in accordance with the changing needs of people. This requires abandoning Hayek's epistemological scepticism about the possibility of any social design and his uncritical affirmation of capitalism as the

---

[42] Polanyi, K. (1957), *The Great Transformation*, Beacon Press, p. 58.
[43] Hayek (1976), p. 37.

only model for a free society. Instead of implementing a policy of non-interference to *protect* freedom, the state should adopt a positive role to *promote* freedom. These are the sketches of how advocates of the positive view would challenge the negative view.

Chapter 2

Constraints on Freedom

The main issue of debate among defenders of negative freedom is the scope of constraints on freedom.[1] Can interventions render one unfree, or is unfreedom merely the result of prevention? What kind of threats constrains freedom? Can omissions as well as acts limit one's freedom? What about social and economic factors? Do all cost-imposing acts reduce freedom? In this chapter, I will critically evaluate how Steiner, Oppenheim and Miller answer these questions.

This discussion will reveal the inadequacy of a purely descriptive account of free action. I will argue that Miller's account is superior to others in so far as he introduces the normative dimension of freedom by presenting moral obligations as the criterion of freedom. Nevertheless, Miller's account is problematic because it confuses criteria that apply at different levels. Analysing the difficulties in Miller's attempt to extend the scope of constraints while remaining within the framework of the negative view will reveal the limits of the negative view.

1. Unfreedom versus Inability

Since negative freedom is defined as the absence of external impediments, a clear definition of negative freedom requires specifying the boundaries of unfreedom, or the scope of constraints on freedom. In the previous chapter, we have seen that Hayek's account of freedom starts with the distinction between various obstacles to action. According to him and for Berlin, whilst natural and social obstacles are not relevant to freedom, deliberate interference by others is the only kind of constraint on freedom.[2] Other advocates of the negative view preserve this distinction in another form, by distinguishing between obstacles created directly by human arrangements from those that depend on people's lack of certain talents and material resources, which are products of the unintended consequences of the

---

[1] The reason why I prefer the terminology of constraints rather than coercion is because the latter is too restrictive; it refers only to one type of constraints that are deliberately imposed on another. Other constraints on freedom include those that arise unintentionally, because of omissions, economic constraints and internal constraints on freedom.

[2] Hayek (1991), pp. 82-5.

actions of many individuals. Only the former are claimed to be relevant for freedom.

Another way to express this distinction is by referring to the difference between 'can' and 'may'; the former denotes ability and the latter signifies liberty.[3] For example, a person who has enough money *can* buy illegal drugs but he *may not* lawfully do so. On the other hand, anyone *may* buy an expensive car but most people *cannot* actually buy it with their limited income. If we apply both of these notions in the same example, lacking the economic means to buy alcohol and being deprived of the liberty to buy alcohol because of prohibition laws have different implications on freedom.[4]

On the one hand, I want to refrain from identifying freedom with effective power since this would imply that the disabled, poor and ignorant are unfree, regardless of whether they have civil rights or not. On the other hand, I disagree that equality before the laws and having civil rights ensure equal freedom for all. The distinction between 'formal freedom' and 'effective freedom'–having the means to exercise formal freedom– can be helpful in solving this dilemma.

Machlup argues that having knowledge, power and opportunity transform formal freedom into effective freedom. Formal freedom is important even without the effective power to exercise it because it gives people new aspirations and ambitions to achieve the means that are necessary to exercise the unused freedoms.[5] He gives the following example. If the maximum speed my car can reach is much slower than the speed limit then I may be motivated to buy a faster car to exercise my freedom to go faster. In his words, 'having money neither gives nor implies freedom; it merely enables you to exercise more of the existing freedoms'.[6] We can give another, more historical example. Workers used the legal freedom of association to form pressure groups and achieved the right to vote, increasing their political power and effective freedom with the addition of democracy to liberal society in late 19th century.[7] This social change not only enabled greater exercising of the existing freedoms but also introduced new freedoms by extending the scope of civil rights. So, formal/legal freedoms are valuable also as instruments to increase effective freedoms.

---

[3] Feinberg has another interpretation. He claims that the distinction between 'can' and 'may' corresponds to the difference between freedom (as the ability to act in a certain way) and liberty (as the authoritative permission to do so). Feinberg, J. (1998), 'Freedom and Liberty', *Routledge Encyclopedia of Philosophy* (ed. Craig, E.), vol. 3, p. 753.

[4] Machlup, F. (1969), 'Liberalism and the Choice of Freedoms', *Roads to Freedom: Essays in Honour of F. A. von Hayek* (ed. Streissler, E.), Routledge & Kegan Paul, pp.125-6.

[5] *Ibid*, p. 130.

[6] *Ibid*, p. 126.

[7] Macpherson, C. B. (1972), *The Real World of Democracy*, Oxford University Press, pp. 9-10.

2. Source of Constraints

There are three main theories about which obstacles form constraints on freedom. All of them start from the conviction that if one's freedom is constrained then there is somebody responsible for that. The first view that is held by Hayek and early Berlin, links the responsibility of the coercer with his deliberate imposition of an obstacle. Neither the unintended consequences of one's actions that create an obstacle, nor the failure to remove an obstacle can constrain freedom. This is based on the assumption that the responsibility of coercion arises only when one has bad intentions. Such a notion of responsibility is too narrow because it excludes the unintended yet predictable consequences of one's actions that would impose an obstacle on another as irrelevant to freedom.

According to the second view, the criterion of constraints is *causal responsibility*. For Oppenheim, 'any obstacle for which human agents are in some way or other causally responsible should be regarded as a constraint on freedom'.[8] According to his view, only acts –whether deliberate or not– can be constraining, not omissions such as failing to remove an obstacle. But as Miller points out, there isn't a clear distinction between acts and omissions. Miller gives the following example. 'If I allow trees to grow on my land which prevent you from driving your car into your garage, have I blocked your drive or merely failed to keep it clear? Either description of my behaviour –as an act or as an omission– seems about as plausible as the other.'[9]

Oppenheim's conception of unfreedom is too narrow since deliberate omissions do not count as constraints, and it is also too wide because accidental acts can be coercive thanks to the causal link. For example, if X cries for help on a mountain and this triggers an avalanche which confines Y under the snow then X is causally responsible for confining Y. This constrains Y's freedom to move, and it is different from the case of a natural disaster that makes him unable to move but not unfree to move.

Miller rightly claims that the causal responsibility view fails to make constraints attributable to human agency since people can coerce others without willing, intending or being able to foresee the result.[10] Although Oppenheim argues that the advantage of his account is in giving a descriptive, morally neutral conception of freedom, this is at the price of impairing the link between coercion and the coercer's awareness of it, thereby divorcing coercion from moral responsibility.

The third view is the *moral responsibility view* that was first introduced by Benn and Weinstein and later developed by Miller. It considers an obstacle as a constraint on freedom if and only if somebody else 'can be held morally

---

[8] Oppenheim, F. (1984), ' "Constraints on Freedom" as a Descriptive Concept', *Ethics*, vol. 95, p. 306.
[9] Miller, D. (1983), 'Constraints on Freedom', *Ethics*, vol. 94, p. 73.
[10] Miller, D. (1984), 'Reply to Oppenheim', *Ethics*, vol. 95, pp. 310-313.

responsible for the existence of the obstacle'.[11] One is rendered unfree if somebody imposes an obstacle deliberately, negligently, or fails to remove it although he has such an obligation. This view holds one responsible for all the foreseeable consequences of his actions that constrain another's freedom, whether they be acts or omissions, imposed deliberately or unintentionally.[12] Miller defends a wide notion of moral responsibility according to which what we owe each other is not merely non-interference; we also have positive obligations such as removing barriers in front of others by making sure that their basic needs are satisfied and not exploiting others.[13]

An implication of Miller's view is that it makes freedom a contestable moral notion. Judgements about freedom would vary with respect to one's notion of moral responsibility and maybe there is no way to resolve such debates. For example, a person with a wide notion of moral responsibility can claim that everybody is responsible for the non-removal of obstacles to effective freedom such as poverty and ignorance. Oppenheim criticises Miller's view by arguing that a moral responsibility view of freedom has the danger of reducing all inabilities to unfreedoms. He claims that the distinction between acts and omissions is helpful in limiting the notion of responsibility so as to preserve the inability versus unfreedom distinction.[14] Miller answers that he both keeps the above-mentioned distinction, as well as enlarging the scope of constraints on freedom.[15]

A possible way to solve the acts-omissions dichotomy is to accept that acts that impose obstacles always constrain freedom, whereas omissions that fail to remove obstacles constrain freedom unless it would be 'too costly' to remove the obstacle.[16] However, it is unclear when an omission is too costly; it depends on the goals, values of the person or the state. Furthermore, it is not clear who is responsible for the omission, whether it is specific people, state, or other institutions. Let us give an example. A passer-by X sees Y beating Z in the middle of an empty street. Y is morally (and legally) responsible for constraining Z's freedom, but what about X? Isn't he morally responsible because of his failure to remove the constraint on Z's freedom (imposed by Y)? X could have interrupted their fight but this could have been 'too costly' since he could have been beaten. He could have called the police but then he thinks this would also be 'too costly' since he then might have to give a testimony and will probably miss his appointment. So, he continues to walk as if he had seen nothing, thinking that he has no moral obligation in this case. We can reconstruct another example in which X sees the seriously wounded Z alone in the street.

It is strange that an individual is often claimed to be morally and legally responsible (and blameable) for killing a person, but not for letting him die.

---

[11] Kristjansson, K. (1992), 'Social Freedom and the Test of Moral Responsibility', *Ethics*, vol. 103, p. 104.
[12] Miller (1983), p. 72.
[13] *Ibid*, p. 83.
[14] Oppenheim (1984), p. 306.
[15] Miller (1983), p. 68.
[16] Machlup (1969), p. 132.

Similarly, one could (and maybe should) be held responsible not only for constraining somebody's freedom but also for letting him be deprived of his freedom. Hence, we need a wider, positive notion of moral responsibility that goes beyond the legal responsibility of non-interference, and which transcends the acts-omissions dichotomy.

This is one of the reasons why I think Miller's view is better than its rivals. On the basis of a positive notion of moral obligation, it has the flexibility of encompassing omissions as well as acts, effective freedom besides formal freedom, without giving up the distinction between inability and unfreedom.[17] Secondly, whereas other rival positions take natural and social conditions as constants, as the given background that does not affect freedom[18] Miller's view considers social institutions as variables that can effect freedom. It also provides a suitable framework in which the historical evolution of freedoms can be analysed. The increase in our control over the natural and social environment produces an enlargement of the foreseeable consequences of actions. This leads to an increase in the domain of moral responsibilities and a corresponding decrease in the scope of mere inabilities. The increase in our expectations from the state and others makes us feel unfree and motivates us towards action that aims at liberation. The more we demand the removal of these obstacles and to the extent that these demands are satisfied, the scope of formal and effective freedoms increases through history. So, the moral responsibility view can help us to reconstruct the unfreedom-inability distinction on a historical basis.

In the light of the above discussion let us reconsider if disabled, ignorant or poor people are free or not. It is not their inabilities that render them unfree but rather certain social and economic policies are (morally) responsible for not remedying these deprivations. If an ill person cannot be healed merely because he does not have enough money, or a person cannot continue his education because of the same reason, then from the assumption that it is the moral obligation of the state to provide health and education as public services it follows that ignorant, ill, or disabled people are being deprived of their freedom to develop themselves, because of the state's failure to perform its duties. Overcoming such obstacles would not be 'too costly' with the advanced means and the immense wealth that could have been directed to solve an enormous waste of human capacities.

3. Degree of Constraints

In the previous section I have argued that an obstacle becomes a constraint on freedom when it is attributable to humans by a special type of causal link, that is through moral responsibility. But how large must an obstacle be to count as a constraint on freedom? This criterion should be as narrow as to exclude obstacles that make an action merely less desirable for the agent, and also it should be as

---

[17] Miller (1983), p. 75.
[18] For example, Oppenheim rejects that 'impersonal constraints (or capitalism)' can constrain freedom. Oppenheim (1984), p. 306.

wide as to allow some interventions to be constraining freedom, by not limiting constraints to total prevention.

There are mainly three rival answers to this question. Hobbes and his successor Steiner argue that only obstacles imposed by others that make an action physically impossible render one unfree because freedom is merely the absence of 'external impediments of motion'.[19] Typical examples of unfreedom are imprisonment with walls or chains. Hobbes and Steiner claim that threats and other interventions do not constrain freedom because they can only make an action less desirable; threats cannot make an action necessary, inevitable or predictable.[20]

Steiner argues that one always has the freedom of disregarding a threat. If a person were unfree when he is threatened not to do x, but he does x, then he would have done something that he was not free to do; this contradiction proves that threats do not render one unfree.[21] This argument is not valid because it can at most show that the coerced person's action is never totally determined by another, a conclusion we already know from Hayek as discussed in chapter 1. It is one thing to say that one can always choose to disregard a threat (by accepting its costs), another thing to say that threats do not constrain freedom. For example, Oppenheim accepts the former but rejects the latter proposition.[22] Steiner's view does not have many supporters because it is too narrow; most defenders of the negative conception of freedom agree that threats can constrain freedom.

Nevertheless, Steiner has put forward an interesting question that no advocate of the negative view can ignore. How can we distinguish threats from offers? Steiner gives the example that being put in a prison cell in winter can be an offer to a homeless person. If freedom means acting with respect to present intentions, then both offers and threats would be constraining freedom by changing a person's intentions.[23] Voluntary consent is not an adequate sign that shows offers to be non-coercive. There may be coercive offers that abuse one's vulnerable position. For example, offering a dangerous job with a low wage is a coercive offer, an offer that is hard for a poor person to refuse.[24]

The second view defended by Oppenheim considers some threats as limitations on freedom and also tries to preserve the objectivity of the first view, by not evaluating constraints with respect to their subjective effects. For Oppenheim, the criterion of coercion is strict or 'practical impossibility [that is] making it so difficult or unpleasant or costly or risky for any actor in normal circumstances (thus not for a specific person) to do x that he has practically no choice but to abstain'. He takes 'punishability' as an 'additional condition on unfreedom'.[25]

---

[19] Hobbes (1996), p. 204.

[20] Steiner, H. (1991), 'Individual Liberty', *Liberty* (ed. Miller, D.), Oxford University Press, pp. 133-4.

[21] Steiner, H. (1994), *An Essay on Rights*, Blackwell, p. 8.

[22] He says the 'threat of punishment may deter someone from acting in a certain way, but does not make him unfree to disregard the threat'. Oppenheim (1984), p. 308.

[23] Steiner (1991), pp. 127, 131.

[24] For more discussion of this issue, see chapter 4, section 3.

[25] Oppenheim (1984), p. 307.

Oppenheim defines penalties with respect to a 'normal agent' which he claims to be an empirical assertion about what 'average people' refrain from rather than as a subjective feeling of deprivation that may vary from person to person.[26]

The notions of 'normal' agent and 'average' people are very problematic because they reduce humans to passive natural beings, which merely respond to external stimuli in predictable ways, rather than as moral agents with free will. As we shall see in chapters 6 and 7, the positive view is strongly against such a naturalistic account of humans. Both Steiner's and Oppenheim's accounts of freedom are inadequate because they deny the normative and subjective aspects of freedom.

Miller defends the third view by claiming that punishments are sufficient but not necessary to constrain freedom. One may constrain another unintentionally or as the result of an omission, which does not involve a punishment.

In order to find out in what sense threats reduce freedom we should focus more on punishments. Punishment is a special way of imposing costs on an action that constrain freedom; but not all costs are relevant to freedom. For example, a parking charge of £10 does not constrain one's freedom to park there but a parking fine of the same amount does. So, we cannot deduce if something is a constraint merely by comparing the size of the obstacles because a £5 fine constrains freedom but a £15 charge does not constrain freedom in the same way.

For those who conceive freedom as the absence of obligations, parking fines constrain liberty by imposing an obligation not to park, whereas a parking charge does not impose such an obligation, which is why it does not reduce freedom.[27] In my opinion, one may argue that a parking charge also imposes a conditional legal obligation to the potential customer, in the form of 'if you want to park here you ought to pay'. We should allow excessive prices to be at least as coercive as (if not more than) small legal fines.

On the other hand, Miller argues against the above explanation that relates constraints on freedom with the existence of obligations. He claims, 'mild threats reduce freedom in just the same way as small legal penalties, despite the fact that there is no obligation to comply with threats. Someone who threatens me to take ten pounds from me if I park my car at a certain place reduces my freedom precisely the same extent as a legal authority which imposes the ten pound fine'.[28] This is an example of a case where freedom is reduced although there is no intention to penalize.

I think that there is an importance difference between the threat and the legal fine in the above example; whereas the former is an unjustified coercion, the latter is a justified coercion and this makes a difference in our evaluation of the constraint. We are more outraged by unjustified coercion, and it seems to restrict our freedom more than the predictable and morally justified coercion, which might

[26] Oppenheim, F. (1995), 'Social Freedom and its Parameters', *Journal of Theoretical Politics*, vol. 7, p. 412.
[27] Miller (1983), pp. 76-9. See also Oppenheim (1995), p. 409.
[28] Miller (1983), p. 79. Hayek would object to this conclusion and argue that an unpredictable threat coerces freedom whereas the predictable legal prohibition does not.

be necessary to prevent greater harm either to others, or to the environment. In contrast to Miller, I believe that the threat constrains our freedom more than the legal fine. However we can construct another example in which the legal fine is not justified, and a threat may have a justified reason behind it.

Furthermore, effects of threats or penalties may differ from one person to another depending on their assets and goals. For example, 'a poor taxi driver considers a small parking fee prohibitive but that a millionaire considers it insignificant'.[29] To take another example, if the state prohibits travelling abroad, this would be coercive to a person who wants to go abroad but not for a person who does not have such a wish or an opportunity. This is why Miller claims that the 'extent of a person's freedom should depend not only on the number of options open to him but on the importance to him of each of these options'.[30]

In the final analysis, if we accept Miller's argument then the debate between negative and positive conceptions of freedom boils down to the conflict between different theories of moral obligation. Judgements about freedom are never morally neutral[31] even though most advocates of the negative view claim to have a purely descriptive conception of freedom. The negative view emphasises legal obligations and argues that the less these obligations are, the wider would be the scope for negative freedom. The main legal obligation is non-interference with the rights of others. According to their critics, the increase in moral obligations of the state and of people can enhance freedoms by encouraging people to support each other as well as not violate the rights of others.

Let us summarize the conclusions of this chapter. We have found out that not all obstacles constrain freedom. Obstacles to action become constraints on freedom if they satisfy the following criteria. If we focus on the *source of the obstacle*, X constrains the freedom of Y to do an action if:

1. X has intentionally imposed the obstacle (Hayek) or,
2. X is causally responsible for the obstacle (Oppenheim) or,
3. X is morally responsible for the obstacle (Miller).

On the other hand, with respect to the *size or the effects of the obstacle*, Y is unfree to do an action if:

1. Y is prevented from doing the action, in the sense that it is a case of physical impossibility (Steiner) or,
2. It is a case of interference in the form of 'practical impossibility' in which the action becomes ineligible for a 'normal agent' or involves a punishment (Oppenheim) or,

---

[29] Oppenheim (1984), p. 307.

[30] Miller (1983), p. 67. In another article, he elaborates those conditions: 'The degree of one's freedom depends on such factors as the severity of the sanction, the probability of its application, the difficulty of surmounting the obstacle and the number of alternatives closed'. Miller (1984), p. 308.

[31] Miller (1983), p. 68.

3. It is a case of interference in the form of penalization, threat or omission to remove an obstacle, provided that the effects of the obstacle are evaluated with respect to Y's assets and goals (Miller).

I have argued that Miller's account of freedom is the most promising one mainly because it is wide enough to explain how social conditions affect freedom, and also it involves the subjective aspect of freedom. In the next section, I will apply the above-mentioned criteria to the issue of economic obstacles to freedom. We will see that the negative view either denies that there can be economic obstacles to freedom on the basis of a narrow conception of coercion, or it accepts that some economic obstacles can constrain freedom, but fails to give an adequate account of this issue.

4. Economic Constraints on Freedom

The Effects of Price Rise on Freedom

So far we have examined four different views on the criteria of unfreedom. Firstly, those who argue that only deliberate acts of others can be coercive consider the notion of economic obstacles to freedom with great suspicion. According to them, the lack of economic resources to buy something implies a case of inability, for which no one is responsible; it is not a case of unfreedom. So, even excessive prices that make one unable to satisfy his basic needs are not relevant to his freedom.[32]

On the other hand, Steiner who represents the second view holds that *all* price rises make *everyone unfree* to buy the item at the old price, yet *anyone is free* to buy it unless the new price exceeds his total budget. This seems like a tautology but when we examine it closer, it is self-defeating. First of all, the requirement that the new price should not exceed his budget is superfluous since he is free to go against the law and steal this money so that he can buy the item at the new price. Hence, in Steiner's sense of freedom as physical possibility (or as absence of complete determination of an action by another) anybody is free to buy nearly anything by resorting to crime. By a similar argument, it is physically possible that one buys it at the old price, by threatening the shopkeeper for example. This refutes Steiner's claim that everyone is unfree to buy it at the old price.

The most important counterintuitive implication of Steiner's proposal is that a poor person is as free as the rich to buy an expensive thing because an obstacle either makes everyone equally unfree or does not affect their freedom at all. For Steiner, freedom does not have degrees and it is independent of any subjective elements (such as the person's goals and assets).

---

[32] Although these thinkers acknowledge that monopolies can constrain freedom, they consider these to be exceptional cases; freedom is not constrained in all other economic transactions.

The third option is Oppenheim's theory of causal responsibility according to which a price rise implies unfreedom if it makes one in 'normal conditions' (in this case it is an 'average consumer' with an average income) practically unable to buy the item. Oppenheim links freedom or unfreedom of everybody to the situation of the average consumer. If he is free then so is any other person including those who cannot afford to buy it. Conversely, if the average consumer is unfree to buy it then even the richest person is unfree. I think such an implication is enough to reveal the implausibility of Oppenheim's view, besides the fact that the 'average consumer' is a problematic term. Although Oppenheim does not deal with economic obstacles explicitly, he gives the following example. If the same weight is put on the back of an athlete and a disabled person they are equally unfree because unfreedom is determined with respect to the capabilities of normal agents; the disabled person suffers more because of this deprivation. [33]

Whereas for Steiner all price rises constrain everybody's freedom and Oppenheim argues that some price rises constrain everybody's freedom, for Miller some price rises constrain some people's freedom. Miller's account is better than its rivals because he takes into account both the subjective and objective aspects of freedom. On the one hand, he admits that the same obstacles can have different effects on different people; this is the subjective aspect of freedom. On the other hand, achieving a consensus on the content of moral responsibility could explain the objective aspect of freedom.

Nevertheless, Miller fails to reconcile these two aspects of freedom because he uses several criteria of unfreedom that are in tension. On the one hand, he wants to argue that economic transactions do not usually constrain freedom because they impose costs that are not freedom-relevant. On the other hand, he claims that a monopolist and a shopkeeper who has increased the price of a commodity that is a 'basic need' constrain the freedom of those who cannot afford to buy it.

According to Miller, most economic costs are not freedom-relevant because in economic transactions no one tries to penalise the other (i.e. there is no 'intention to deter') and everyone acts within the limits of his legal rights. Due to these reasons, the shopkeeper who increases prices after an increase in wholesale prices is not morally responsible for the price rise and therefore customers are not unfree to buy even when they are unable to buy. [34] So, in the case of *acts* that impose obstacles or costs on other people's action, Miller uses two criteria to distinguish whether these costs make them unfree or not: the intention to deter and doing something which one does not have a right to do (violation of legal obligations). [35]

For those *omissions* that have failed to remove an obstacle Miller uses two other criteria to distinguish between freedom and unfreedom. These are the moral obligations of making sure that people's basic needs are met –if one can foresee that a consequence of his omission would be the suffering of another in this way – and the moral obligation of 'fairness' or the obligation not to exploit others. This is

---

[33] Oppenheim (1995), p. 412.
[34] Miller (1984), pp. 77-9.
[35] We should recall that these correspond to Hayek's first and third criteria of freedom, which are discussed in the first section of chapter 1.

why Miller argues that a shopkeeper who has increased the price of a basic need (without his supplier having increased the price) is morally responsible for rendering the poor who cannot afford it unfree to buy because the shopkeeper can foresee the destructive effects of the new price on the poor. When it comes to the monopolist, he is morally responsible for violating the 'obligation of fairness' and thereby rendering everyone who is dependent on his goods unfree.[36]

Although Miller claims that he uses only the criterion of moral responsibility to distinguish between freedom and unfreedom, the following four implicit criteria help us to understand his notion of moral responsibility. For Miller, the presence of any of these four conditions is sufficient to conclude that it is a case of unfreedom. X is rendered unfree by Y if Y has acted with the intention to deter X, or if Y has done something which he was not legally entitled to do, or if Y imposed an obstacle that prevented X from satisfying one of his basic needs, or if Y has violated his moral obligation of fairness.

Let us apply these criteria to the case of parking fines and parking charges. A parking fine restricts freedom because it involves an intention to deter him from parking at a specific place. On the other hand, a parking charge does not directly intend to deter a person from parking there although one may claim that it deters him from parking there unless he pays the money. Moreover, the owner of the car park has the legal entitlement to demand payment from those who want to park, because of his property rights. And since parking at that specific place is nobody's basic need, that criterion does not suffice to claim that a parking charge makes one unfree to park.

What about the last criterion, namely the moral obligation of fairness? Miller claims that price rises render one unfree when they are above the 'fair price, that is the price in normal circumstances' which he defines as 'what the customer would pay if he were not in need or what the supplier could charge if forced to compete with other suppliers'.[37] In my opinion, 'fair price' is an ambiguous notion, and an anachronistic term that applies to pre-capitalism but is not adequate in explaining how prices are determined in a complex market economy.

Justification of Constraints and Levels of Unfreedom

My argument is that Miller's four implicit criteria do not apply in the same level of unfreedom. The first two criteria (the intention to deter and the violation of legal entitlements) refer to unfreedom of a person because of the actions of others, within a given socio-economical system. However, the latter two criteria (the failure to act in accordance with the moral obligations of satisfying basic needs and the obligation of fairness) signify that one is unfree in capitalism relative to an

---

[36] Miller does not clarify whether the monopolist makes rich and poor unfree to the same extent. If so, then his position on this issue is not much different from that of Steiner and Oppenheim. It should be remarked that since monopolies and oligopolies provide not only consumer goods but also basic inputs to all industries, their high prices also affect the basic goods sector, which the poor consume.

[37] Miller (1984), p. 83.

alternative system in which these moral obligations are backed up by certain socio-economic institutions. For example, excessive prices and monopolies would not render one unfree with respect to the institutions and laws in capitalism since they are legitimate; they would make a person unfree from the point of view of a non-capitalist society. Indeed, Miller uses the last two criteria to compare the freedom of people in different societies. He argues that workers in welfare capitalism are more free than those in laissez-faire capitalism because their basic needs are satisfied; they are the most free in socialism since they are not exploited, so 'the moral obligation of fairness' has been actualised.[38]

In short, the first two criteria show that one is unfree because of another agent, but the latter two signify that one is unfree because of the socio-economic system. Miller's attempt to unite these two different levels with the notion of moral responsibility makes individuals responsible for those features that they are powerless to change. This is why his notions of 'fair price' and the 'obligation of fairness' hang in the air. It gives the impression that if each individual fulfilled those moral obligations then there would be no economic constraints on freedom in capitalism.

For example, the monopolist is not violating a universal moral obligation of fairness; he is only doing what the economic rules allow him to do. His action is fair in so far as it conforms to the rules of a competitive market society. Moral obligations are not universal but relative to one's responsibilities in a given system. In order to challenge how the logic of the economic system affects individual freedoms, we need something more than the individualistic and abstract notion of moral responsibility.

Miller's confusion between two levels of freedom is also related with his failure to distinguish between those criteria that separate freedom from unfreedom and the criteria to distinguish between justified and unjustified unfreedom. Miller's argument implies that moral responsibility serves both of these purposes.

For him the shopkeeper who has increased prices in accordance with the increase in wholesale prices has not rendered anyone unfree because he is not morally responsible with regards to those four criteria. By a similar reasoning, it can be claimed that a judge who has imprisoned a person as the result of a fair trial has not rendered him unfree, because the judge was not morally responsible. However, it is more plausible to argue that the judge has in fact rendered him unfree, and is morally responsible for that; it is simply a case of justified unfreedom. Somebody else may claim that these laws on the basis of which he was executed were themselves unfair. For example, if these laws were prohibiting freedom of speech of certain radical ideas, then the imprisonment can be claimed to be a case of unjustified unfreedom. Although there are different levels of justification that may conflict with each other, the fact that the prisoner is unfree remains the same with respect to all of these.

The above-mentioned four criteria not only demarcate two levels of freedom but also correspond to different levels of justification with respect to individual

---

[38] *Ibid*, pp. 84-5.

intentions, legal and moral obligations. An unfreedom, which is justified with respect to one level, can be unjustified with respect to another level of justification, as we have seen in the previous example of the prisoner. Whether one considers a case of unfreedom as justified or unjustified depends on which level of justification he takes as fundamental.

In the final analysis, we have seen that Steiner's and Oppenheim's descriptive accounts of freedom are unsatisfactory because they fail to explain the normative and subjective aspects of freedom. Miller's account is better in incorporating these dimensions of freedom. Still, one needs to go beyond the negative view and embrace a positive conception of freedom in order to explain how a socio-economic system restricts individual freedom. So far, we have focused merely on the conditions of free action and now it is time to explore what it means for a person, and a society to be free.

Chapter 3

Free Action, Free Person and Free Society

In this chapter, I will first argue that the negative view has difficulties in deriving adequate conceptions of a free person by taking an aggregate of free actions. As Taylor claims, any notion of a free person assumes that some freedoms are more significant than others, which implies the normative dimension of freedom. Negative freedom cannot be a value-free, neutral conception of freedom, as it claims to be.

Secondly, I will briefly consider various attempts to reconcile the conflicting liberties of people, from natural right theories, to utilitarian and social contract views and will argue that the 'measurement' of the freedom of a person is very difficult, if not impossible, because of the incommensurable criteria of freedom.

After showing the inadequacy of Steiner's and Oppenheim's evaluations of the notion of a free society, I will focus on another attempt, as hinted by Hayek, that grounds free society on voluntary exchange relations and freedom of contract. This will provide the main arguments for capitalism as a free society, which I will criticise in the next chapter.

1. Conflicting Liberties and Incommensurable Criteria of Freedom

Comparisons between freedoms of different people and societies require that there are some criteria to pass from freedom of actions to freedom of persons. This is one of the most problematic aspects of the negative view. Steiner puts forward a simple criterion, and claims that one is free to the extent that his particular actions are free. In other words, the greater the number of one's free actions, the freer he is. There are two important flaws in this argument. Firstly, the number of one's free actions is indefinite because one cannot individuate actions in a uniform way[1], and they are also potentially infinite. One can conclude that since they are both indefinite and infinite, talking about the 'number of (free) acts' is meaningless.

---

[1] In Gray's words, 'individuation of actions is in significant part conventional, so that a piece of behavior may be appropriately characterized by many different act descriptions'. Gray, J. (1989), 'Liberalism and the Choice of Liberties', *Liberalisms: Essays in Political Philosophy*, Routledge, p. 145.

Secondly, not all of these actions have the same significance; it would be unfair to count them as contributing the same to the overall freedom of an agent. According to Taylor, we should refer to the significance of actions in order to have any notion of a free person and to find out the ways in which one can become freer. In his words, 'we make discriminations between obstacles as representing more or less serious infringements of freedom. And we do this, because we deploy the concept against a background understanding that certain goals and activities are more significant than others.'[2] But such an approach carries us outside the framework of negative freedom, towards hybrid and positive theories of freedom.

The issue of 'measurement' of freedom is closely related to the conflict and choice among liberties, which is an unavoidable problem for liberalism.[3] Almost all proponents of the negative view agree that there necessarily exist tensions between liberties of different people; these can only be reconciled through law. Laws secure 'the right of each to the maximum freedom compatible with equal freedom for all others'.[4] Laws are not neutral; they assume that some liberties (or rights) are more significant than others.

Within the framework of liberalism, there are two possible explanations of the sense in which laws can *legitimately* constrain some liberties. These are the 'liberty principle' and the 'harm principle'. Libertarians refer to the liberty principle and claim that some liberties can legitimately be restricted only to advance 'a more extensive liberty', but not for furthering any other value. Utilitarians claim that liberties can legitimately be restricted by the 'harm principle' as well as the 'liberty principle'. Neither the liberty principle nor the harm principle can solve which liberties are more significant than others; 'more extensive liberty' is a vague notion, and the content of 'harm' depends on one's moral theory.

The liberal understanding of freedom is often expressed by using Mill's words. 'The only freedom which deserves the freedom is that of pursuing our own good in our own way, so long as we do not attempt to deprive others or impede their efforts to obtain it.'[5] This formulation is merely formal; it cannot prescribe a concrete method of how to solve the conflicting liberties of people. It requires assuming a particular hierarchy of freedoms, according to which some freedoms are means and others are taken as ends that have intrinsic value.[6] How to choose between a conflicting set of liberties depends on one's notion of well-being. For example, when libertarian property rights and welfare rights conflict, a negative theory of freedom gives priority to property rights, whereas a positive theory of freedom proposes welfare rights as ends and other rights as means.[7]

According to Gray, there are three approaches to resolve conflicts between liberties. For the natural right theorists, we can enlist a set of basic liberties which

---

[2] Taylor (1991), p. 149.
[3] Gray (1989), p. 158.
[4] Machlup (1969), p. 136.
[5] Mill (1985), p. 72.
[6] Machlup (1969), p. 129.
[7] Bellamy, R. (1992), *Liberalism and Modern Society: A Historical Argument*, The Pennsylvania University Press, pp. 2, 255.

do not conflict with each other and which can be secured without any economic costs. Freedom of speech and property rights are claimed to be among such basic liberties or rights. Gray is correct in claiming that there is no guarantee that these do not conflict with each other. Furthermore, these rights cannot be secured without any economic costs because this requires at least police forces, courts and prisons, which absorb a substantive portion of any national budget.

Secondly, for utilitarians, conflicts between liberties of different people such as the freedom of the rapist and that of his victim should be resolved in a way that maximizes the 'total amount of happiness'. This position is in contrast with a moralized notion of freedom according to which, no liberty is lost when laws close the 'option of rape'. However, there is something odd about the utilitarian claim because it does not seem fair to balance the pleasure the rapist derives as against the pain he inflicts on others.

Thirdly, for those who defend a social contract view such as Rawls, there exists a rational decision procedure by which all free and equal people in the 'original position' would agree on the same set of basic liberties, based on the assumption that they share a common human nature. Gray claims that this is the most feasible option if one can flesh out the theory of human nature on which it is based, by making it more socio-historical.[8] But then one can argue that the set of basic liberties would be relative to society and to compare freedom of different societies would be almost impossible since they will have different (and probably incommensurable) criteria to evaluate the freedom of people.

On the other hand, Machlup tries to give a list of basic freedoms that are universal, what he calls a 'catalogue of freedoms' as economic liberties (freedom of work, enterprise, trade, travel, migration, contract, markets, competition, choice of consumption, occupation), political liberties (of coalition and association, assembly, vote, free speech and privacy), intellectual or moral liberties (of non-conformity, teaching, learning, religion and conscience).[9] However, these liberties are far from being universal and although they can count as significant freedoms, not all of them can be guaranteed by laws, or correspond to legal rights even in liberal societies.

Machlup notes that freedoms in his list can conflict and there are two tendencies among different groups of liberals to sacrifice one set of liberties to promote another set. According to him, the main tension between liberalism is between 'intellectual liberals' who claim that free enterprise and markets can be restricted for promoting social justice and the 'economic liberals' who can constrain freedom of speech, being afraid that people may be attracted to alternative ideologies. However, his proposal is not satisfactory at all when he claims that the above mentioned groups are only half or 'fuzzy' liberals, a true liberal would value liberty above all other social goals.[10] He thereby fails to address the question of which liberty should be prior, when they do conflict with

---

[8] Gray (1989), pp.147-58.
[9] Machlup (1969), p. 138.
[10] *Ibid*, p. 144.

each other. It seems that, in the final analysis, we have not found a feasible liberal solution to the problem of conflicting liberties.

Indeed, this is what Oppenheim and Berlin agree upon. They claim that those liberties are incommensurable and cannot be aggregated into a total freedom of an individual or of a group.[11] We can grasp why not only the liberties, but also the criteria to assess them are incommensurable by having a glance at Berlin's list that includes very diverse considerations. In Berlin's words,

> The extent of my freedom seems to depend on: how many possibilities are open to me; how easy or difficult each of these possibilities is to actualise; how important in my plan of life...these possibilities are when compared with each other; how far they are closed and opened by deliberate human acts; what value not merely the agent, but the general sentiment of society in which he lives, puts on the various possibilities.[12]

As we have seen in the previous chapter, various advocates of the negative view disagree on which of the above-mentioned criteria are appropriate; some of these criteria refer to freedom, whereas others denote the conditions for 'feeling free', or the value of freedom for a specific person. Oppenheim argues that the value of any option for the individual is not relevant to how free he is. For example, if US citizens are allowed to travel anywhere but Cuba and North Korea then all of them are relatively free (if we compare it with the number of countries which they are allowed to go) and an agent who attaches great value to travelling to Cuba is no less free than others.[13] We should draw attention to an internal inconsistency of Oppenheim; he contradicts the above claim by saying elsewhere that 'the degree of the actor's deprivation is another dimension of his unfreedom...the degree of X's deprivation and unfreedom increases with his desire to do x.'[14]

If we return back to the main issue of the non-aggregatability of particular liberties into a total freedom, here is Oppenheim's reason for it. He argues that the extent of one's freedom depends on the magnitude and the probability of impediments and punishments. So, one may be more free with respect to one criterion and less free with respect to another. In that case we can neither hierarchically rank those criteria, nor aggregate their opposing effects on the freedom of an agent. Oppenheim gives the following example. 'If fines for speeding are higher in Italy, but better enforced in France, we cannot affirm that the drivers in either country are more unfree to speed than in the other, unless we specify: as measured by the amount of fine or the probability of its application.'[15] In the final analysis, the various ways in which the negative view attempts to derive the freedom of a person from the freedom of his actions, or compare freedoms of people seem to have various problems.

---

[11] Oppenheim (1995), p. 417.
[12] Berlin (1969), p. 130.
[13] Oppenheim (1995), p. 415.
[14] Oppenheim, F. (1961), *Dimensions of Freedom: An Analysis*, St. Martin's Press, p. 192.
[15] Oppenheim (1995), pp. 411, 417.

2. Free Society: Descriptive, Normative or Meaningless?

What about the notion of a free society? Is there a way in which the negative conception of freedom can have a coherent notion of a free society? There are three main roads available for the negative view. First of all, it can claim that a free society is a *descriptive term* denoting a society made up of free people. Hence, claiming that a society is freer than another means that it has more members who are free. This is in parallel with their understanding of a free man as someone most of whose actions are free, and it faces similar difficulties, which I will not repeat here. In short, these are problems about how to add up incommensurable liberties of different people into a sum that denotes the total net amount of freedom in a society.

On the other hand, Oppenheim exemplifies the second approach. He argues that unlike the notion of negative freedom that can only be predicated of actions, 'free society' is a *normative term* signifying a society 'whose members are free to do what they ought to be left free to do and unfree with respect to those activities which should be made impossible and punishable.'[16] In other words, a free society is a system-in which unjustified unfreedom is minimised. However, since the criteria of justification vary and can even be incommensurable, free society is a contestable notion. Oppenheim accepts that freedoms of different societies are not comparable because each system creates some liberties and restricts some others pertaining to different types of action. In the end it becomes impossible to claim that one system provides more total freedom than the other.[17]

Steiner holds the third view, which argues the notion of a free society is not meaningful. Freedom of a society cannot be increased (or maximized) because it always remains constant; it can only be redistributed. This conclusion follows from Steiner's conception of freedom as the 'physical possession of the components of one's action'. He claims that if somebody loses some of this possession then necessarily another person gains it. As the 'law of conservation of liberty' states, within the universe of agents there is no absolute loss or gain of individual liberty. According to Steiner, this shows the vanity of the projects for 'widespread emancipation and increasing personal liberty'.[18]

In order to reject Steiner's argument and its conservative conclusion, it suffices to reject his initial characterization of freedom as the physical *possession* of the components of one's action. Freedom is rather related to widening of the domains of meaningful choice; an increase in one's freedom in this sense does not imply a decrease in another's freedom. In contrast, more freedoms can flourish in a society where people do not compete with each other to possess the 'constant amount of freedom' as much as possible, but create new domains of freedom together by political and other forms of participation.

Most importantly, Steiner's argument has the absurd consequence that liberty is not greater in a society where slavery is absent than the one in which it exists,

---

[16] Oppenheim (1961), p. 207.
[17] Oppenheim (1995), p. 418.
[18] Steiner (1994), p. 52.

assuming that the two societies are alike in all other respects. For him, we can appraise the former society not because it has greater freedom, but only because it has a more equal distribution of freedom. In my view, abolishing slavery adds new freedoms in addition to providing an egalitarian distribution of freedom.

MacCallum claims that these three views are the only feasible options to define a free society. For him, what one means by a free society should either be a society in which 'there is no activity in which men in that society are not free to engage, and no possible restriction or barrier from which they are not free.'[19] Since it is obvious that this is not a feasible situation, either those who talk about a free person and a free society are confused about what freedom means, or what they mean by a free person is someone who is free in doing a variety of significant, valuable actions which is a contestable value judgement.[20]

In the final analysis, none of the versions of negative freedom we have considered can derive an adequate account of a free society. It is now time to consider an alternative basis for this notion, which already has hints in Hayek's account of freedom.

3. Freedom of Contract and Freedom of Exchange as the Basis of a Free Society

An individual is free if he is not constrained in his relations with others and if his freedom of action (within legal limits) is not constrained by the state. Negative freedom starts with the assumption that the individual is *naturally free*. All individuals are self-responsible with the power and knowledge to improve their lives.

This natural freedom is sometimes expressed as 'self-ownership'. One is the sole owner of his labour power and property, and is free to engage in voluntary exchange relations with others, to further his self-interest. Such economic freedom is taken as an essential component of negative freedom. Voluntary, non-coercive relations between people are modelled after the image of market relations.

Market relations of exchange are non-coercive because they conform to Hayek's three criteria of freedom, as discussed in the first section of chapter 1. Firstly, the intentions of both the seller and the buyer are to advance their self-interest, rather than to restrict the freedom of each other, or to do harm. Secondly, both parties benefit from the exchange since it is based on voluntary consent. They are free to exchange with others if they do not like the other party's offer. So, the effects of this relationship deprive neither of them of 'what he considers to be valuable', which was Hayek's second criterion of freedom. Thirdly, the exchange relation is a legally legitimate action and nobody violates the legal rights of the

---

[19] MacCallum (1991), p. 116.

[20] *Ibid*, p. 117. As we shall see in the second section of chapter 10, acknowledging the essential normative aspect of freedom enables the positive view to give a better account of the relationship between the notions of freedom of action, freedom of a person and free society.

other. Hence, competitive market society consists of voluntary co-operative relations between people with equal rights. In Friedman's words,

> The possibility of co-ordination through voluntary co-operation rests on the elementary proposition that both parties to an economic transaction benefit from it, provided that the transaction is bi-laterally voluntary and informed. Exchange can therefore bring about coordination without coercion.[21]

Such a defence of freedom of contract implies that only the two concerned parties should decide the terms of the contract, and the state should not interfere with this voluntary, free relation. From the assumption of the legitimacy of absolute property rights and a self-regulating free market, it follows that only a minimal state with negative duties is necessary to protect individual rights to 'life, liberty and property' through police, army and courts. If a government has more powers and imposes progressive income tax, provides public housing, makes minimum wage laws and establishes a pension system then it restricts individual liberty.[22] For example, minimum wage legislation constrains both the freedom of the worker to sell his labour power at any price, and the freedom of the employer to hire labour with a lower wage. Progressive income tax restricts the freedom of the rich to spend their money, as they like. The rich can be encouraged to help the poor only on a voluntary charity basis, but not through enforcement by the state, in the form of obligation to pay taxes.

Other defenders of the negative view accept that the state should have some positive duties to promote the welfare of its citizens, although they believe this to be at the price of restricting freedoms of some people. In contrast to the positive view, the negative conception of freedom takes freedom and economic equality to be incompatible.

Capitalism is usually characterised by three defining features: free markets (formation of prices through supply and demand, without government intervention), wage labour (labour power as a commodity) and private property (private ownership of the means of production).[23] Let us see how these three components are compatible with, and necessary for negative freedom.

Free markets provide the model for a free society because personal coercion is eliminated in 'freedom of contract' between citizens with equal rights. Impersonal market forces may foster some inequalities of income and wealth and thereby can constrain the scope of freedom of choice for the poor. Nevertheless, this is not a constraint on negative freedom because nobody is responsible for it. The economic order is the 'unintended consequence of the actions of many people each seeking his own interest'.[24] Friedman firmly believes that only legitimate inequalities arise out of market relations.[25]

---

[21] Friedman, M. (1974), *Capitalism and Freedom*, The University of Chicago Press, p. 13.

[22] *Ibid*, p. 162.

[23] Schweickart. D. (1993), *Against Capitalism*, Cambridge University Press, p. 4.

[24] Friedman, M. (1980), *Free to Choose: A Personal Statement*, Secker & Warburg, p. 14.

[25] Friedman (1974), p. 162.

Wage labour is the basis of a free person, who is able to choose how to lead his life. In pre-capitalist societies, individuals were submerged in their society, and had fixed social roles within hierarchical societies. Slaves were the property of their owners and serfs were bound to the land and their lord. Self-ownership was applicable only to privileged classes and groups. One of the greatest achievements of capitalism is to give everybody the equal freedom of self-ownership, which liberates them from relations of personal dependence that prevailed in pre-capitalist societies. Everyone is the sole owner of his labour-power and can decide with whom to exchange it, what job to choose and what items to consume.

The right to private property is the third and maybe the most important component of capitalism. The first justification of the 'intrinsic' right to property goes back to the 17th century, when capitalism was developing in England. Locke argued that the right to private property is not a conventional right, but an inalienable right; this justification was based on his labour theory of value. According to this principle, one has a right to all the products of his labour.[26] Nozick makes a contemporary defence of absolute rights to private property, by arguing that if the initial appropriation of property is legitimate, then the entitlement principle allows one to legitimately own what he has acquired through exchange relations. Other justifications of private property emphasize the incentive it gives to people, which is necessary for a competitive market economy. Based on the justification of absolute property rights, it follows that the private ownership of the means of production is legitimate. On the basis of such arguments, the negative view proposes capitalism as the model for a free society. I will challenge this claim in the next chapter, by exploring the ways in which capitalism restricts people's negative freedoms.

---

[26] Locke (1996), p. 320.

Chapter 4

Limits of Negative Freedom
in Capitalism

After considering the defence of capitalism as a free society, let us now evaluate various critiques of these arguments that link freedom with private property, wage labour and free markets. Cohen claims to give an internal critique; his aim is to show that capitalism does not provide negative freedom to all people, by comparing private property with communal property, and by establishing the 'collective unfreedom' of the wage labour. He argues that capitalism does not maximize liberty (negative freedom) for all; some are free at the expense of others. Problems with Cohen's arguments will reveal the inadequacies of an internal critique.

Secondly, I will evaluate whether free markets enhance individual freedom, from the point of view of an external critique. We will see that although freedom of contract is based on voluntary consent, this does not imply free choice for those who have bargaining disadvantages.

Lastly, in order to explain some of the unfreedoms produced by certain capitalist institutions, I will concentrate on the limits of freedom within the realms of production and consumption by evaluating the freedom of contract between the worker and the capitalist, and investigating the limits of the cherished consumer freedom.

Cohen starts his argument by situating his project of making an internal critique of capitalism in comparison with rival approaches. According to him, egalitarian liberals criticize capitalism by granting that it maximizes freedom but arguing that if the price of unrestricted freedom is poverty and insecurity for many people, it is not worth it. So, for them, freedom should be legitimately restricted to enhance social justice and equality. On the other hand, 'revolutionary socialists' argue that capitalism can only provide 'bourgeois freedom', not 'real freedom'. Cohen finds both of these views to be unsatisfactory. The former is wrong in supposing that capitalism maximizes negative freedom for all, and the latter view is ineffective by condemning capitalism on the basis of another kind of freedom, which is not persuasive because a defender of capitalism can argue that 'he prefers freedom of the known variety to an unexemplified and unexplained rival'.[1] However, if one

---

[1] Cohen, G. A. (1981), 'Freedom, Justice and Capitalism', *New Left Review*, no. 126, pp. 7-8.

argues that capitalism is not the best system with respect to negative freedom then this is a challenge that defenders of capitalism cannot ignore. This is the way, which Cohen promises to explore.

1. Private Property

Cohen argues that to defend capitalism as a realm of freedom is to see only one side of the picture; it is a realm of freedom for some and a realm of unfreedom for others. Private property is 'a particular way of distributing freedom and unfreedom'[2]; it gives freedom to the owners but restricts the non-owners' freedom to use these goods. Some are free at the expense of the unfreedom of others. Here, Cohen takes Nozick as a target because Nozick claims that as long as private property is just (in the sense that the original appropriation and the procedure for transferring property are fair) no one restricts the freedom of another within exchange relations. According to Cohen's interpretation of Nozick, 'as long as people do only what they are entitled to do, no one can be unfree as a result.'[3]

According to liberals, such as Nozick, one has absolute property rights over anything that he owns through a series of voluntary exchanges. The root of this argument that attempts to justify the institution of private property goes back to Locke. He gives one of the first justifications of the transfer of land from communal to private ownership. God has given the earth to mankind in common but as long as land is under communal property, it remains 'wasted and uncultivated'; mankind cannot benefit from it. Therefore, the earth was given 'to the use of the industrious and rational' who can achieve the greatest productivity. This requires the land to be appropriated as private property, provided that there is enough and as good left to others. Locke soon drops this limiting condition for the historical periods after the invention of money, because he thinks that consenting to money implies mankind's consent to the inequalities it brings.[4]

There are two problems with the above argument as Marxists point out. On the one hand, the original appropriation of land and other resources is illegitimate, since it is based on coercion, rather than on voluntary consent. Colonial history is full of ample evidence that the original appropriation of land and precious metals was done by force, without the consent of the inhabitants living in the newly discovered lands.[5] The colonialist acquisition of land as well as the forcible expropriation of peasants from their lands through enclosures were the coercive

---

[2] Cohen, G. A. (1991), 'Capitalism, Freedom and the Proletariat', *Liberty* (ed. Miller, D.), Oxford University Press, p. 170.

[3] Cohen, G. A. (1988), 'Are Disadvantaged Workers Who Take Hazardous Jobs Forced to Take Hazardous Jobs?', *History, Labour and Freedom: Themes from Marx*, Clarendon Press, p. 252.

[4] Locke (1996), pp. 319-26.

[5] For a vivid portray of the roots of the initial accumulation of capital, through colonization and exploitation of Latin America, see Galeano, E. (1997), *Open Veins of Latin America: Five Centuries of the Pillage of a Continent*, Monthly Review Press.

means of transforming communal ownership into private property; this was the basis of primitive capital accumulation, as Marx explains in *Capital*.[6]

On the other hand, freedom of contract based on voluntary consent is not merely a fair procedure for the transfer of property; it is at the same time a relationship of exploitation, in which the worker gets only a small portion of the value he produces whereas the owners of the means of production appropriate the surplus value.[7]

Cohen's internal critique refers to neither of these points, and maybe this is the reason why it cannot accomplish what it promises to do. On the basis of a single example he argues that communal ownership can provide more negative freedom for all people, when compared with private ownership. His comparison of private and communal ownership of household tools leads him to conclude that it is more 'rational' to contract into communal property because it provides more 'tool-using liberty' when compared with the case in which each person has private ownership of some of the tools. He argues that people fail to see the advantages of communal property because the capitalist ideology leads them to have strong attachments to private property.[8]

As Gray argues, Cohen cannot show that communal property provides more freedom than private property because it opens up a different set of freedoms and restricts some others. For example, under common ownership of household tools people are unfree to sell these things or give them as gifts and they cannot engage in 'long-term planning of their tool use'.[9] In order to decide which system of property increases freedom, we first have to decide which set of options and freedoms are more valuable. Cohen cannot do this because he assumes a value-free negative conception of freedom.

On the other hand, Gray is wrong in claiming that communal property yields just another way of distributing freedom and unfreedom. He misses the fact that communal property provides a more equal distribution of freedoms and unfreedoms in comparison with private property. If an equal distribution of freedom has intrinsic value, then we have reason to incorporate communal property as a viable option, as well as private property. This is the most we can get from Cohen's internal critique.

But does Cohen really make an internal critique in his defence of communal ownership? Gray is right in arguing that Cohen does not make an internal critique when he claims that communal property increases tool-using freedom of each, because he then shifts from freedom as non-interference to freedom as the non-restriction of options.[10] The latter is not a negative conception of freedom, but

---

[6] Marx, K. (1947), *Capital*, vol. 1, International Publishers, pp. 761, 775.

[7] The individual freedom in the 'realm of exchange' is based on relations of concealed oppression in the 'realm of production', as we shall explore in chapter 11.

[8] Cohen, (1981a), 'Illusions About Private Property and Freedom', *Issues in Marxist Philosophy* (ed. Mepham, J. and Ruben, D.), vol. 4, Harvester Press, pp. 236-8.

[9] Gray, J. (1988), 'Against Cohen on Proletarian Unfreedom', *Social Philosophy and Policy*, vol. 6, p. 81.

[10] *Ibid*, p. 83.

rather corresponds to the hybrid view, which we will explore in the next chapter. Whenever Cohen wants to argue that an alternative set of institutions would serve better in providing negative freedom, he has to transgress the boundaries of an internal critique. Another example is when Cohen switches from the liberal definition of economic freedom (freedom to sell what one owns and buy what one can afford) to another one (freedom to use goods and services). He argues that in capitalism, everyone is free in the first sense of economic freedom but not in the second sense of the term, because the poor have less economic freedom than the rich. With this move he diverges from an internal critique by changing the definition of economic freedom given by the advocates of negative freedom.[11]

We have seen that Cohen cannot achieve much with his 'internal critique' and he tends to shift from an internal to an external critique to arrive at more substantial conclusions.

2. Wage Labour

According to Cohen, the worker is free as a wage labourer and unfree because of the 'collective unfreedom' he has due to his membership of the proletariat. He is free to make a contract with the capitalist and sell his labour power. The worker is not only free to sell his labour power with respect to the serf and the slave, but also he is free in comparison with somebody without a work permit.[12] Cohen asks: 'If the worker is not free to sell his labour power, of what freedom is a foreigner whose work permit is removed deprived?'[13]

Cohen thinks that the worker is both free and forced to sell his labour power. He gives a linguistic argument claiming that being free and forced are not only compatible, but also being forced to do something entails being free to do it.[14] In my opinion, we can make sense of the claim that the worker is both free and forced to do something not by a conceptual analysis, as Cohen does, but by interpreting these terms in different levels. As we shall explore in chapter 11, the worker is free with respect to the serf or is legally free but his freedom is constrained because of a limited freedom of choice in determining the terms of the contract because of his limited bargaining power with respect to the capitalist.[15] Cohen argues that the 'Rightist' is right in claiming that the worker is free to sell his labour power and

---

[11] Cohen (1981a), pp. 229-30.

[12] Cohen (1988), p. 243.

[13] Cohen (1981a), p. 224.

[14] He claims that, one cannot be forced to do what he is not able to do, and being able to do something implies that one is free to do it. *Ibid*, p. 223. I am not convinced by this argument which seems to conflict with Cohen's claim that the foreigner whose work permit is removed is not free to sell his labour power. Since the foreigner can find a way of working illegally, he is able to work and thereby also free to sell his labour power.

[15] In capitalism, capitalists are more free than workers because of their extensive freedom of choice with respect to the terms of the contract. Cohen, G. A. (1988a), 'The Structure of Proletarian Unfreedom', *History, Labour and Freedom: Themes from Marx*, Clarendon Press, p. 274.

the 'Leftist' is also right in arguing that the worker is forced to sell his labour power. He gives Marx his due, by remarking that for Marx 'the period of time for which he is free to sell his labour power is the period of time for which he is forced to sell it'.[16]

We have seen that for Cohen, being forced entails being free, although it seems to be a minimal freedom with a very restricted freedom of choice. But we have not yet considered his arguments for claiming that the worker is forced to sell his labour power under capitalism. First, by a conceptual analysis he 'clarifies' under which conditions somebody is forced to do an action. Afterwards, he argues that even when the worker is not forced to sell his labour power, he suffers from 'collective unfreedom'.

One is forced to do A if he has another alternative B different from A, but when there exists no 'acceptable or reasonable alternative'. Cohen gives the following example. One's having another alternative is necessary for it to count as *his* action; otherwise, for example, if he is dragged out of a room by physical force, then he is not forced to leave the room but is thrown out.[17] He is forced to leave the room only when somebody threatens him by saying for example that 'either you go out, or I will beat you'. This alternative is not 'acceptable' because it is usually too costly for him to choose the option of being beaten.

Let us apply this analysis to the situation of a worker, whose options are accepting a hazardous job, begging, or escaping out of the proletariat by some luck and skill. Is he then forced to take a hazardous job?[18] Rightists deny this because they count other alternatives as acceptable and Cohen agrees that each worker is free to escape from the proletariat since we can find such examples of workers who set up their own business and escape from the proletariat. Those who cannot escape are still free, thanks to the distinction between unfreedom and inability.

Cohen predicts some possible leftist objections to his argument. The first objection might argue that if workers' educational deprivation makes them incapable of leaving the proletariat then others can be held responsible for that. So, the workers are not only unable but also unfree because of such denied opportunities. According to the second possible objection, since 'capitalism requires a substantial hired labour force' which would not exist if more than a few workers left the proletariat, workers are not free to leave the working class and are thereby forced to sell their labour power.[19]

Mandel and Reiman can exemplify these critiques that Cohen has predicted.[20] Mandel claims that if it were possible that after a few years of selling their labour

---

[16] Cohen (1988), p. 244.

[17] *Ibid*, pp. 245-9.

[18] Cohen remarks that he is oversimplifying the case by assuming that the worker knows about the hazards of the job that he is offered, which is not usually the case in real life situations where 'much hazard is revealed only after the contract has been signed, and a certain amount of managerial effort is directed at preventing its revelation'. *Ibid*, p. 250.

[19] *Ibid*, p. 249.

[20] Mandel, E. (1976), *An Introduction to Marxist Economic Theory*, Pathfinder Press, p. 33;

power, workers could rise to petit bourgeoisie then they would not have been forced to continue selling their labour power. However, the accumulation of capital and wealth in relatively few hands takes away that option, by making it more and more costly for them to start their own enterprise. Reiman makes a similar point by arguing that workers are not overpaid so it is very hard, almost impossible to save and be a petit bourgeois.

As a reply to this point, Cohen argues that workers do not try to escape from the working class, not because of their lack of objective opportunities but because of various internal motivations. So, they are not objectively forced to sell their labour power. According to Cohen, workers either think that leaving the proletariat is too difficult or costly to try, or they do not favour personal escapes because of the 'sentiment of solidarity'. In other words, workers do not want to rise above the working class but want to rise with them, as Eugene Debbs has expressed.[21] In my opinion, this sentiment of solidarity is too weak to counteract the dominant ideology that encourages workers to find individual escapes from the proletariat.

Rejecting the Marxist arguments that explain the unfreedom of workers, leads Cohen to invent another notion 'collective unfreedom' to explain the sense in which workers can be considered as unfree. He argues that even though each worker is individually free to leave the proletariat, they are 'collectively unfree', or unfree as a member of the working class. This is because each is free to escape only on the condition that others do not exercise this freedom, since the number of exits is small with respect to the number of workers.[22] Collective unfreedom is not the unfreedom of a group, but the unfreedom of individuals because of their membership of a group. 'As soon as enough people exercise the coexisting individual freedoms, collective unfreedom generates individual unfreedoms. If, though free to do A, I share in a collective unfreedom with respect to A, I am less free than I otherwise would be.'[23]

Gray gives the following counterexample to show that 'collective unfreedom' is not a useful notion to explain unfreedoms specific to capitalism. 'We do not usually suppose that, unless any subscriber to a telephone system can use it at the same time as every other or most other subscribers, then the entire class of telephone users is rendered unfree by the system'.[24] On the other hand, if collective unfreedom is a pervasive property of all social institutions, then it loses its significance in the arguments against capitalism. Gray's analogy is misleading because Cohen's point is not that all workers cannot leave the proletariat *at the same time*. In principle, a telephone system can function even when there are no subscribers, but capitalism cannot exist without a significant number of workers.

Cohen remarks that not all unfreedoms are lamentable, on the basis of his value-free conception of negative freedom. 'It is what this particular collective

Reiman, J. (1987), 'Exploitation, Force and the Moral Assessment of Capitalism', *Philosophy and Public Affairs*, vol. 16, p. 37.

[21] Cohen (1988a), pp. 263-5.

[22] *Ibid*, pp. 264-6.

[23] *Ibid*, pp. 269-70.

[24] Gray (1988), p. 91.

unfreedom forces workers to do which makes it a proper object of regret and protest. They are forced to subordinate themselves to others who thereby gain control over their productive existence'.[25] It is because workers are forced to work for the capitalists that collective unfreedom is bad. But he has no separate argument to show why workers are forced to sell their labour power; he establishes it only with the help of his argument about collective unfreedom. This is the point where everything becomes confused and even circular.[26] Gray is right in claiming that this problem arises from the irreconcilability of Cohen's normative account of force and his value-neutral account of freedom. In Gray's words,

> The logic of Cohen's argument requires him…to accept that the proletarian is forced to sell his labour power even though he is free to refuse to do so. This is so, at least in part, because 'force' unlike 'freedom', is for Cohen a normative concept. It embodies standards of desirability and acceptability. It is only the conjunction of value-free notion of collective unfreedom with the value-laden notion of force that gives Cohen his conclusion that workers are nontrivially unfree under capitalism.[27]

In so far as Cohen makes an internal critique, he cannot demonstrate that capitalist institutions provide less freedom than other possible alternatives such as socialism. Negative freedom analyses freedom in personal relations, within a given framework of institutions. As soon as one starts questioning the effects of this framework on negative freedom, he goes beyond a purely negative conception of freedom.[28] This is the main problem with all internal critiques of negative freedom.

It seems that Cohen has proposed his notion of collective unfreedom as an alternative to the Marxist notion of exploitation.[29] Cohen says 'there is a freedom, namely to escape the proletariat which workers have, and which Marx said they lacked.'[30] His argument is invalid because the fact that *some* workers are able to escape from the proletariat does not imply that *each* worker is free to escape.

Furthermore, Cohen's notion of collective unfreedom conflicts with the Marxist argument that even when workers are individually unfree, they are collectively more free because of the power of worker collectives in challenging or reforming

---

[25] Cohen (1988a), p. 272.

[26] Gray (1988), p. 99.

[27] *Ibid*, pp. 99-100.

[28] This was the source of Miller's confusion about the criteria of unfreedom as we have seen in chapter 2, section 4.

[29] According to Mason's interpretation of Cohen, collective unfreedom is not undesirable because it makes workers vulnerable to exploitation, but because 'it excludes the possibility of a desirable state of affairs –one in which all workers exercise their individual freedom to leave the proletariat'. Mason, A. (1996), 'Workers' Unfreedom and Women's Unfreedom: Is There a Significant Analogy?', *Political Studies*, vol. 44, p. 79. In my opinion, this argument is begging the question and cannot explain why collective freedom is a desirable state of affairs, within the framework of negative freedom.

[30] Cohen, G. A. (1985), 'Are Workers Forced to Sell Their Labour Power?', *Philosophy and Public Affairs*, vol. 14, p. 104 .

the capitalist system. Cohen admits that this is the weakest part of his argument.[31] Yet, there is another way in which the unfreedom of workers can be explained, by referring to the problems about the freedom of contract between parties with unequal powers, as we shall investigate in the next section.

3. Free Markets

Free markets refer to a system of voluntary exchange relations and 'freedom of contract' between employer and employee, without the intervention of the state. For its defenders, competitive free markets have historically evolved on the basis of 'the natural propensity to truck, barter and exchange'[32] which reflects the universal human motivation to improve one's material well-being. It is claimed that such natural and universal competitive motives have given rise to division of labour and local markets, which then extended to national and international trade once political barriers (state interventions) were removed.

Polanyi challenges this evolutionist account of free market society.[33] He distinguishes between societies with markets and the market society, in which production is mainly for exchange and profits, and which is competitive. Non-competitive local markets and long-distance trade were historically prior to competitive national markets. The latter did not evolve from either of the former, but was fostered by extensive state regulation and intervention. Hence, it is a myth that free market and state regulation are always antagonistic.[34]

The mercantilist state aimed at getting rid of the 'particularistic restrictions' and prohibitions of feudal society, but also extended the scope of regulation.[35] Only after the development of the factory system, which made land, labour and money 'fictitious commodities', that the society was subordinated to the laws of the 'self-regulating markets'.[36] Polanyi agrees with Marx's view that the emergence of competitive market society is not through the spontaneous development of voluntary exchange relations but through forcible means, such as the peasants being deprived of their land through enclosures in Britain.

Furthermore, the competitive acquisitive drive is neither natural, nor universal. It is not the initial source of market society, but rather a relatively recent product of market society. The voluntaristic element in bargain was not dominant in previous

---

[31] *Ibid*, p. 105. Because of such reasons, I find the Marxist notion of exploitation to be a more coherent and useful notion to explain the unfreedom of workers, as we shall explore in chapter 11.

[32] Smith, A. (1981), *The Wealth of Nations*, Liberty Classics, pp. 25-7.

[33] Polanyi (1957), p. 58.

[34] *Ibid*, pp. 60, 63.

[35] *Ibid*, pp. 66-7.

[36] *Ibid*, pp. 71-2, 76. Polanyi considers land, labour and money as 'fictitious commodities' since they are not produced for sale. The solution he proposes to the perils of the 'commercial society' is to de-commodify these items, which he thinks is already taking place to some extent, through state regulation of these markets since the 19th century.

historical periods when exchange relations were bound up with customary relations of reciprocity and redistribution by the social authority.[37]

As Sayers illuminates, free markets have both a liberating and a coercive aspect. By dissolving traditional communities and transforming self-sufficient peasants into wage labour, the emergence of free markets has forced individuals into a 'new and wider network of relations', making them more interdependent and universal beings who have a greater range of activities and abilities. Its coercive aspect refers to both the forcible creation of wage labourers by depriving them of their traditional means of livelihood, as well as the inability of capitalism to employ new conditions and possibilities in a way that would increase the well-being of all.[38] This requires the perspective of an immanent critique, which will be explored in chapter 11.

Freedom of Contract and Impersonal Constraints on Freedom

How free are individuals that voluntarily consent to the terms of the contract? In other words, does freedom of contract imply free individuals? As Atiyah argues, those who take voluntary consent as the sign of individual freedom confuse free will (or voluntary consent) with free choice. It is the same fallacy Hobbes had committed when he argued that any action follows from free choice even when a person is threatened and acts out of fear.[39] Other defenders of negative freedom accept that merely having a motive for complying does not imply the existence of fully voluntary consent, or the absence of coercion. On the basis of a broader notion of constraints, they distinguish between threats and offers; both may give a person a motive for complying, but only threats constrain freedom. If it can be shown that freedom of contract is to the advantage of both parties, then it would be similar to an offer, rather than a threat. This would be the basis on which the negative view can argue that freedom of contract does not constrain the freedom of the involved parties.

According to the classical distinction between offers and threats, offers make a person 'better off' with respect to his 'baseline' (the initial conditions) so they are not coercive. Threats are coercive because they make a person 'worse off' with respect to his baseline. However, this position leads to a *reductio ad absurdum* as follows.

> Since one is not coerced when one is advanced from a baseline, it turns out that the worse off in absolute terms a person is, the more difficult it is to coerce him. The range of his voluntary acceptance seems to increase when we would ordinarily think of such an individual as being especially vulnerable to coercion.[40]

---

[37] *Ibid*, pp. 60-61.

[38] Sayers, S. (1992), 'The Human Impact of the Market', *The Values of the Enterprise Culture* (ed. Heelas, P and Morris, P.), Routledge, pp. 126-33.

[39] Atiyah, P.S. (1979), *The Rise and Fall of Freedom of Contract*, Clarendon Press, p. 43.

[40] McGregor, J. (1989), 'Bargaining Advantages and Coercion in the Market', *Philosophy Research Archives*, vol. 14, p. 27.

As McGregor argues, a relative improvement of one's situation with respect to his baseline is not enough to distinguish coercive from non-coercive proposals; the appropriateness of the baseline position should also be considered. Offers one cannot refuse can be coercive to somebody who is in a desperate situation. 'With threats, the coercer puts one in a vulnerable position...whereas with coercive offers the proposer finds his victim in a vulnerable position.'[41]

Let us apply the insights gained from the above considerations, to the case of freedom of contract. The scope of one's free choice is related with his bargaining advantages, which are directly proportional to the scope of alternatives, one's knowledge of the terms of negotiation, one's wealth (which makes him less risk averse), and the abilities he possesses that others want.[42] Great inequalities between bargaining positions put the weak party in a vulnerable position, since the stronger party may take advantage of his weakness. Hence, even when freedom of contract makes both parties 'better off', due to unequal bargaining advantages, it does not follow that this relation is non-coercive.

McGregor claims that, most defenders of negative freedom disregard the effects of bargaining advantages on freedom of contract because they assume the ideal model of a perfectly competitive market, where nobody has bargaining advantages over another.[43] The 'impersonal operations of market forces' may make an individual's bargaining power weak in comparison with his needs, so that it would form a suitable condition for others to force him into exploitative deals.[44] As a result, the negative view ignores impersonal economic factors that constrain freedom.

As we have explained before, Cohen operates with a restricted notion of freedom, according to which being free to do something does not imply being free not to do it.[45] In my opinion, for a course of action to be the result of a free choice, one should be both free to do it and free not to do it. In other words, the right to dissent is essential to have freedom of choice. For example, selling one's labour power is a free choice only if he is free to sell it and also free not to sell. Capitalism provides the former freedom but restricts the latter to a great extent. On the one hand, it liberates people with respect to previous historical forms by adding new freedoms (via introducing new legal rights); on the other hand, by depriving workers of the means of production, it forces them to sell the only thing they have, their labour power, and thereby constrains their freedom of not selling their labour power.[46] In other words, capitalism gives all people 'formal freedom' but deprives

---

[41] *Ibid*, p. 45.

[42] *Ibid*, p. 31.

[43] *Ibid*, p. 27.

[44] *Ibid*, p. 39.

[45] Cohen argues as follows: if one is initially free to do A, and free not to do A and then forced by somebody to do A, this force only removes the latter freedom (not to do A), but not the former (to do A). Cohen (1981a), p. 224.

[46] Mandel (1976), p. 34.

most of them of 'effective freedom', the means to use this freedom to shape their lives as they choose.[47]

When there are immense inequalities of assets (wealth, skill, and knowledge) between parties then it is not a free choice of the weak party to decide with whom to contract and he has almost no power in determining the terms of the contract.[48] Hence, under conditions of social and economic inequality, freedom of contract turns into a 'freedom' to exploit and be exploited.[49] Now, I will exemplify these points by considering freedom of contract in the realm of production and will give a panoramic view of the conflicting freedoms of capitalists and workers, which will be further elaborated in chapter 11.

Free Contract Between the Worker and the Capitalist

The voluntary consent of the worker does not imply a free choice because having no other means to earn a living, he is forced to make a contract with the capitalist; most of the times he has no other reasonable alternative. He needs the capitalist more than the capitalist needs him. His options in choosing with whom to contract are very limited and he cannot contribute to the determination of the terms of the contract because there is concentration of capital and wealth in the hands of the owners of means of production, which puts them in a superior social position vis a vis a large number of workers and unemployed. As Marx calls it 'a reserve army of labour' or many unemployed people are waiting to take his job if he does not accept it.

There are two situations in which the workers can have considerable bargaining power. The more they are qualified and the more they are organized into worker collectives and trade unions, the more power they could have in determining the terms of the contract. However, both ways have certain limitations because the former requires a certain level of higher education, which is often beyond the reach of most children of poor families, and the latter requires an institutional set up, such as laws that establish the right to strike. Even when such legal rights are available, workers may lack enough knowledge, skill and money to organize into worker collectives or they avoid political activism because of the immediate threat of unemployment they face.

---

[47] For the distinction between formal and effective freedom, see chapter 2, section 1. I will argue that effective freedom (power for self-determination) is an essential element of the positive view in chapter 10.

[48] Schweinitz, K. (1979), 'The Question of Freedom in Economics and Economic Organization', *Ethics*, vol. 89, p. 341.

[49] According to 'UN's latest 'Human Development Report', the total wealth of the top 358 'global billionaires' equals the combined incomes of 2-3 billion poorest people (45 per cent of the world's population.' Bauman, Z. (2000), *Globalization: The Human Consequences*, Polity Press, p. 70. As Amin argues, 'in the peripheries of the capitalist system, poverty and unequal distribution of income are not negative effects produced by specific circumstances or mistaken policies. They are the product of the system's logic, the logic of world polarization immanent in the system itself.' Amin, S. (2000), *Capitalism in the Age of Globalization: The Management of Contemporary Society*, ZED Books, p. 16.

Moreover, the contract between worker and capitalist is not as free, as uninterrupted as it is claimed to be. On the one hand, the state guarantees profits and 'redistributes the national income in favour of the leading monopolistic groups...by distribution of subsidies, tax reductions and by granting credits at reduced interest rates'. On the other hand, it controls the increase in wages and transforms the role of trade unions into a 'guarantor of stability'.[50]

The ideological justification of this policy is the assumption that economic progress is better both for rich and poor.[51] As the argument goes, an increase in wages could imply a decrease in profits, which would be a disincentive for capitalists. This would in turn lead to closing off of some enterprises, an increase in unemployment rates and in the final analysis everybody would be worse off. This argument does not apply to late capitalism in which the main problem is overproduction in developed countries, which could be partially solved by increasing the demand through increasing wages, as Keynesian economic policies suggest.[52]

This is one of the greatest paradoxes of capitalism: it creates poverty amidst overproduction. Butter mountains and milk lakes that are created to keep prices high coexist with starving masses. 'The unemployed die of hunger not because there is too little to eat but because there is relatively too great a supply of foodstuffs'.[53]

As a result, freedom of contract in the realm of production is a myth because it is made between parties of unequal power and the state continuously interferes to protect the rich, rather than to compensate the poor. State intervention is often not for harmonizing interests of workers and capitalists, but to provide the best possible conditions for capitalists to increase their profits.

Furthermore, it should be remarked that in the age of globalisation, states have limited power to change this state of affairs because if they impose some restrictions on capital in order to enhance social welfare (ranging from minimum

---

[50] Mandel (1976), pp. 73, 77.

[51] For Adam Smith, only rapid economic growth and scarcity of workers can increase their wages. This kind of reasoning lies behind Malthus' suggestion that the solution to poverty is in the hands of the poor; if they reproduce less they would be richer. This hides the fact that poverty stems from unfair distribution, rather than from excessive population. Galbraith, J. K. (1969), *The Affluent Society*, Houghton Mifflin Company, pp. 24-6.

[52] An alternative way to dampen the effects of such periodic crises would be by a social security system that would prevent the sudden decrease in demand when some factories begin to close. Mandel (1976), p. 76.

[53] *Ibid*, p. 52. Another aspect of that paradox is food aid that is used not to help those in need but to increase imports. For example, Britain in 1985-86 instead of aiding 'the most widespread famine Africa has ever known...chose to aid countries such as Turkey and Mexico which, unlike the countries in Africa, have the money to buy British manufactured goods...US Department of Agriculture admits that American food aid is a means of creating a demand for imports from the US'. At the Bretton Woods Conference in 1944, 'aid was institutionalized as the industrialized world's principal tool of economic colonialism.' Goldsmith, E. (1995), 'Development Fallacies', *The Future of Progress: Reflections on Environment and Development*, Green Books, pp. 68-70.

Freedom

wages, social security to progressive income taxes) then capital runs away to other countries where it can earn more profit. The mobility of the capital and the limited mobility of wage labour is another factor that turns free contract into an unequal exchange.

The rights of multinational corporations are protected and extended by international institutions such as the International Monetary Fund (IMF), The World Bank and the World Trade Organisation (WTO), while national laws that protect human rights are overridden.[54] Multinational corporations are legally accepted as persons, with immense rights and almost no obligations, which practically put an end to the freedom of contract between two *individuals* with *equal* rights.

On the one hand, corporations use cheap labour and natural resources of underdeveloped countries and impose certain 'structural adjustment plans' on those countries for them to be attractive to foreign investment and to manage their immense foreign debts. This results in the denial of national policies for sustainable development and destroys their chance of collective self-determination.[55] On the other hand, the flow of capital and investments to those countries has bad implications for the conditions of workers in their own developed countries. Either wages in developed countries decrease or they cannot compete with the cheap labour of immigrants, 'sweat shops' abroad and unemployment at home. The global collaboration between corporations results in a global impoverishment, sustained through the competition between workers, and the absence of solidarity among them. In Miller's terms,

> Our current problems are rooted in the forced competition required by the structure of market society, with its carefully crafted artificial scarcities of opportunity for co-operative and mutually satisfying activity. This forced competition for scarce educational, work, housing and other opportunities is the basis for dividing the majority of people against one another by sex, race, age and ability. A ruling minority depends on a divided majority for its security and privilege. [56]

---

[54] Trade Rights in Intellectual Property reinforces not competition but the power of monopolies, 'GATT-WTO, for instance, wants to forbid Third World manufacture of inexpensive pharmaceutical products, which are of vital importance, in order to protect the massive profits of monopolies in this sector'. Amin (2000), p. 29.

[55] Barriers to foreign investment are overcome by various repressive means, even by using military force to overthrow democratically elected governments, which was the case in Guatemala in 1954 and in Chile in 1973. 'These need not be terribly cogent, because the electorate in the (democratic) home country is little affected by repression abroad. Indeed, many among the electorate benefit from the less expensive goods that these policies yield'. Schweickart (1993), p. 191.

[56] Miller, W. (1999), 'Social Change and Human Nature', *Monthly Review*, vol. 50, p. 45. For the creation of artificial scarcities and the encouragement of competition in the Third World, see Norberg-Hodge, H. (1995), 'The Pressure to Modernize', *The Future of Progress: Reflections on Environment and Development*, Green Books, pp. 97-103.

Limits of Consumer Freedom

The paradigmatic example of freedom in capitalism is consumer's freedom of choice. Capitalism has extended the scope and importance of consumption in comparison with pre-capitalist societies by creating new needs in the realm of consumption. This implies a new area of unfreedom for the poor, through increasing the gap between needs and the material means for satisfying them.

Consumer freedom is often expressed as 'consumer is the king' (or sovereign) in market society. There are two senses of 'consumer sovereignty'. First of all, consumers are claimed to be the best judges of their desires, know them before coming to market and the only motive behind consumption is to 'maximize their utility'. This is why, liberty requires protection of a private sphere in which 'external social authorities' (such as central planning by the state) cannot interrupt or shape people's private desires.[57] Secondly, consumer is sovereign because producers respond to consumers' expressed preferences; it is the consumers who decide what is to be produced through their demands.

These claims do not correspond to reality. As Dobb claims, utility theory assumes that each individual has a free range of opportunities and makes his choice after surveying the range of all alternatives. This cannot be postulated because alternatives depend on the economic and social position of the individual.[58]

Secondly, it is not the desires of consumers that shape what is to be produced, but conversely it is the corporations, which shape consumer desires through various sales promotion techniques and advertisements. These do not only shape desires but also increase the intensity of those desires. 'Advertising and marketing, for example, by intervening substantively and culturally through images, styles, psychology and so on, result in a kind of artificial urgency of desire: consumers will want a particular good at any price'.[59]

In a broader sense, people have never been fully free to define their own needs because individual needs are always a part of the 'system of needs' of one's society. Defenders of free market or consumer society give the false impression that one achieves such freedom in capitalism. This leads to an 'illusion of freedom' which hides the fact that choices are no longer constrained by traditions but by more complicated manipulative mechanisms that teach people what they need and desire.

An implication of the above considerations is that an increase in the number of commodities does not automatically imply an increase in consumer freedom. A consumer's freedom of choice is not only related to the scope of commodities, but

---

[57] Whereas the state is conceived as an external social authority that has the power to threaten individual liberties, market forces are conceived as impersonal forces, which are merely the unintended consequences of the actions of millions of consumers and producers. They are neither conceived as social authorities, nor as institutions that may limit freedom. Slater, D. (1997), *Consumer Culture and Modernity*, Polity Press, p. 41.

[58] Dobb, M. (1960), *Political Economy and Capitalism*, Routledge & Kegan Paul, p. 169.

[59] Slater (1997), p. 50. On how logos affect people's lives see Klein, N. (2000), *No Logo*, Flamingo.

also to his purchasing power and his ability to make informed choices. In the final analysis, overemphasis on consumer freedom fosters an extremely individualistic account of freedom that eclipses the social, economic and political aspects of freedom.

In this chapter, we have shifted the unit of analysis from freedom of action to freedom of choice and explored how the negative view ignores the effects of the distribution of wealth on individual freedom. To incorporate these elements requires investigating the goal of freedom. Is freedom merely freedom *from* personal constraints *to* satisfy one's arbitrary desires, or does it involve more than that? This question is the starting point of the hybrid view that will be discussed in the next chapter.

Chapter 5

The Hybrid View

Whereas the negative view takes freedom of action as the unit of analysis and focuses exclusively on the objective constraints on freedom, what I have called the 'hybrid view' has emerged from the inadequacy of the negative view in explaining the goals and the subjective uses of freedom. It lies in the middle ground between negative and positive conceptions of freedom and incorporates those thinkers who try to extend and revise the negative conception of freedom so that it will include both the internal constraints on freedom as well as a richer conception of the self.

We can trace back the origins of the hybrid view to J. S. Mill's account of freedom that considers freedom as the pursuit of one's own good in his own way. This introduces a subjective and normative dimension of freedom. He also gives the clues of the objective and rational aspects of freedom by distinguishing between 'higher' and 'lower' pleasures and linking freedom with making informed choices towards the objective goal of self-realization. As we shall see in this chapter, the first version of the hybrid view develops the objective and rational aspect of free choice, whereas the second version explores the subjective and moral aspect, related with free agency.

MacCallum's triadic scheme is helpful in understanding differences and similarities between the negative and hybrid views. According to this schema, any adequate conception of freedom can be expressed in terms of a relation between three variables: x is free from y to do, or to become z, where 'x' ranges over agents, 'y' refers to constraints, and 'z' ranges over actions or circumstances.[1]

The negative view exclusively deals with 'y', which is reduced to the universal external constraints, and it considers the goal of freedom 'z' to be a mere subjective preference of the agent 'x'. In other words, for the negative view, freedom is the absence of universal constraints so that any agent may pursue any of his desires. As we shall see in the first section, taking freedom as the satisfaction of one's arbitrary desires gives rise to the 'paradox of the contented slave', which leads the first version of the hybrid view to reconsider the goal of freedom, or the content of 'z'.

This consideration illuminates that constraints on freedom cannot be determined without specifying goals of freedom. We have already encountered this

---

[1] MacCallum (1991), p. 102.

fact in chapter 2, when it was exposed that the same obstacle may have different effects on people depending on their different goals.

The first version of the hybrid view (late-Berlin, Benn and Weinstein) revises z to be the satisfaction of actual or possible desires, and takes y as constraints on the scope of choice, which gives rise to a notion of freedom as non-restriction of options by human arrangements. This view emphasizes conditions of free choice and the possibility of 'illusion of freedom'. We shall explore in the first section whether this account is sufficient to solve the 'paradox of the contented slave.'

On the other hand, the second version of the hybrid view (Frankfurt, Dworkin, Watson) reveals that the utilitarian model of the self underlying the negative view is too restricted to explain the fact that one's freedom can be constrained by his own desires that he fails to control. Furthermore, if others manipulate one's choices then he is not free although he seems to be satisfying his desires. These observations lead the second hybrid view to define the goal of freedom 'z' as the satisfaction of 'second-order desires' or as doing what one values. This modification extends scope of constraints so that it also involves internal constraints, as well as external, personal constraints. It also introduces the notion of an internally complex self, free agency, and the normative aspect of freedom, which serve as a bridge between hybrid and positive conceptions of freedom.

1. The First Version of the Hybrid View: Choice and the Illusion of Freedom

The negative conception of freedom can be formulated as freedom *from* external constraints *to* satisfy one's desires. This implies a subjective criterion of freedom that will be abbreviated as the 'Desire Thesis', according to which 'the amount of freedom a person possesses varies directly with the extent to which his desires are satisfiable under the options available to him.'[2] The Desire Thesis cannot be associated exclusively with either the negative or the positive conception of freedom. On the one hand, Hobbes who is widely accepted to be the father of the negative view claims that freedom is the absence of external impediments so that one can do what he wills or desires. On the other hand, Rousseau who is probably the founder of the positive view claims the key to freedom and happiness to be the proportion between one's desires and abilities. The insight that underlies the Desire Thesis is the wish to construct a notion of freedom that would include both the objective aspect of being free and also the subjective aspect of feeling free.

The Paradox of the Contented Slave

Let us focus on two objections to the Desire Thesis made by advocates of the negative view. Steiner is against the Desire Thesis because he wants to exclude all subjective factors in order to reach a descriptive and 'morally neutral' account of freedom. According to him, what one desires is irrelevant in figuring out whether

---

[2] Arneson, R. (1985), 'Freedom and Desire', *Canadian Journal of Philosophy*, vol. 15, p. 431.

he is free or not because one might have a freedom that he does not want to use. This is why we should carefully distinguish between being free and feeling free. Somebody is free if there are no external constraints on his action, whereas one feels free if he is free to do what he desires to do.[3] Hence, feeling free is not necessary for being free.

Steiner denies any link between freedom and desires, or the agent's intentions. But this makes freedom irrelevant to an agent because constraints on freedom are then objective and universal but not related with one's particular goals and aspirations. Denying the normative aspect of freedom and making it merely descriptive leads to an inability to explain why we value freedom. It does not solve the problem of how to relate objective and subjective aspects of freedom, but only avoids it.

Berlin's objection to the Desire Thesis is based on a different reason. He argues that the association of freedom with actual desires leads to a *reductio ad absurdum* of the negative conception of freedom. His argument goes as follows. If freedom is the absence of constraints to do whatever one desires, one way to increase freedom is by repressing some of one's desires and desiring only things within his reach. This is what Berlin calls the 'Stoic strategy', which leads to the 'paradox of the contented slave' that threatens the basic assumptions of the negative conception of freedom. If the Desire Thesis is true then it implies that the contented slave is free[4]; but a slave is the paradigm case of unfreedom for the negative theory. So, that contradiction compels one to reject the Desire Thesis and to find an alternative description of the goal of negative freedom.[5] Yes, negative freedom is the absence of external constraints, but to do what?

In the final analysis, Steiner claims that feeling free is not necessary for being free and Berlin argues that feeling free is not sufficient for being free. So, what is the relation between being free and feeling free? In other words, how are the objective and subjective aspects of freedom related?

Freedom as the Non-Restriction of Options and Reasonable Choice

Berlin becomes one of the founders of the hybrid view, by revising the definition of negative freedom into freedom as the absence of constraints 'to satisfy one's actual and potential desires and choices', in the new introduction he has written ten years after his defence of the negative view.[6] Benn and Weinstein develop this idea into freedom as the 'non-restriction of options'.[7]

---

[3] Steiner (1991), pp. 125-6.

[4] In fact, the Desire Thesis does not deny the objective aspect of freedom. So, from the Desire Thesis we can at most infer that the contented slave is more free than the discontented one because the former has more subjective freedom than the latter and the objective aspect of their freedom are the same (they are both slaves).

[5] Berlin (1969), p. xxxviii.

[6] *Ibid*, p. xl.

[7] Benn, S. I. and Weinstein, W. L. (1971), 'Being Free to Act, and Being a Free Man', *Mind*, vol. 80, p. 201.

As we have seen in chapter 3, section 1, comparing the freedom of people by the quantity of available options is not possible because of the problems in individuating the courses of actions available to people; they are indefinite and infinite. As Christman notes, 'If freedom consists in unrestrained possible desires, then the concept of liberty becomes vacuous due to the impossibility of enumerating restraints'.[8] Furthermore, since every choice implies giving up of other alternatives, it is not clear whether 'non-restriction of options' is possible at all.[9]

Taylor argues that all conceptions of freedom need a background of what kind of actions are more significant, in order to compare freedoms of people. In other words, the normative aspect of freedom is crucial and freedom involves the absence of obstacles to 'significant action'.[10] Advocates of the hybrid view seem to agree with Taylor's remarks. Benn and Weinstein argue that any meaningful proposition about freedom is in the following form. Being free from X implies that X is contrary to one's interest, and being free to do Y requires that Y is 'an object of reasonable choice'. So, 'our conception of freedom is bounded by our notions of what might be worthwhile doing'.[11]

Let us try to clarify the relation between freedom and the scope of options. A person is free to do some action only if he is also free not to do it; the existence of another 'reasonable choice' is the first condition of free action. For instance, one is not free if somebody has manipulated his options, so that there is only one reasonable alternative. In general, threats reduce freedom by reducing the number of reasonable choices, whereas offers increase the number of such options. However, there may be irresistible offers that reduce freedom. For example, as we have seen in the previous chapter, the abuse of one's weak bargaining power is a case of unfreedom if turning down the offer would lead him 'to suffer real deprivation'.[12]

Defining unfreedom as the absence of reasonable alternatives has problems because of the vagueness of the notion 'reasonable'. Either what constitutes a 'reasonable alternative' changes from one person to another and we cannot find an objective yardstick, or it depends on how much pressure and sanction is enough to force a 'normal' agent into a single course of action.[13]

Benn and Weinstein seem to accept the latter interpretation by claiming that it is a 'prudential defence' and does not exclude that extraordinary people may

---

[8] Christman, J. (1991), 'Liberalism and Individual Positive Freedom', *Ethics*, vol. 101, p. 353.
[9] In Sartre's words, 'To be finite, in fact, is to choose oneself –that is to make known to oneself what one is by projecting oneself toward one possible to the exclusion of others. The very act of freedom is therefore the assumption and creation of finitude'. Sartre, J. P.(1957), *Being and Nothingness*, Methuen, p. 546.
[10] Taylor (1991), pp. 149-50.
[11] Benn and Weinstein (1971), p. 195.
[12] *Ibid*, p. 202.
[13] This is the path Oppenheim takes, as we have analyzed in chapter 2, section 3. I will not repeat here the problems about defining unfreedom objectively with respect to the motivations of a 'normal agent', which is too ambiguous to be helpful.

disregard threats or legal sanctions. So, one may freely do what he is unfree to do. For instance, 'criminals freely commit crimes they are not free to commit'.[14] This seemingly paradoxical claim is justified as follows. On the one hand, we should accept that criminals act freely or voluntarily; otherwise they would not have been responsible for their choices. On the other hand, they are unfree to commit crimes, because its sanction is too severe to constitute a 'reasonable' option for a 'prudent' person. The authors try to establish an objective standard for the evaluation of options, while preserving the subjective choice of the agent to obey or disobey any law, threat or pressure.

The criterion of free choice is claimed to be the ability to make a 'reasonable' choice based on a 'realistic' understanding of the alternatives. The meaning of a reasonable choice can be based on an internal, counterfactual or an external rationality condition. It is a common feature of the hybrid view to reject the external rationality condition, which they attribute to the positive view and to use a 'minimal, internalist rationality requirement'.[15] The external rationality criterion is supposed to argue that for a choice to be reasonable, it should be based on true beliefs, and the agent should choose the most effective means for his ends.[16] This seems to me more similar to the 'rational choice theory' rather than being related to the positive conception of freedom.

According to the internal rationality condition, giving 'sufficient' or 'good' reasons for one's choice is enough to conclude that it was a reasonable choice. But what constitutes sufficient or good reasons? If the contented slave asserts that he chose to remain a slave since this makes him happy, is this a good, legitimate reason? The internal rationality condition's defect is not being able to separate real reasons from rationalizations. So, nearly all choices are reasonable, with respect to the subjective standards of the chooser. This is why the hybrid view fails to admit that the contented slave is unfree, unless it finds an evidence of some explicit manipulation by another person.

Mill tries to find an objective basis for reasonable choice by introducing what can be called as a counterfactual rationality condition. This is based on the assumption that people with a similar quality of experience will agree on what a reasonable choice involves. I am here referring to Mill's argument that those who have enjoyed both 'lower' and 'higher' pleasures will prefer the latter. So, a reasonable choice is something, which those who have engaged in higher activities and who have tasted higher pleasures would choose. Whereas the 'normal' agent views, such as that of Benn take the average, prudent person as the yardstick of reasonable choice, Mill takes intellectual elites as the paradigm of reasonable choice. By linking reasonable choice with informed choice, Mill puts forward an objective rationality criterion to be a free chooser. In other words, one's freedom is directly proportional to the extent that his choices are based on knowledge and critical deliberation.

---

[14] *Ibid*, p. 206.
[15] Christman (1991), p. 350.
[16] *Ibid*, p. 349.

Mill argues that making choices has an intrinsic and developmental value, which is different from the instrumental value of choices in satisfying one's desires. One becomes a free chooser by actually making choices; 'the opportunity to make choices enables us to grow and develop as persons'.[17] Mill takes choice making as an indicator of one's degree of individuality and contrasts it with the attitude of conformity or submission to customs. Even when customs are good, conforming to custom as such does not educate or develop distinctively human qualities.

> The human faculties of perception, judgement, discriminative feeling, mental activity, and even moral preference are exercised only in making a choice. He who does anything because it is the custom makes no choice. He gains no practice either in discerning or in desiring what is best. The mental and moral, like muscular powers, are improved only by being used.[18]

Since exercising freedom by making choices is what makes us distinctively human, for Mill nobody has the right to give up his freedom. This introduces a further addition to the harm principle, in drawing the boundaries of personal freedom. A person is free to do anything that would not harm others, and he should never give up his freedom by submitting to another person.

Conditions for Being a Free Chooser

Benn and Weinstein give the following criteria for being a 'free or autonomous chooser'. Firstly, a minimum degree of rationality is necessary to have a realistic understanding of the alternatives. Secondly, one's choice should not be completely determined by another person's decision, or proposal. It should be remarked that this condition does not exclude choosing through being persuaded and influenced by advertisements. Thirdly, one should be capable of criticising and rejecting proposals. For this, he should have access to non-manipulated information; the coercer should not control the source of information. On the basis of these criteria, the authors argue that a person who has sold himself to be a slave and those who use addictive drugs disqualify themselves as choosers.[19]

The authors exclusively focus on the internal constraints on freedom that diminish one's capacity as a chooser. They give three examples in which the actors are disqualified from being a free chooser. Forms of insanity diminish one's responsibility as a chooser, by preventing him from having a realistic understanding and evaluation of the alternatives. Similarly, hypnotised or brainwashed subjects are not the owners of their choices. The last and the most interesting example is the case of a submissive partner who 'cannot squarely contemplate the possibility of doing otherwise than to obey'.[20] Prejudices,

---

[17] Mills, C. (1990), 'Choice and Circumstance', *Ethics*, vol. 109, p. 157.
[18] Mill (1985), p. 122.
[19] Benn and Weinstein (1971), p. 211.
[20] *Ibid*, p. 210.

limitation of one's imagination and the impaired capacities for critical thinking due to her upbringing may lead to fatalism and thereby form internal constraints on freedom. The submissive wife forms a more concrete and common version of the contented slave example. In order to understand whether the first version of the hybrid view can solve the paradox of the contented slave, let us focus on this example of the submissive wife.

But this is related with the issue of the relativity of social roles and cultural norms. If one can judge a submissive wife to be a diminished chooser, then what about another woman who has internalised her social role as a sexual object, and as a 'man-hunter'; is she also a diminished chooser? Both women have internalised the norms of their different cultures and aspire to opposite role models that describe what it means to be a woman. Which woman is a more equipped chooser?

In order to answer this question, we have to compare the costs they have to pay if they disobey cultural norms. In other words, what is the price they have to pay to use the right to dissent? For example, if the submissive wife is living in a fundamentalist Muslim society, infidelity may be punished with death penalty, and similarly in a traditional Hindu community women are explicitly encouraged to burn themselves with the corpses of their dead husbands. We cannot talk of the right to dissent in these cultural settings; they do not have other 'reasonable' options than to obey.

On the other hand, social pressures in a Western society are milder, and individuals not conforming to social norms do not face such severe sanctions. Nevertheless, even if the submissive wife is a member of a Western society, it is still difficult for her to choose a non-submissive life especially if she has no job that would enable her to live an independent life after the divorce.

These cases show that internal and external constraints on freedom are inseparable in more common examples. We may label a phobia, or a mental disease as an internal constraint on freedom, but we cannot do this so easily with social factors that diminish the capability of choice of disadvantaged individuals. The hybrid view overemphasizes the former exceptional cases, but does not consider how becoming a competent chooser requires living in a society in which 'reasonable' alternatives are available. The capacities required to be a free chooser can only flourish on the basis of objective social opportunities, as the positive view argues. The objective social context of free choice is a fundamental difference between the hybrid and the positive conceptions of freedom.

Failing to acknowledge the social conditions of free choice makes the hybrid view impotent in explaining why the contented slave or the submissive wife has impaired freedom. It is the social and economic factors that force people to give up their freedom; the so-called internal constraints are intimately related with objective social conditions.

We have started this section by a comparison of the Desire Thesis with the hybrid view of freedom. Let us conclude by giving another example which demonstrates that doing what one wants to do is not sufficient to be free and that the existence of other reasonable options is crucial for free choice. Feinberg gives the following example that clarifies the difference between negative freedom and hybrid freedom as the non-restriction of options. John Doe can do a thousand things but not what he most wants to do. On the other hand, Richard Roe can only do one thing, which is what he most wants to do.[21] Who is more free? Negative freedom, by emphasizing doing what one wants without intervention, claims Richard Roe to be more free, whereas the hybrid view claims John Doe is more free. We do not have to choose between those two views; the ability to do what is significant for the person (or feeling free) and the availability of genuine alternatives are both components of an adequate notion of freedom.

Christman gives the following example by modifying the contented slave example.

> Imagine that the 'happy slave' is a Tibetan Monk who has spent the last several years in the same room meditating and sitting quietly…and from which he will never desire to move. If chains are then put on the door of the room, a room he does not want to leave, then his freedom of action is simply unaffected by these chains.[22]

In contrast to Christman, I want to argue that a person who is forced to do what he most wants to do is not free, because this violates Benn and Weinstein's third criterion of free choice that is having the right to dissent. As Rousseau has remarked, when tasks we voluntarily choose to do are imposed on us as duties by external force, we become less free.[23] The monk is less free than before although he may not feel less free because he does not mind these external obstacles. He has less 'breathing space' because his counterfactual freedom is reduced. In other words, if he wanted to change his mind, he would not be able to go out. Furthermore, his self-imposed obligation of not leaving the room has now become an externally imposed obligation that restricts his freedom. The right to dissent and change one's mind is crucial to have freedom of choice.

What conclusions can be drawn from these various evaluations of the 'paradox of the contented slave'? Firstly, since feeling free, or being content[24] is not sufficient for being free, happiness and freedom do not always imply each other. One may be happy yet unfree, or free but not happy. Secondly, one is not always the best judge of his freedom; he may have illusion of freedom'. This may be either because of his ignorance of the other reasonable alternatives, or because he is unaware of the constraints. For example, somebody who is unaware that the door

---

[21] Feinberg, J. (1973), *Social Philosophy*, Prentice-Hall Inc., p. 7.

[22] Christman (1991), p. 354.

[23] In the 6th Reverie Rousseau says, 'I saw with good pleasure, it was necessary that I should act freely, without constraint, and that to take from me all the sweetness of a good deed, it sufficed that it should become a duty for me' Miller, J. (1984), *Rousseau: Dreamer of Democracy*, Yale University Press, p. 190.

[24] Although Berlin uses feeling free and feeling content interchangeably, as the existentialists claim feeling free can lead to feelings of anguish instead of contentment, and as Fromm claims people may 'escape from freedom' and the responsibilities it brings. For simplicity, I have assumed that feeling free is an enjoyable feeling and implies contentment but it does not necessarily imply being totally satisfied or happy.

of his room is locked may feel free due to his ignorance of this constraint on his freedom.[25]

If the contented slave has an illusion of freedom, then he is less free than a discontented slave, who has a better, more realistic grasp of his situation. As Ancsel says 'no one is bound by tighter chains than a man who believes himself to be free when he is not. Yet the tighter these chains the less people are aware of them. The oppressed must be rid of the illusion of freedom because...it only deepens their subjection.'[26]

On the other hand, in exceptional cases, the contented slave might have good reasons to choose slavery. For example, if he is involved in a blood feud between two families, and if the master protects him from getting killed, he may prefer that security to freedom. In more standard cases, his contentment may emerge out of ignorance, in the sense that he believes that he was born a slave and it cannot be otherwise, or through manipulation by his master, or by his voluntarily choosing escapism and retreating back to his 'cave' and being content there, rather than fighting for his freedom which may involve taking great risks. In the first and second cases of ignorance and manipulation, since his contentment is not based on informed choice, his freedom is impaired. In the third case, he may voluntarily choose to remain a slave, because of the high costs of fighting for his freedom but it would be wrong to describe this choice given under social oppression as a free choice.

In the final analysis, subjective and objective aspects of freedom overlap only if there is freedom of choice and the absence of an illusion of freedom. The first version of hybrid theory introduces the possibility of an illusion of freedom that is absent in the negative view. However, it explores the conditions for freedom of choice from a purely individualistic and limited perspective, emphasizing the internal constraints on freedom but disregarding the impersonal social constraints.

As Benn claims free action requires the possibility of choice, which presupposes a chooser, a free agent, who can be 'qualified as the subject of a free act'.[27] We will now investigate who is that free agent, which is explained by the second version of the hybrid conception of freedom.

2. The Second Version of the Hybrid View: Values and Free Agency

The second version of hybrid theory has not emerged from an attempt to solve the paradox of the contented slave, which was the root of the first version. It has targeted another problem about taking desire-satisfaction as the goal of freedom. Since desires may conflict with each other and we cannot satisfy most of our desires due to limitations in time, talents and opportunities, the satisfaction of which desires are more important for the achievement of freedom? In other words, which desires are most crucial for one's identity as a free agent? As we shall see in

---

[25] Feinberg (1973), p. 5.

[26] Ancsel, E. (1978), *The Dilemmas of Freedom*, Akademiai Kiadu Budapest, p. 36.

[27] Benn and Weinstein (1971), p. 209.

the following pages, Frankfurt and Watson answer these questions by replacing the utilitarian notion of the self with an internally complex self. They argue that a particular subset of desires, or values with which the person identifies is the root of free agency. I will compare their views with those of Taylor, who directly addresses Frankfurt's views and has many similarities with Watson's position, although he is a representative of the positive conception of freedom.[28]

Frankfurt on Free Will and Second-Order Desires

Frankfurt starts his analysis by focusing on a particular feature that distinguishes humans from animals. Both animals and humans strive to satisfy their desires, but only humans are capable of forming 'second-order desires', or desires about desires. For example, a person may both desire smoking and also has a second-order desire for stopping the desire to smoke. Why don't we express this in simpler terms and claim that he has two conflicting first-order desires, in the sense that he desires to smoke and also desires to stop smoking? This simpler expression would not show us which desire is more important for him, with which desire he identifies. However, having a second-order desire means that a person identifies with that desire; he wants that desire to be his will, to motivate him into action. A person's second-order desires reflect his aspirations and ideals.[29]

'The capacity for reflective self-evaluation that is manifested in the formation of second-order desires' is the distinctive feature of humans.[30] This is different from the utilitarian notion of the self, for which the self always wants to satisfy the strongest desire, and reason is concerned with finding the best means to achieve this fixed goal. The choice between different desires is based only on the calculation of pleasure and pain they would yield.[31] By contrast, in Frankfurt's model, second-order desires can be based on non-hedonistic motivations because people have ideals other than the maximization of pleasure.

The crucial difference between the two models is that, the utilitarian self's will is determined by his strongest desire, whereas Frankfurt's self has a free will, which can choose not to satisfy the strongest first-order desire. This is why Frankfurt claims 'the essence of being a person lies not in reason but in will'.[32] The existence of a free will presupposes that its owner is a rational being, but the converse is not true; not all rational beings have free will. Frankfurt constructs such a hypothetical entity, called a 'wanton' that has desires, can reason but does not

---

[28] I will elaborate Taylor's views about the socially embedded self in chapter 9.

[29] Frankfurt remarks that second-order desires are not necessarily moral, they may be 'capricious and irresponsible'. Frankfurt, H. (1971), 'Freedom of the Will and the Concept of a Person', *The Journal of Philosophy*, vol. 68, p. 13.

[30] *Ibid*, p. 6.

[31] Even though Mill is a utilitarian, he distinguishes between higher and lower pleasures. However, this falls short of an internally complex self because he believes that a person who has tasted both kinds of pleasures would naturally favor higher pleasures; so in his picture, there is no conflict between two kinds of desires of the same person.

[32] *Ibid*, p. 11.

have a free will. As opposed to a self-evaluating person, a wanton 'does not care about his will. His desires move him to do certain things, without its being true of him either that he wants to be moved by these desires or that he prefers to be moved by other desires.'[33]

Animals and very young children are examples of wantons but humans can also act wantonly. A wanton is indifferent about what he wills; he is indifferent to the enterprise of evaluating his desires and motivations. He takes them as given and just acts on his strongest desire. He does not have long-term goals and his self does not have a self-imposed unity. As Sayers reminds us, this is similar to what Plato calls the 'democratic personality'. 'Without the unifying direction of reason the self is fragmented and disordered. It haphazardly pursues any and every 'unnecessary' desire that it happens to feel and is never satisfied. An integrating influence is essential for happiness.'[34] This idea is fully developed by Hegel who argues that freedom essentially involves the ability for reflective self-consciousness.[35] Unlike Plato and Hegel, Frankfurt tries to achieve a unified self not by introducing a separate faculty of reason, but by referring to the power to evaluate desires and the notion of a free will.

In contrast to a wanton, a 'person' cares about what he wills. He takes a side when considering the relative worth of his various desires, identifies with a subset of his desires and conceives other conflicting desires as alien forces to be controlled. The second-order desires with which he identifies enable him to have a relatively enduring identity. He should also have a strong will so that he would be motivated by his second-order desires into action and could resist temptations towards immediate pleasure that might conflict with his goals.

Frankfurt compares an unwilling drug addict with a wanton. The unwilling addict takes a side about his conflicting desires by identifying with one of them, and conceiving the other as an alien force against his will. A wanton may suffer a similar conflict but he does not take a side, since he has no standpoint to compare these conflicting desires.[36] This is why a wanton neither has free will, nor lacks free will. 'It is only because a person has volitions of the second order that he is capable of enjoying and of lacking the freedom of the will.'[37] The unwilling addict is capable of having free will, but as long as he cannot live in accordance with his standards and give up drugs, he lacks free will.

The conflict between desires is not sufficient to form an internal constraint on freedom because making a choice always requires giving up other options.

---

[33] *Ibid*, p. 11. Plato was the first one to use the term 'wanton' in his *Phaedrus* (237e-238a) to describe a situation in which desires rule irrationally towards pleasure. He named that rule as 'wantonness', and contrasted it with 'temperance', which is the result of judgements guiding one rationally. Watson, G. (1975), 'Free Agency', *The Journal of Philosophy*, vol. 72, p. 208.

[34] Sayers, S. (1999), *Plato's Republic: An Introduction*, Edinburgh University Press, p. 77.

[35] I will devote chapter 8 to a detailed analysis of Hegel's account of freedom, which is one of the most satisfactory versions of the positive view.

[36] Frankfurt (1971), p. 13.

[37] *Ibid*, p. 14.

However, the contrast between second-order desires and the strongest first-order desires establish an internal constraint on freedom by motivating the self in opposite directions. For example, a smoker has internal constraints on his freedom only after he decides to stop smoking. As a result, one's goals provide a yardstick to distinguish constraints on freedom. If we can imagine a person without any sustaining goals, like a wanton, then he would not have any internal constraints on his freedom.

I think that Frankfurt identifies free will with a strong will. One has free will if he is moved by his second order desires. Defenders of the negative conception of freedom miss this aspect of freedom, by identifying freedom with the freedom of action. According to Frankfurt, freedom has two components: freedom of action (freedom to do what one wants to do) and freedom of the will (freedom to will what one wants to will). Freedom of action and freedom of the will do not imply each other. For example, animals enjoy freedom of action without having freedom of the will, and a person who is unaware of the constraints on his freedom of action still has free will although he lacks freedom of action. Frankfurt also argues that there is nothing more to freedom than the conjunction of both. [38]

In contrast to the negative view, Frankfurt relates freedom with self-mastery and self-discipline. The difference between Frankfurt's views and the positive conception of freedom is that the latter group links self-mastery with rational self-determination, whereas Frankfurt refrains from incorporating the notion of an active reason in his model of the self, in which free will and second-order desires are the key elements.

I will now consider three main criticisms of Frankfurt. Dworkin points out that a person whose second-order desires are manipulated is not fully free. So, autonomy is the third component of freedom, in addition to freedom of action and freedom of the will. Watson raises the infinite regress problem and proposes a change in terminology, by replacing second-order desires with values. Taylor is concerned with the objectivity problem, which refers to the possibility of error in one's evaluations. Let us take a closer look at these critiques.

Dworkin on the Procedural Account of Autonomy

Dworkin accepts Frankfurt's account of freedom but adds a 'formal or procedural account of autonomy', which is missing in Frankfurt. Even when an agent identifies with his second-order desires, it is possible that those desires are manipulated and not authentic. Dworkin introduces certain criteria of 'procedural independence', which would eliminate manipulated second-order desires and would ensure that a person's evaluations are based on informed choices.

He contrasts his notion of formal autonomy with the substantive account of autonomy that underlies the positive conception of freedom. If an autonomous person is one who gives meaning to his life, and who is the owner of his choices,

---

[38] *Ibid*, pp. 14, 15, 17.

then autonomy should be a 'weak and contentless notion'.[39] Otherwise, it would impose particular ends on people and thereby violate the independence criterion of autonomy. He defines autonomy as 'the capacity to reflect upon one's motivational structure and to make changes in that structure'.[40] This links autonomy with the structure of desires since it is related to the capacity to satisfy second-order desires rather than the first-order ones, and the source of the choice. If a person's actions are based on a choice, which is not manipulated by others, an informed choice that is the result of critical thinking then he is said to be autonomous. Interfering with a person's liberty against his second-order wishes interferes with his autonomy.[41]

This is called a 'procedural account of autonomy' because whether someone is autonomous is decided by analysing the procedure, which generates his motivations and the changes in his preferences. It is not related with the content of his choice but depends on how the choice is made. This is why self-imposed restrictions do not decrease one's autonomy. For example, a person may autonomously choose to restrict his freedom and autonomy. In Dworkin's words, 'a person who wishes to be restricted in various ways, whether by the discipline of the monastery, regimentation of the army, or even by coercion is not, on that account alone, less autonomous'.[42] Later in his book, Dworkin makes his point more provocatively.

> There is nothing in the idea of autonomy that precludes a person from saying 'I want to be the kind of person who acts at the commands of others. I define myself as a slave and endorse those attitudes and preferences. My autonomy consists in being a slave'.[43]

I do not agree with Dworkin's conclusion. Although one may freely or voluntarily decide to be a 'slave' because he values other things such as security more than he values autonomy, one's autonomy cannot consist in being a slave. A wife, who quits her job and becomes a housewife just because her husband requires so, is a person who submits voluntarily and gives up at least a part of her autonomy. She may claim it back after some time and rebel against the husband's impositions, even accepting the possibility that her husband would not allow her to work and they will get divorced, but until then she is less autonomous since she has lost control over an important dimension of her life. Autonomy requires one to take the responsibility of her choices. A woman who says, 'I quit my job because my husband wanted it' is less autonomous than another wife who says, 'I quit my job because my husband's salary is enough for both of us'. In the first case her will is dependent on the will of others, but in the second case she has an independent reason. I have pursued this line of thought in the previous section when considering the case of the contented slave and submissive wife, which I will not repeat here.

---

[39] Dworkin, G. (1988), *The Theory and Practice of Autonomy*, Cambridge University Press, p. 31.
[40] *Ibid*, p. 108.
[41] *Ibid*, p. 16.
[42] *Ibid*, p. 18.
[43] *Ibid*, p. 129.

As a result, autonomy does not have a definite content so an autonomous person is not necessarily one who acts morally or someone who chooses self-realization. One can autonomously commit crimes and evil acts. However, one can choose any content to his autonomy within the limits of some boundary conditions. Actions that fall outside those boundaries are not autonomous. Examples of those boundary conditions are submission to other people and not accepting the responsibility for one's life.

Watson on the Internally Complex Self, Values and Free Agency

Watson makes another critique of Frankfurt's theory by referring to the problem of infinite regress. He questions the specific status of second-order desires as the basis of free will and free agency. If one can be a wanton with respect to his first-order desires, then it is also possible that a person can be a wanton with respect to his second-order desires. Would such a person have free will? It can be argued that being a wanton about second-order desires would diminish one's freedom. Even if we can make sure that he is a person and not a wanton with respect to second-order desires, what about his status with respect to third-order desires, and so on. This is the problem of infinite regress. In other words, in order to make sure that a person has free will we have to refer to an endless series of higher-order desires. Frankfurt acknowledges this infinite regress problem but evades it by claiming that the 'decisiveness of the commitment' in the level of second-order desires makes it unnecessary to refer to higher-order desires.[44]

Watson finds this solution arbitrary. According to him, the notions of 'decisive commitment' and 'identification' that Frankfurt introduces may be useful, but they are different from second-order desires because identification can be first order (to courses of action that make up one's conception of good life, rather than with desires). Hence, referring to second-order desires is superfluous.[45] There is no reason to assume that second-order desires represent the 'true self' better. Frankfurt cannot give an adequate account of which desires are more truly our own and how an agent can be unfree with respect to his own will.[46] This is why Watson shifts the debate on personhood and freedom from an analysis of higher-order desires to the difference between desires and values; with this crucial change in terminology, new doors open.

Watson starts his analysis by distinguishing free action from intentional action. Intentional action is necessary but not sufficient for free action. For example, when somebody acts under the pressure of a threat, when his choices are manipulated, or if he has an addiction or phobia his action is still intentional but not free. His action is then caused by external factors, rather than based on reasons of his own.

If we want to characterise free action in terms of doing what one wants, we have to distinguish between two possible interpretations. Doing what one wants can either mean following one's strongest desire or doing what one values, what

---

[44] Frankfurt (1971), p. 16.
[45] Watson (1975), p. 219.
[46] *Ibid*, p. 217.

one thinks to be good.[47] For example, when an alcoholic who wants to give up alcohol keeps on drinking, does he act as he wants? The answer is 'yes', if we accept the former sense of wanting, but the answer is 'no' if we follow the latter interpretation. It makes more sense to claim that he can be more free if he acts not on his strongest desire (for alcohol in this case), but when he acts on his most significant desire, what he thinks would be good for him.[48]

These two different meanings of 'doing what one wants' are based on there being two different sources of motivation: desires and values. Of course, desires and values are intimately connected since one's values colour his desires. If a person values a certain state of affairs, then he also desires to achieve that ideal. The converse is not always true; desiring an object does not necessitate that the agent values it. Irresistible desires, cravings, addictions one wants to get rid of are examples of such cases. Hence, desires and values are relatively independent; a person may have desires that conflict with what he values most.[49] As Watson claims: 'The problem of free action arises because what one desires may not be what one values, and what one most values may not be what one is finally moved to get...evaluation and desire may diverge.'[50] How does this situation affect freedom?

For Watson, the possibility of freedom depends on this duality of the sources of motivation. The question of freedom does not arise either for God or for animals that have only one source of motivation.[51] God (and also the Devil) immediately do what they value and animals immediately do what they desire. Mediation of desires is necessary for free agency. Freud's tripartite division of the human soul can be taken as exemplifying such a mediation of desires. The ego mediates between the super-ego (that roughly corresponds to values) and the id (that is the seat of desires) and reconciles them in a creative way through sublimation. Otherwise, an unbalanced domination by either the id, or the super-ego results in mental problems and can establish internal constraints on freedom.

If the possibility of free agency and free action depends on this duality of motives, the actuality of free action requires reconciliation, but not an elimination of this duality.[52] The struggle to make one's desires and values converge to each other can be taken as a struggle for liberation through achieving self-mastery. The more one's actions are in conformity with his values, the more unified would be his self so the more free he would be and feel. As Neely claims, the notion of a free

---

[47] *Ibid*, p. 216.

[48] It should be noted that for his action to be free, this significant desire should be his own, not manipulated by others. This does not mean that the desire is independently formed, not influenced by what others say. It just means that it is a result of critical self-evaluation.

[49] Values provide subjective and inter-subjective reasons for action but desires do not always provide reasons, even for the agent himself. One may think that satisfaction of desires and appetites is a worthwhile and valuable activity but this does not imply that one values the particular objects of those desires. *Ibid*, pp. 208-9, 213.

[50] *Ibid*, p. 209.

[51] *Ibid*, p. 220.

[52] *Ibid*, p. 215.

agent implies that there is some coherence between his various desires and goals. One who is 'torn between alternatives…is less a free agent than he might be because he is less a single agent…From the point of view of one of these agents, the others are external circumstances tending to frustrate the efforts of the one'.[53] This idea of unity and harmony goes back to Plato's notion of an internally complex self, which has three parts. As Sayers argues, 'Freedom for Plato is connected with the idea of the harmony of the self. It does not consist in the mere absence of restraint –the liberty to satisfy any and every desire.'[54]

We can draw two conclusions from Watson's account. Firstly, it is more fruitful and realistic to divide the self into relatively independent sources of motivation (as Plato does) rather than distinguishing between higher and lower order desires as Frankfurt has done. This is because our evaluations are usually first-order. The 'initial practical question' is not 'what desires should I pursue?' but it is rather 'which course of action is most worth pursuing?'[55] In other words, reflective evaluations are not higher order preferences but are 'practical judgements regarding what constitutes a good way to live' which are also open to rational inter-subjective justification.[56]

Secondly, the notion of a free agent implies a moral being whose values establish a yardstick to rank his desires. The free agent is a person who can 'translate his values into action', who is motivated to act by what he values. A person's values stem from his identity. 'One cannot dissociate oneself from all normative judgements without forfeiting all standpoints and therewith one's identity as an agent'.[57] This is what Taylor calls the indispensable 'horizon of evaluation' that we will discuss soon. What is missing in Frankfurt and Watson is a discussion of the issue whether one's reflective evaluations can be mistaken, or the possibility of error. Is the normative dimension Watson introduces purely subjective, or does it have an objective component? It is Taylor who sheds some light on these issues.

Taylor on Strong Evaluations and the Objective, Social Context of Values

Taylor agrees with Frankfurt that the capacity for reflective self-evaluation of desires is central for humans. There can be two sorts of evaluation. In 'weak evaluations', a person compares various desires with respect to their outcomes and prefers the option with the greatest utility. The choice between a relaxing holiday in the south and an exhilarating holiday in the north is based on a weak evaluation; it is merely a subjective preference, desiring something constitutes its sole justification. On the other hand, in 'strong evaluations' one makes a qualitative distinction between desires and compares his alternatives contrastively by referring

---

[53] Neely, W. (1974), 'Freedom and Desire', *The Philosophical Review*, vol. 83, p. 39.

[54] Sayers (1999), p. 139.

[55] Watson (1975), p. 219.

[56] Stern, P. (1986), 'Translator's Introduction', Tugendhat, E., *Self-Consciousness and Self-Determination*, MIT Press, p. xxiv.

[57] Watson (1975), p. 216.

to his ideals and insights about the good life.[58] For example, choosing to visit ancient civilizations because it is a 'more humanly uplifting experience' involves a strong evaluation. The 'strong evaluator' is more articulate about his preferences since he can express what he values in a richer language.[59]

In the final analysis, a weak evaluation involves an assessment of 'objects in the light of our desires' and a strong evaluation entails the assessment of the desires themselves.[60] For Taylor, the capacity for strong evaluation is the essential feature of a person or a 'human subject'.[61] Weak evaluations refer to what we value as living organisms, such as the absence of pain and the drive to survive. On the other hand, strong evaluations denote what we value as subjects, by articulating the distinctively human ideals.[62]

According to Taylor's interpretation, utilitarians conceive people only as 'weak evaluators'. In contrast, for Taylor all people are strong evaluators, although they sometimes choose between certain options through weak evaluation. It is almost impossible to conceive a person without any strong evaluations. Taylor finds the utilitarian account of human motivation inadequate in explaining distinctively human capacities and aspirations because it portrays people as lacking 'depth' [63] The ability to evaluate and normatively rank motivations enables one to distinguish the strongest from the most worthwhile desires.

Watson has expressed a similar idea by distinguishing desires and values as two separate sources of motivations. Instead of assuming such a duality, Taylor takes emotions as the source of all motivations. Emotions are neither immediate nor transparent to the subject. Self-awareness and the articulation of emotions and values are achieved in various degrees, through a process of self-interpretation that takes place in a social medium. All emotions are embodied in an interpretive language that involves 'import-ascriptions'. In other words, emotions are value-loaded. For example, considering a situation as shameful, humiliating or courageous requires a specific interpretation of reality. A person who does not have these concepts will have a different experience. Certain modes of experience are not possible without certain self-descriptions.[64] Taylor gives the following example: 'If someone for instance thought that there was nothing higher than life

---

[58] Taylor, C. (1977), 'What is Human Agency?', *The Self: Philosophical and Psychological Issues* (ed. Mischel, T.), Basil Blackwell, pp. 106-7.
[59] *Ibid*, p. 113.
[60] Taylor, C. (1986), 'Self-Interpreting Animals', *Human Agency and Language: Philosophical Papers*, vol. 1, Cambridge University Press, p. 33.
[61] Taylor (1977), p. 117.
[62] Taylor (1986), p. 60.
[63] 'Someone is shallow in our view when we feel that he is insensitive, unaware or unconcerned about issues touching the quality of his life which seem to us basic or important. He lives on the surface because he seeks to fulfill desires without being touched by the 'deeper' issues, what these desires express and sustain in the way of modes of life' Taylor (1977), p. 115.
[64] *Ibid*, p. 126.

and the avoidance of pain, and believed that no one would sanely and responsibly think otherwise, he would have no place in his vocabulary for physical courage.'[65]

Our self-interpretations are partly constitutive of our experience and the medium of these assessments is the social language in which we articulate our emotions. The capacity for strong evaluations makes communication possible by referring to aspirations that have meaning for members sharing the same language. This is why Taylor argues that strong evaluations are necessarily connected to one's identity. These form the 'indispensable horizon or foundation out of which we reflect and evaluate as persons. To lose this horizon, or not to have found it, is indeed a terrifying experience of disaggregation and loss'.[66]

We can distinguish between two senses of 'identity'. Objectively, it is how others classify us with respect to our nationality, ethnicity, gender, class and occupation. Subjectively, our identity is established by how we interpret ourselves, our aspirations, the factors shaping who we are. Taylor's view has similarities with the existentialist position because he claims that factuality does not determine how we evaluate it. One's upbringing may shape him in a certain way, but still he has the power to evaluate those influences and recreate his identity within certain limits.

Strong evaluations form a socially embedded horizon of evaluation, which is not the product of individual choice but rather is the basis and the background of any choice. They are articulations of our sense of what is worthy human conduct. Taylor remarks that strong evaluations are not necessarily ethical, they may be aesthetical or related to 'personal style', such as the tastes that are related to our conception of the good life.[67]

Nevertheless, there is possibility of error in our strong evaluations. They may be wrong, distort reality as well as make something accessible and inaccessible in new ways.[68] For example, one may have an irrational fear or an inappropriate shame. Taylor gives the example of a black man who is initially ashamed of his background, and lacks confidence. After reflecting on this, he realises that 'apologizing for his existence is senseless. So he goes through a revolution like that expressed in the phrase 'black is beautiful''.[69] With this 'transvaluation' both his shame disappears, and also he conceives his previous feelings of shame as distorting reality. Since there is always room for re-evaluation, we are responsible for our strong evaluations although we do not choose them.[70]

The richness of the language in which we evaluate our desires opens the possibility of a wider scope of experience. Not only do the emotional lives of people from different cultures vary, but also in the same culture, people with different vocabularies have different experience. 'Consider two people, one with a single love/ lust dichotomy for the possible types of sexual feeling, the other with a

---

[65] *Ibid*, p. 114.
[66] *Ibid*, p. 125.
[67] Taylor (1986), p. 68.
[68] Taylor (1977), p. 130.
[69] Taylor (1986), p. 69.
[70] Taylor (1977), p. 130.

very variegated vocabulary of different kinds of sexual relations. The experience of sexual emotions of these two men differs.'[71] These are not two equally valid articulations but the man with more refined distinctions has a better assessment of his experience. Taylor's claim that strong evaluations have depth can be understood as illuminating the possibilities of humans as a species.[72] Since humans are self-interpreting animals, the more articulate is their reflective self-evaluation, the richer is their experience and they become more fully human subjects.

Some qualities such as shame, dignity, courage, honour, humiliation cannot be defined objectively and universally. They are meaningful only for persons who already understand their 'emotional meaning', that is, people with specific aspirations and self-interpretations. In Taylor's words, 'something is humiliating for me by virtue of…the way I see myself and aspire to appear in public space'.[73]

Taylor's thoughts are inspired by Hegel's views. Hegel argues that some feelings like honour are specific socio-historical products. Ancient Greeks did not have a notion of honour; it emerged with the development of individuality and subjectivity in the 'romantic' period, which changed people's self-interpretations.[74]

This last point is similar to Taylor's point about humiliation being intimately connected with a specific self-interpretation. Hegel emphasizes that those self-interpretations are social, cultural products and Taylor claims that they depend on the richness of the language one uses to articulate his feelings. 'Human motivations are reflexively constituted by our interpretations and therefore are deeply embedded in culture'; they cannot be reduced to universal and natural goals of survival and reproduction.[75]

Persons are beings for whom things have specific significance. They do not start with the raw material of desires and then order their preferences or interpret

---

[71] Taylor (1986), p. 71.

[72] This has similarities with Marx's account of 'emancipation of the senses', as we shall expand in chapter 11.

[73] *Ibid*, p. 57.

[74] Honour cannot be derived from the anger one feels due to physical injury as in the case of Achilles who is angry at Agamemnon who 'treats him disgracefully and publicly deprives him of respect among the Greeks, since the injury does not pierce into the very heart of personality as such, so that Achilles is satisfied by the return of the share of which he had been deprived'. Hegel, G. W. F. (1975), *Aesthetics: Lectures on Fine Art*, vol. 1, Oxford University Press, p. 557. Hegel continues, 'In honour, therefore, man has the first affirmative consciousness of his infinite subjectivity…The measure of honour thus does not depend on what the man actually is but on what this idea of himself is.' *Ibid*, p. 558. In an interesting article, Berger compares how the pre-modern notion of honour and the modern notions of dignity and individual rights reflect two different relations between the individual and society. Honour refers to a self socially situated within a hierarchical ordering, whereas dignity belongs to the self whose identity is independent of his social position. Berger, P. (1987), 'On the Obsolescence of the Concept of Honour', *Liberalism and Its Critics* (ed. Sandel, M.), Basil Blackwell, pp. 150-54.

[75] Taylor, C. (1986a), 'The Concept of a Person', *Human Agency and Language: Philosophical Papers*, vol. 1, Cambridge University Press, p. 111.

some as higher, others as lower; rather 'interpretation is constitutive of the feeling'.[76] Strong evaluations are central for being a human subject because humans are self-interpreting animals. This process of self-interpretation and re-evaluation can take place only in a community with a language that is rich enough to articulate these distinctively human emotions. There are 'peculiarly human ends' and our recognition of these goals distinguishes us from animals.

Although Taylor does not discuss the implications of his views on freedom, I think that self-awareness and critical re-evaluation of one's goals and values lead to a human being with a variety of experiences and refined senses. Having more articulate evaluations transforms one's experience by adding new ways of perceiving the world. In this way, the self-transformation and enlargement of the self leads to an enrichment of one's freedom.

In the final analysis, Taylor, as an advocate of the positive conception of freedom, criticises the hybrid view in the following way. Firstly, he brings into focus the objective aspect of freedom. He argues against Frankfurt and Watson that one can be mistaken in the evaluation of his desires or in his normative judgements. The hybrid account of freedom faces the same problem as the negative conception of freedom; it has a tendency to reduce freedom to its subjective aspect by associating freedom with doing whatever one values. However, as we have seen in the first section when discussing the possibility of an illusion of freedom, one can be mistaken about whether he is free or not. Taylor introduces an objective criterion (the degree of articulation of one's evaluations) to assess whether one's values distort the reality or not.

Secondly and most importantly, Taylor emphasizes the social dimension of free agency. Values are not merely products of individual choice but are chosen against the background of a social horizon of evaluations. In the next part, especially in chapters 6 and 9, I will elaborate this notion of a socially embedded self, which is fundamental for the positive conception of freedom.

Although the hybrid view extends the set of constraints to include internal constraints, and shifts the focus of analysis from freedom of action to free choice, autonomy and free agency, it is still not an adequate theory of freedom in so far as it fails to conceive poverty and ignorance as restricting the effective exercise of choice. This defect leads us towards the positive conception of freedom.

---

[76] Taylor (1986), p. 63.

PART II

THE POSITIVE CONCEPTION OF FREEDOM

Chapter 6

Green's Notion of Freedom

Freedom has both a negative aspect (not submitting to the arbitrary will of another) and a positive aspect (rational self-determination and self-activity). The historical roots of the positive conception of freedom goes back to Rousseau's idea of 'moral freedom' as the obedience to self-imposed laws, and 'general will' as linked with the political freedom of the members of a self-legislating community. Kant develops the first theme by arguing that being free is identical with being rational and moral (chapter 7). Hegel situates moral agency within its social context and argues that the moral development of an individual takes place through the process of socialisation; one becomes a moral agent by actively participating in concrete social institutions with others (chapter 8). Green is a leading exponent of British Idealism that makes a new synthesis of the themes introduced by the above-mentioned thinkers.

The positive conception of freedom defines freedom as rational self-determination and the power for self-determination. The core argument of the positive view is the following. Freedom involves self-consciousness (or the ability to make second-order choices). This is what moral agency means, and it requires an active reason. These abilities can develop only through social relations. Hence, freedom is not a natural given but is a social achievement. Individual freedom ultimately requires a free society. In this chapter, I will establish how Green pursues this line of thought.

On the one hand, Green shows the inadequacy of the conception of the self that underlies the negative view. He puts forward the view that the self is internally complex and socially embedded, in contrast to the view that the self is simple and atomistic. This enables us to grasp the positive and social aspect of freedom that is based on moral agency. On the other hand, he criticises the view that takes free market society grounded on 'freedom of contract' as the model of a free society. Green puts forward the notion of a 'common good' to argue that the state has positive duties to promote the social conditions for freedom. Individual freedom is not only something to be protected against the possible interventions by others, but also, more importantly, freedom should be actively promoted by the state, which should act in accordance with the aspirations and needs of the people.

Green defines positive freedom as 'the positive power or capacity of doing or enjoying something worth doing...and something that we...enjoy in common with others'.[1] According to this definition, freedom has three aspects. Firstly, freedom is intimately connected with self-realization. The goal of freedom is 'to make the most and best of ourselves',[2] in contrast to the negative view that considers the goal of freedom as the satisfaction of arbitrary desires. As we shall consider in the first section, the ideal of self-realization presupposes an internally complex self (who is both a natural being and a moral agent) as opposed to the utilitarian account of the self, given by the negative view.

Secondly, freedom is something that we enjoy with others; no one can be free at the expense of restricting another's freedom to develop himself. In contrast to the negative view, which takes the conflict between individual freedoms as inevitable, Green thinks that there can be a social order (organised around a the notion of a 'common good') in which the positive freedoms of people would not conflict. The social nature of freedom follows from the view that the self is always socially embedded.

Thirdly, Green relates freedom with the power to achieve self-development and thereby challenges the distinction between unfreedom and inability that is a fundamental presupposition of the negative view (see chapter 2, section 1). It follows that freedom as self-development has objective social conditions.

Green argues that the negative aspect of freedom is necessary but not sufficient for an adequate account of freedom. For example, he says that freedom is not '*merely* freedom from restraint or compulsion', power is also necessary; and that freedom is not '*merely* freedom to do as we like irrespectively of what it is that we like'.[3] Green formulates a notion of socially valuable freedom by imposing further conditions on the constraints and uses of freedom; he enlarges the former and restricts the latter. Internal and impersonal constraints can limit freedom as well as the external personal constraints, and freedom cannot be used to harm oneself or the social good.

1. The Internally Complex Self and Moral Agency

Green associates the purely negative freedom with a naturalistic view of humans (as driven only by impulses), and an atomistic view of society (as merely an aggregate of individuals) that is unable to explain concrete social relations adequately. He shares the views of Plato, Rousseau and Kant that human action has both natural and spiritual/moral motives and the self usually stumbles between these two conflicting aspects. It is in this sense that the self is internally complex. The degree of one's freedom is in parallel with the extent of his rational ability to achieve control over the natural part of his self; this refers to positive freedom as involving rational self-determination. Like Hegel and Bradley, Green thinks that people cannot be fully free when they run after disconnected desires and when they

---

[1] Green, T. H. (1991), 'Liberal Legislation and Freedom of Contract', *Liberty* (ed. Miller, D.), Oxford University Press, p. 23.

[2] *Ibid*, p. 22.

[3] *Ibid*, p. 21.

are motivated mainly by pleasure. This is why the absence of external constraints is not sufficient to be free; willing the 'right' objects is also necessary. What make some objects 'right' are not their intrinsic properties; it depends on people's motives that lead them to those objects. If their only motive is obtaining pleasure then these objects cannot be 'right' because in this case the self only acts as a natural being, rather than as a moral agent.[4]

For Green, humans can get closer to 'self-perfection' when the objects of their will tend to correspond to the objects of universal reason. Reason is always in the pursuit of self-realization or self-perfection. Obeying what reason commands is the only way in which a self-conscious human being can be self-satisfied.[5] Green's notion of active reason that motivates action is in contrast to with Hume's idea of passive reason, which 'is and ought to be the slave of passions'.[6] Like other advocates of the positive view, Green takes reason to be the basis of moral agency and freedom.

He distinguishes between the possibility and the actuality of freedom. The possibility of freedom stems from free will.[7] Although external factors can directly constrain one's actions, they cannot reduce the freedom of his will. To put it differently, the will is free to refuse any content. One does not merely make choices by following his strongest desires, but also he can make second-order choices by evaluating which courses of action are more significant than others. However, this does not mean that the will is free to choose any content. The objects of the will are inseparable from the person. The will is always already determined; it is the person as directed to a particular object.[8] There is no contentless will that can choose between motives, 'an unmotivated will is a will without an object, which is nothing...in being determined by the strongest motive...man is determined by himself'.[9]

---

[4] Green, T. H. (1921), 'On the Different Senses of Freedom as Applied to the Will and to the Moral Progress of Man', *Lectures on the Principles of Political Obligation*, Longmans, Green & Co., pp. 3, 17-8. So, the extent of individual freedom depends on how one relates with the world; whether it is a one-dimensional relation based merely on consumption, or whether it involves articulate emotions, fundamental projects and reflective self-interpretations makes a difference as we have seen through Taylor's comparison of weak and strong evaluations in the previous section.

[5] *Ibid*, pp. 20-21. This Kantian idea is also an important theme for Hegel who claims 'only a rational (which is for him also a moral) will is free. The arbitrary will, wanting incompatible things is necessarily frustrated time and again.' Plamenatz, J. (1980), *Man and Society*, vol. 2, Longman, p. 219.

[6] Hume, D. (1985), *A Treatise of Human Nature*, Penguin Books, p. 462, (section 2.3.3).

[7] Green (1921), p. 22.

[8] *Ibid*, p. 14. It seems that Green has anticipated Heidegger's notion of Dasein, being-in-the-world, a century before him. Green's views on the intentional nature of consciousness are similar to those of Brentano who was a contemporary of Green.

[9] *Ibid*, pp. 12-13. Elsewhere, Green expresses this as follows: 'The idea of self-determination is active... 'Always obey the stronger motive', but my character makes it stronger, and character...could not be formed without the action of *self*, at once distinguishing itself from wants and pleasures which determine it, and forming them to a

Self-determination is a result of free will and it is 'not a subject of value for it is empty of any moral content: it is formal freedom'.[10] Defenders of negative freedom conceive freedom as self-determination in the sense that one's actions are not being determined by the compulsion of another. Whether one has negative freedom or not is not connected with the kind of motives underlying his actions. It does not matter whether the subject aims at 'satisfaction of animal appetites' or his action is a 'heroic self-sacrifice', whether he acts out of impulse or duty.[11] The negative view considers freedom as the immediate link between one's preferences and actions, without exploring how the nature of one's preferences is an integral part of one's moral character.

In contrast, the defenders of the positive view claim that the nature of one's strongest motive or dominant interest determines the kind of freedom he has. One's character is expressed by his dominant interest, which changes in parallel with one's moral development. In this sense, freedom is intimately related with moral agency. More valuable kinds of freedom are associated with 'higher' interests or more spiritual motives. Positive freedom is a morally loaded conception of freedom that identifies freedom with a particular kind of self-determination, namely rational self-determination. In other words, the actuality of freedom is related to the self-conscious choice of a particular motive aimed at self-realization. As we shall see now, Green takes the transformation of the potential freedom into actual freedom as overlapping with the moral development of an individual, through the process of socialization.

2. Stages of Moral Development and the Subjective Conditions of Freedom

Since the self-conscious person is equivalent to his will, educating the will towards the 'right' objects can only be achieved by cultivating people of 'character', who act morally. The transformation of natural impulses, which guide one's actions into self-conscious and spiritual motives, is achieved through the medium of social institutions. The autonomous will is reached not by destroying or repressing the natural impulses but by 'fusing them with higher interests'.[12] By supplying people with concrete interests and giving content to their ideals of self-perfection, social institutions tend to 'rationalize and moralize the citizen'. In other words, like Rousseau and Hegel, Green conceives socialisation as a process of 'moral liberation'.[13] For him, social progress can be measured by the 'historical growth in freedom' which is also in parallel with the moral development of individuals

---

totality.' Green, T. H. (1999b), 'Fragments on Moral and Political Philosophy', *Lectures on the Principle of Political Obligation and Other Writings* (ed. Harris, P. and Morrow, J.), Cambridge University Press, p. 312.

[10] Simhony, A. (1991), 'On Forcing Individuals to be Free: T. H. Green's Theory of Positive Freedom', *Political Studies*, vol. 39, p. 308.

[11] Green (1921), p. 15.

[12] *Ibid*, p. 21.

[13] *Ibid*, pp. 7-8.

towards self-perfection. The attainment of freedom 'is the end of all our effort as citizens'.[14]

Green argues against the social contract view that people are free in the 'state of nature', prior to society. Even if we can imagine a pre-social man, his independence does not mean that he is free because he would be 'slave to his natural appetites', not much different from an animal. Freedom is necessarily social because 'the full exercise of the faculties with which man is endowed' requires social relations.[15] This follows from taking the self as socially embedded and taking self-realization as the goal of freedom. Green agrees with Rousseau and Hegel that submission to society is the first step in 'true freedom'.[16]

Personal and moral identities are constructed in and through specific relations with others; social roles one performs and aspires to are crucial in this process. One learns the meaning of and the concrete ways of self-realization through the socialization process. The subjective aspect of freedom is enhanced through a process of moral development starting with the habitual internalisation of conventional morality and culminating in the reflective, self-conscious pursuit of self-realization. Green speculates on the stages of moral development of a person and claims that those who can complete the following process can reach full moral freedom.[17]

Firstly, one internalises the 'conventional morality' of society so that his actions and mode of self-satisfaction are in accordance with the expectations of others.[18] Through reflection, he transforms this feeling of social conformity into a conception of universal duty; 'rational recognition of duty' is the second step in moral development. Although he is bound by duties, he also feels free because he does not conceive duty as imposed on him from without, externally.[19] The person conceives those duties as enlarging his self, by uniting his reason with the 'practical reason, as operating in previous generations of men' and thereby uniting his good with the good of others. Green calls this stage the 'reconciliation of reason with itself', because it enables the individual reason to partake in the objective substantive reason; reason finds its true identity.

Those stages are not adequate for complete moral growth because the individual is still ultimately motivated by pleasure and pain, which is replaced by a higher motive only in the third stage. In this last stage, the individual desires self-perfection for its own sake and thereby attains autonomy in a 'higher sense'

---

[14] Green (1991), pp. 21-2. Such a connection of the development of freedom with that of consciousness and moral progress is a very Hegelian theme; Green and Hegel have similar notions of the Spirit as the source of this teleological progress.

[15] *Ibid*, p. 22.

[16] Rousseau, J. J. (1988), 'On Social Contract', *Rousseau's Political Writings* (ed. Ritter, A.), Norton & Company, p. 95 (Book 1, chapter 8). Hegel, G. W. F. (1977), *Phenomenology of Spirit*, Oxford University Press, pp. 111-19 (the section 'Independence and Dependence of Self-Consciousness: Lordship and Bondage').

[17] This account directly follows from Hegel's views on the historical evolution of the 'ethical life', as we will discuss in chapter 8, section 3.

[18] Green (1921), p. 24.

[19] *Ibid*, p. 25.

because the objects of his will become self-expressions of his own idea of self-perfection.[20] Obeying laws that he has imposed on himself for the goal of self-perfection, he achieves full 'moral freedom' or autonomy.

Can such moral development take place in any society, or does it require a free society that promotes freedom for all its members? Green seems to accept the latter formulation. The purely negative conception of freedom refers to a society in which only some people are free at the expense of others. In such a society, individuals run after antagonistic material interests and conceive each other as barriers or merely as a means for their selfish goals. Green thinks this to be a unsatisfactory situation, which ought ultimately give way to a higher stage in which all people would be positively free to realise themselves.[21] This requires a society organised around the notion of a 'common good' achieved through people's recognition that they have shared interests and goals.

Since every social individual needs to be recognised by others, a society of mutual recognition entails that people will consciously grasp that their own self-development is intimately connected with the development of others. In other words, self-realization can take place only in a society of mutual recognition, as Hegel proposes. Such a free society would consist of individuals who have reached (or at least could reach) the highest stage of moral development described above. Green thinks that in this case there will not be any conflicts between the positive freedoms of people because of the following reasons.

Firstly, Green replaces the 'harm principle' that reconciles the antagonistic negative freedoms of people with the notion of a 'common good'. Whereas the 'harm principle' asserts that we are free to do anything that would not harm others, the common good principle declares that we are free to do anything that would not harm the common good. This could prohibit using others as a means as well as the violation of civil rights. So, common good principle includes and goes beyond the harm principle.

Secondly, Green argues positive freedom to be not a competitive but a cooperative good; one's positive freedom presupposes and supports the positive freedom of others. In other words, this positive freedom is not possessive but relational. Positive freedom is not something that one owns (as one owns a private sphere to exercise his negative freedom), but which can only be sustained and exercised in and through specific mutually supportive social relations.

We can draw an analogy between this socially *valuable* freedom and a *good* friendship. Though a friendship may be built on any motive, a good friendship has objective and subjective preconditions. Objectively, it should be a relation between two equal people, in contrast to a relation between a master and a slave. Subjectively, friends should conceive and treat each other as equals, respect their

---

[20] *Ibid*, p. 26.

[21] Simhony describes Green's account of the stages of freedom as follows: 'Negative freedom –not being interfered by others– is a first stage in the process of self-development of the individual, whereas positive freedom (in the sense of self-control) is a higher stage in the same process.' Simhony, A. (1993), 'Beyond Negative and Positive Freedom: T. H. Green's View of Freedom', *Political Theory*, vol. 21, p. 37.

individuality, go beyond selfish motives and put some effort to sustain and contribute to the friendship as a value in itself. Similarly, it is possible to achieve individual freedom at the expense of harming others, but this cannot produce socially valuable freedom, which requires one to respect and sustain the freedom of others. It is worth quoting Green at length to illuminate his idea of a free society.

> Civil society may be, and is, founded on the idea that there being a common good, but that idea in relation to the less favoured members of society is in effect unrealised because the good is being sought in objects which admit of being competed for. They are of such a kind that they cannot be equally attained by all. The success of some in obtaining them is incompatible with the success of others. Until the object generally sought as good comes to be a state of mind or character of which the attainment, or the approach to attainment, by each is itself a contribution to its attainment by everyone else, social life must continue to be one of war –a war, indeed, in which the neutral ground is constantly being extended and which is itself constantly yielding new tendencies to peace, but in which at the same time new vistas of hostile interests, with new prospects of failure for the weaker, are as constantly opening.[22]

Although Green does not explicitly refer to Marx, there is a striking similarity between Marx's formulation of a free society as a place where 'the free development of each is the condition for the free development of all'[23] in the 'Communist Manifesto' (1847) and Green's description of the ideal society in which the attainment of positive freedom 'by each is a contribution to the attainment by everyone else' as quoted from 'Prologomena to Ethics' (1883). Both Marx and Green agree that becoming a free individual ultimately requires the existence of a free society. However, as we shall see in the last section of this chapter, Green and Marx propose different ways in which this goal can be reached. Whereas Green thinks that it can be achieved through the welfare state capitalism, Marx argues that a fully free society requires the transcendence of capitalism.

In the final analysis, Green invites us to think about the meaning and policies of 'valuable freedom', which is ignored by the defenders of pure negative freedom. The negative view claims that the content of valuable freedom is subjective; it is just a matter of personal taste and arbitrary preference that does not require discussion and consensus. In this sense, Green highlights the crucial normative aspect of freedom by focusing on the question of why we value freedom and what kind of freedoms are valuable. Furthermore, whereas the negative view takes the conflict between the self and others as natural, and inevitable, Green argues that it is specific to societies where competitive goods such as accumulation of wealth, is praised more than anything else. If we can imagine another society in which people desire self-realization and have adequate means to pursue this path, only in such a society would there be no conflicts between positive freedoms.

---

[22] Green, T. H. (1999), 'Prolegomena to Ethics: Selections', *Lectures on the Principle of Political Obligation and Other Writings* (ed. Harris, P. and Morrow, J.), Cambridge University Press, p. 279.

[23] Marx, K. (1962), 'Manifesto of the Communist Party', *Karl Marx and Frederick Engels Selected Works*, Foreign Languages Publishing House, Moscow, vol. 1, p. 54.

3. Objective Social Conditions of Freedom and the Positive Role of the State

The negative view claims freedom to be something one naturally owns and thereby thinks of policies to *protect* freedom from the 'inevitable' threats of others. On the other hand, Green devises social policies that would *promote* freedom because he conceives positive freedom not as naturally given to the individual, but as a social product, which needs to be supported actively by the state. Whereas the negative view conceives the basic function of the state as preventing interference with individual liberties, Green argues that the state should make positive reforms to 'promote the conditions favourable to moral life'.[24]

People have duties to each other and the state has obligations to its citizens, all referring to the common good. Whereas people have a moral obligation to contribute to the perfection of themselves and others, the state has a political obligation to serve the common good, by devising policies that correspond to common needs and aspirations of people. We can expect from people to fulfil their moral obligations only when the state fulfils its political obligations.

Green criticises the actual societies in so far as they violate the background conditions for these moral and political obligations. In contemporary society, which factors prevent most people from the pursuit of self-realization? Green's answer is that either people do not know how to develop themselves because of their ignorance of the various options, or there are not enough social opportunities for self-development, especially for the poor. This is why Green considers ignorance and poverty as the main barriers for self-realization, and as fundamental constraints on positive freedom.

Green's emphasis on social and economic constraints on freedom is intimately related with his critique of freedom of contract. In opposition to the negative view, he argues that freedom of contract based on voluntary consent does not automatically imply freedom for both parties. People, who do not have the material means to satisfy their basic needs, are in a vulnerable position, which may force them to accept dangerous jobs or extremely long working hours. Contracts may force the weak party to submit to the conditions set forth by another, whatever they may be.

Green draws an analogy between voluntary slavery and wage-labour. As slavery is not morally acceptable even when it is voluntarily accepted, similarly for Green, 'No contract is valid in which human persons willingly or unwillingly, are dealt with as commodities, because such contracts of necessity defeat the end for which alone society enforces contracts'.[25] For Green, this end is the common good, or the self-realization of all. But from this quote, we should not infer that Green is against wage-labour; Green wants to prevent extreme poverty and ignorance mainly because of their negative effects on moral development. As a result, for Green freedom of contract is valuable not in itself but only in so far as it is

---

[24] Green, T. H. (1999a), 'Lectures on the Principles of Political Obligation', *Lectures on the Principle of Political Obligation and Other Writings* (ed. Harris, P. and Morrow, J.), Cambridge University Press, p. 21; §18.

[25] Green (1991), pp. 23-4.

compatible with the goal of positive freedom, i.e. 'the liberation of the powers of all men equally for contributions to a common good'.[26]

Since some barriers to self-development are insurmountable by individual action, state should actively regulate 'freedom of contract' and prevent the poor from being oppressed by the rich. The 'sanitary regulations of factories, workshops and mines, ...prohibiting the labour of women and young persons beyond certain hours...and compulsory education' are necessary to prevent 'the lowering of the moral forces of society...Without a command of certain elementary arts and knowledge, the individual in modern society is effectually crippled as by the loss of a limb or a broken constitution'.[27] These ideas demonstrate the extent to which Green's views had formative influences on the development of the welfare state in 19th-century-Britain.

We should note that for Green, the state's duty is mainly negative, to 'hinder hindrances to autonomy' rather than actively encourage a particular type of good life. In Green's words, 'any direct enforcement of outward conduct...does interfere with the spontaneous action...For this reason the effectual action of the state; i.e. the community as acting through law, for the promotion of habits of true citizenship, seems necessarily to be confined to the removal of obstacles'.[28]

However, he sometimes contradicts this principle as in the case where he defends the strict control in the sale and use of alcohol, in the name of guaranteeing that all individuals realize themselves. Whereas Mill distinguishes between actions that only concern oneself and those that concern others, Green considers all individual harm as harming the social good. For example, he defends strict control on the sale of alcohol not only because drunkards create 'social nuisance', but also because every barrier to self-realization is also a restriction of the common good which involves nothing less than the self-development of each individual in society.[29] This particular example leads to the common critique against the positive view that it allows people to be 'forced to be free', which I will answer in the next section.

Another ambiguity of Green is in his use of the notion of common good; sometimes he uses this phrase to refer to the mutually compatible self-realization of all citizens, whereas other times, he simply means the actual shared interests and needs within a community. But how can we make sure that there is really a common good in this second sense? Green argues that even if one cannot articulate what the common good consists in, he habitually has an 'instinctive recognition' of the interests he shares with others.

> Very likely he does not think of it at all in connection with anything that the term 'state' represents to him. But he has a clear understanding of certain interests and rights common to himself with his neighbour –if only such as consist in getting his wages paid at the end of the week, in getting his money's worth at the shop, in the inviolability of

---

[26] *Ibid*, p. 23.

[27] *Ibid*, p. 24.

[28] Green (1999a), p. 161; §209.

[29] Green (1991), p. 29.

his own person and his wife's...It is the fault of the state if this conception fails to make him a loyal subject, if not an intelligent patriot. It is a sign that a state is not a true state– that it is not fulfilling its primary function of maintaining law equally in the interests of all, but is being administered in the interests of classes.[30]

In the above quotation we can see that Green was inspired by Rousseau's idea that for the 'general will' to be expressed, the state should embody the interests of all. Rousseau further argues that the existence a common good requires an egalitarian society. Hegel has a similar idea that a state, which does not satisfy the common needs of its citizens is not legitimate. This is a democratic and a progressive idea; we may call such states as 'citizen-friendly', in contrast with the supposedly 'neutral' state of the liberals – as state that has only negative duties.[31]

For the positive view, the state is legitimate (i.e. citizens have a political obligation to obey its laws) *only if* it has a positive, social content and serves the public good. As a result, establishing social order and security (the negative duties of the state) are not enough to create a political obligation for the citizens to obey the state's decrees. The state can promote the positive freedom of citizens and thereby become a morally and politically legitimate institution only if it also has positive duties, as well as negative ones.

Positive freedom requires social institutions and policies that would guarantee the satisfaction of basic needs for all people, so that they could both have the necessary means to develop themselves and also could be motivated by the pursuit of self-realization. 'Until life has been so organized as to afford some regular relief from the pressure of animal wants, an interest in what Aristotle calls 'living well' or 'well-being', as distinct from merely 'living' cannot emerge.'[32] Furthermore, the state could also encourage certain lines of activity such as arts and sports that could contribute to the self-realization of individuals, as defended by the 'perfectionist liberals' today.[33]

Those who are against the positive duties of the state (what they prefer to call as state 'interference' because of its repulsive connotation) claim that people should be left alone to choose their own good; otherwise people's independence and self-reliance would be restricted. Green has a double answer. Firstly, education and the availability of meaningful options are necessary for people to become good judges of their own good; articulate self-knowledge is not natural and introspective but a social achievement, as Taylor claims (in the last section of chapter 5). Secondly, even when people know their interests they do not always have the adequate socio-economic means to achieve them. Positive legal measures are necessary to rise the 'moral and material well-being' of the 'overworked women,

---

[30] Green (1999a), p. 96; §121.

[31] This point raises large issues on the relation between freedom, equality and democracy, which is beyond the scope of my book. I am mentioning this issue only because I think that combining freedom with equality and democracy serves as a better foundation for the 'citizen-friendly state' when compared with Green's more problematic notion of the 'common good'.

[32] Green (1999), p. 275.

[33] Raz, J. (1988), *The Morality of Freedom*, Clarendon Press.

the ill-housed and the untaught families…Left to itself, or to the operation of casual benevolence, a degraded population perpetuates itself'.[34]

In short, positive freedom has both objective conditions (the social and economic means for self-development) and subjective conditions (the knowledge of common interests and the pursuit of self-development). Whereas the objective conditions of freedom should be promoted by a welfare state, the subjective conditions of freedom are related to one's level of moral development and self-consciousness. The promotion of objective conditions is necessary but not sufficient for the development of subjective conditions.[35] Let us now consider some critiques of Green's views, focusing on Berlin's criticisms of the positive view.

4. Critique of Green

Berlin makes three fundamental criticisms of the positive conception of freedom and explicitly refers to Green in some of these. Firstly, he argues that Green's claim that the positive freedoms of people do not conflict is based on the assumption that there is a unique way of self-realization, true for all people.[36] Berlin tries to refute the possibility of a harmony between positive freedoms by attacking this supposed-basis.

Berlin's charge is not justified because the harmony between positive freedoms follows from Green's assumption of self-realization as a non-competitive good. Green does not presuppose that there is a unique way of self-realization; he rather assumes that various modes of self-realization can be compatible in the ideal society. This follows from Green's implicit premise that links self-realization with moral development rather than with the competitive pursuit of material gains, as well as his definition of self-realization in such a way that it would not harm others (since common good principle includes the harm principle).

Berlin's second criticism is that taking the goal of freedom as rational self-determination presupposes a 'divided self' where the 'lower' self is repressed and dominated by the 'higher self'.[37] It is true that like Hegel, Green presupposes a duality between nature and reason; reason transcends nature.[38] Both thinkers claim that freedom requires that the rational and social part of the self to dominate the

---

[34] Green (1991), p. 27.

[35] This theme goes back to Plato, Rousseau and Hegel for whom there is a 'close connection between the rationality of the individual will and the rationality of the social and political order. The individual can have a coherent and viable system of ambitions and principles only where social and political conditions are favorable' Plamenatz (1980), pp. 219-20.

[36] Berlin (1969), pp. 151, 154.

[37] *Ibid*, pp. 132, 134.

[38] Although it would serve Hegel's purposes better if he could argue that the higher, spiritual self evolves out of the lower, natural self, he cannot do this because of his pre-Darwinian framework. There remains a gap between Nature that repeats itself and Spirit, which is progressive.

appetitive and natural part. In other words, freedom implies bringing our appetites under rational control. This theme goes back to Plato and is shared by Rousseau, Kant and Hegel. However, for Hegel and Green self-discipline and self-mastery requires a *sublimation* of natural desires, rather than a *repression* or denial of them. Hegel characterises the purely negative freedom as caprice, as following any desire and contrasts it with the positive aspect of freedom, which refers to the moral evaluation of desires and integrating them through rational projects.

Simhony argues that Green has a unified rather than a divided self, because unlike Hume who marginalizes the role of reason, and Kant who divorces it from desires, for Green, 'reason and desires are inseparable in that they are constitutive of each other. Desires motivate action...only as organized and structured by reason...desires are not simply natural...and reason is practical'.[39] Although Green does not start from a duality of reason and desire, in so far as his argument is based on the assumption of a hierarchy of motives, Berlin's criticism has an element of truth. But then, this charge also applies to Mill since he relates self-realization with the pursuit of 'higher' pleasures. Instead of calling the self as a divided self (which creates the impression that there is an unbridgeable gap between two parts of the self), we can call it an internally complex self that refers to the possibility of reconciling those two aspects of the self. This is a consistent and rich theory of human nature, providing a concrete alternative to the theory of the atomistic self.

Being 'Forced to be Free'

Berlin's third criticism (the totalitarianism charge) goes as follows. Any argument which claims that the state has positive duties to promote the 'common good', would impose an arbitrarily preferred specific conception of the 'good life' on people, and thereby allow 'totalitarian' policies of freedom, and paradoxes such as 'forcing people to be free' by failing to recognize people as capable of choosing their own good.[40] In short, the charge against the positive view is that a state with positive duties is illiberal, totalitarian and anti-freedom.

I will give four arguments to defend the positive view. Firstly, the state's positive duty is to provide the opportunities for self-development rather than force citizens to develop themselves. Individuals living in a society where there are adequate opportunities for self-realization would have some positive freedom, regardless of whether they self-consciously develop themselves or not. Although those who pursue self-realization have more positive freedom and can be morally praised for Green, others can neither be blamed nor be forced to be otherwise. Everyone is legally free to pursue any life style that would not conflict with the common good. In other words, they have a legal obligation not to prevent others from self-development, which refers to instances of harm, exploitation and possibly gender oppression, as violations of the common good.

The second argument focuses on 'civil liberty' as the right to do what the laws do not forbid and emphasizes the similarities between negative and positive views.

---

[39] Simhony (1991), p. 310.
[40] Berlin (1969), pp. 157-8.

Both sides agree that absolute freedom without any restrictions is impossible in any society. Some limitation of freedom is necessary to ensure the minimum conditions of freedom and a system of laws necessarily limits some freedoms to enable other freedoms, based on a specific hierarchy of freedoms. Whereas the negative view takes absolute property rights as fundamental, the positive view gives priority to welfare rights. No matter which hierarchy of freedoms is assumed, the restriction of some liberties in the name of other more important ones cannot be labelled as being 'forced to be free'. If the US Bill of Rights does not force citizens to be free, then the policies of a welfare state also cannot force citizens to be free.

The third argument deals with moral freedom, as an important aspect of positive freedom, which is neglected by the negative view. If what the liberals consider as a constraint on freedom is indeed something that liberates us, then 'being forced to be free' would no longer be paradoxical.

The negative view assumes liberty and authority/compulsion to be antagonistic; the more of one implies the less of the other. This is why it declares that less government means more individual freedom. In contrast the positive view acknowledges that there is a form of compulsion involved in freedom. Since the achievement of positive freedom is linked with becoming a moral agent, the transformation of the natural will into a moral will in and through society is crucial. Social norms are imposed on the individual in the process of education and socialization, which always has an element of compulsion to it. It is probably in this sense that Rousseau says we can be 'forced to be free'.[41]

Rose argues that the link between liberty and discipline does not arise from a philosophical confusion, in contrast to what Berlin assumes. It is a paradox that 'to make humans free it has been necessary to subject them to all manner of compulsion, from the authority of their parents through compulsory schooling to regulation on food hygiene, sewerage and criminal activity...Freedom is an artifact of government, but it is not thereby an illusion'.[42] The positive view gives a better account of freedom because it accepts this seemingly paradoxical aspect of freedom, whereas the negative view refuses to admit the link between freedom and compulsion.

For example, the negative view assumes that 'free markets' do not involve any compulsion, since they consist of voluntary exchange relations between individuals. However, there is compulsion involved in the construction of 'free markets' because new legal and administrative means such as 'building up prisons, asylums, regulation of hours and conditions of labour, legally enforced medical interventions on sanitary reform and compulsory vaccination' are some of the means used in transforming people into wage laborers, consumers and profit-seeking agents, forcing them to act responsibly. Foucault has noted that the same people who, in the 19th century celebrated liberty also built the prison. 'People were to be 'freed' in the realms of the market, civil society, the family: they were

---

[41] Rousseau (1988), p. 95 (Book 1, chapter 7). In chapter 8, section 3 I will explain Hegel's argument that there is liberation in doing one's duty.
[42] Rose, N. (2000), *Powers of Freedom: Reframing Political Thought*, Cambridge University Press, pp. 62-3, 68.

placed outside the legitimate scope of political authorities, subject only to the limits of the law. Yet the 'freeing' of these zones was accompanied by the invention of a whole series of attempts to shape and manage conduct within them in desirable ways.'[43]

The positive view argues that freedom requires self-discipline through the process of socialization and subjection to political authority. The former component is inevitable but the latter can yield more or less freedom depending on the nature of this political authority. If the state is conceived as alien authority that has arbitrary power over its citizens then citizens do not have political freedom. This is the starting point of the fourth argument that defends the positive view against the totalitarianism charge. Political freedom or collective self-determination is a crucial aspect of positive freedom. People cannot have political freedom if they submit to an external authority, such as 'an enlightened dictator' who claims that he has privileged knowledge of the 'common good'. Whereas a benevolent tyrant can ensure negative freedoms, he can never give people positive freedom, since it is intimately linked with real democracy. Hence, people cannot be 'forced to be free' by external authorities, against their will.

In the final analysis, we have seen that what the negative view conceives as a restriction of individual freedom, indeed contributes to the enhancement of individual freedom. The possession of civil rights is necessary but not sufficient to be free. Freedom also requires that people have equal access to the material means necessary to exercise these civil liberties, this is the positive aspect of freedom. Whereas the negative view is right in emphasizing the requirement of checking state's power over the individuals through civil rights and constitutional checks, the positive view has the merit of explaining the positive function of the state in relation to the positive aspect of freedom.

The Common Good

It is now time to consider some problems about the notion of a common good, which does a lot of work in Green's political theory. Do people have a shared conception of the common good in a class-divided society? Even if we imagine an egalitarian society in which classes are eliminated, wouldn't the religious and the atheists, rightists and leftists, and different ethnic groups have different ideas of the common good? How can we expect to find a comprehensive common good for all, in a complex modern society divided along the axis of class, gender and racial differentiation?

Green would probably answer that the existence of a common good is not incompatible with the individual or social differences of opinion about what constitutes a good life. The notion of common good emphasizes the shared humane interests and needs that go beyond the avoidance of pain and the pursuit of pleasure. The 'harm principle' cannot be the basis of reconciling people's freedoms since it assumes that we do not have anything in common other than the avoidance

---

[43] *Ibid*, pp. 65, 68, 69.

of pain and harm; it reduces our common concerns to those related with our 'natural being'. In contrast, the notion of a common good highlights the interests and needs we share as moral agents, as socially embedded beings. Furthermore, the content of the common good is not static but evolves in parallel with the changing demands and aspirations of people.

Yet emphasizing the common good and shared interests should not blind us to the antagonistic interests between people. Green's argument that positive freedoms of different people cannot conflict because different modes of self-realization are compatible overlooks the deep-rooted conflicts of interests between members of different classes. In other words, Green is not justified in assuming that the 'true' interests of people will converge once everybody is provided with decent living conditions through welfare policies.

Whereas Berlin accuses Green and other advocates of the positive view of being illiberal, we may charge Green with being too liberal. For example, although Green proposes some limitations on the freedom of contract, he embraces 'unchecked freedom of appropriation' although it leads to immense inequalities of wealth. He does not favour re-distributive policies claiming that inequality of property legitimately follows from different talents and efforts of individuals and 'the right of bequest'. He agrees with Locke that the private ownership of land is better than common ownership for the social good. He thinks that workers may become 'small scale capitalists' if the state helps them to get educated and to be self-reliant, and thereby change their 'servile habits'. In contrast to his contemporary Marx, Green thinks that the problem is not with the unlimited accumulation of capital but with the moral condition of workers. It is worth quoting Green at length in order to clarify that he is not against capitalism, but rather against a minimal state.

> It is true that the accumulation of capital naturally leads to the employment of large masses of hired labourers. But there is nothing in the nature of the case to keep these labourers in the condition of living from hand to mouth, to exclude them from that education of the sense of responsibility, which depends on the possibility of permanent ownership. There is nothing in the fact that their labour is hired in great masses by the capitalists to prevent them from being on a small scale capitalists themselves...if they have education and self-discipline...It is not then to the accumulation of capital, but to the condition, due to the antecedent circumstances unconnected with that accumulation, of the men with whom the capitalist deals and whose labour he buys on the cheapest terms, that we must ascribe the multiplication in recent times of an impoverished and reckless proletariat...When we consider all this, we shall see the unfairness of laying on capitalism or the free development of individual wealth the blame which is really due to the arbitrary and violent manner in which rights over land have been acquired and exercised, and to the failure of the state to fulfil those functions which under a system of unlimited private ownership are necessary to maintain the conditions of a free life.[44]

Maybe because of the above account of capitalism, he thinks that the workers and the capitalists share the same common good since 'the interests of capital and

---

[44] Green (1999a), pp. 175-8; §227, 230.

labour are identical'.[45] Although Green has contributed to the debate on freedom by linking the subjective and objective social conditions of freedom, his notion of common good remains one of the weakest parts of his theory. In the next two chapters we will explore the metaphysical foundations of the positive view through Kant's and Hegel's accounts of moral agency and substantive autonomy.

---

[45] Green (1999b), p. 316.

Chapter 7

Kant on Rational Self-Determination

What is self-determination? Is it determination by the self, or determination of the self? In the former sense, what are determined are the objects of various choices, such as what to wear, where to live and which job to have. These are determined by the self, as opposed to being determined by other people, or by the state. This is what the negative conception of freedom understands by self-determination. It is a natural given, provided that nobody interferes with one's choices. In other words, all people are self-determining because they have freedom of choice.

On the other hand, if self-determination were determination of the self, then this would mean the determination of who one is, his tastes, values, beliefs and goals. Since one's identity is shaped by his upbringing, education, culture, it is not evident whether self-determination in this strong sense is possible. Having negative freedom and freedom of choice is not sufficient to claim that one can create and transform his self in this way. As we have seen in chapter 5, the hybrid view argues that in order to be a free agent one should also have self-consciousness and the ability to make second-order choices, so that he can project himself towards an ideal he wants to become. From now on, I will call this strong sense of self-determination rational self-determination, which lies at the centre of the positive conception of freedom.

In this chapter, we will first see how Kant relates freedom, morality and rationality. I will then argue that Berlin's attribution to positive freedom that only virtuous people are free does not apply to Kant because he links freedom, morality and rationality not in the narrow sense, but in an inclusive sense. This will add new insights about the meaning of rational self-determination and its relation to freedom.

Nevertheless, Kant's views imply an unbridgeable gap between the possibility of rational self-determination (grounded in the free will) and rational self-determination as an ideal (linked with the autonomous will) because he divorces morality from politics. In contrast to Green, Kant cannot explain under what social conditions a person with a free will can become autonomous, even though this defect makes Kant's theory immune to the 'paternalism charge'.

1. Free Will, Rationality and Moral Agency

Kant's theory of freedom is based on a duality between Nature and Reason; the former is the sphere of determinism with respect to causal laws and the latter is the seat of the free will. At other times, he refers to this distinction as referring to different 'points of view' from which one can regard himself: as a natural being and as a rational being, which Kant calls belonging to the 'world of sense' and to the 'intelligible world', respectively.[1] As natural beings, like other animals, we are subject to laws of nature; our actions have *causes*. External factors shape our desires and inclinations, and we are motivated mainly by our inclinations and desires that are directed towards achieving pleasure and refraining from pain. In other words, our actions are guided by the 'principle of happiness'.[2] On the other hand, as rational beings, we have a will; our actions have *reasons* and they are guided by the 'principle of morality'.

For Kant, having a will, acting for reasons and being a moral agent are equivalent and denote the distinctive feature of humans. These signify something more than the capacity for intentional action. Intentional action may also be impulsive and require no self-conscious choice. However, when somebody acts for reasons he is to some extent self-conscious of those reasons.

Having a will implies the possibility of having a weak will or a strong will. Kant argues that every human being is a moral agent because people have a sense of morally right and morally wrong actions even when they actually prefer the most pleasant course of action rather than the right one. Anybody can recognise that an action is pleasurable yet wrong, or unpleasant but right. In other words, even those who transgress moral principles know the validity of these principles.[3] Knowing the right course of action but acting wrongly is an exclusive human predicament. This does not imply that people always agree on what is right.

After assuming that all people are moral agents, conscious of moral principles, Kant argues that freedom is a presupposition of morality; 'since there is and must be morality, we must believe in freedom'.[4] In other words, people become conscious of their freedom through their moral consciousness, in an a priori way.[5] As Descartes says, 'I think therefore I am', Kant seems to assert 'I am moral therefore I am free', which is often expressed as 'ought' implies 'can'. The awareness that a person is a moral being means that he is not merely a natural being. Thereby, one becomes aware that his will is not determined by his inclinations and desires since he can always choose to act contrary to his strongest desires.

---

[1] Kant, I. (1997), *Groundwork of the Metaphysics of Morals*, Cambridge University Press, para. 452.
[2] *Ibid*, para. 453.
[3] *Ibid*, para. 455.
[4] Solomon, R. (1988), *Continental Philosophy Since 1750: The Rise and Fall of the Self*, Oxford University Press, p. 37.
[5] Kant, I. (2001), *Critique of Practical Reason*, Cambridge University Press, p. 4.

This capacity to act non-impulsively corresponds to a free will, a will that is not submerged in the 'world of sense'. All natural beings obey laws of nature, but humans alone can make their own laws by determining their will with respect to rational principles, and this is the basis of freedom. It is well known that Kant's theory of freedom was largely inspired by Rousseau's notion of 'moral liberty' as the 'obedience to the law that one has prescribed for oneself'.[6]

This characterization of freedom raises two questions. Firstly, why wouldn't a person be free if his actions were lawless? Secondly, even if one has to obey some rational principles, why isn't it enough if one obeys the moral norms of his society? In other words, why should one make his own laws in order to be free?

As an answer to the first question, Kant would argue that a state of lawlessness is not possible. What would appear as acting randomly, in fact means being swayed by inclinations and this would reduce a person to a mere natural being, which obeys laws of nature non-consciously, although he *appears* to be independent. In other words, even if one's actions don't have reasons, they would still have causes. Secondly, if one obeys the moral norms of his society in an uncritical way, then he would not be free but rather determined by laws and customs of that society. A moral agent can neither discover objective moral laws to guide his conduct (as Plato assumes), nor should uncritically accept the moral authority of his society. Hence, being a moral agent requires becoming a chooser of one's own reasons and moral norms.

Nevertheless, this does not imply that morality is purely subjective and changes from person to person. For a person to claim that he is acting morally, based on reasons, he should be able to argue that those reasons also apply to anybody in similar circumstances. This criterion could distinguish valid reasons from mere rationalizations. For one's subjective reasons to have universal validity, they should not be referring to his particular interests, but to principles that any *rational* being would accept, no matter what their particular interests and inclinations are. On the basis of such reasoning Kant formulates various versions of the 'moral law', which he calls the 'categorical imperative'. All moral principles are rational in the sense that firstly, they can be 'invented' by any rational agent and secondly, they are valid for all rational agents. As a result, the capacity to reason, or what Kant calls 'practical reason' makes both morality and freedom possible.

Morality is the domain of subjective and rational principles that guide action. Free will opens up the possibility of acting on the basis of moral principles and thereby the possibility of being self-determining moral agents. In Kant's words, 'a free will and a will under moral laws are one and the same'.[7] What Kant refers to by the phrase 'a will subject to moral laws' is somebody who recognizes the validity of moral laws, which does not imply that he always obeys these laws and is a virtuous person. But this is how Berlin interprets Kant's views on the inseparability of freedom and morality.

---

[6] Rousseau (1988), p. 96 (Book 1, chapter 8).
[7] Kant (1997), para. 447.

2. Berlin's Criticism and Two Senses of Rationality, Morality

Let us now focus on whether Berlin's criticism of the positive conception of freedom applies to Kant. Berlin interprets the link between freedom, morality and rationality as implying that only rational actions are good and only good actions are free. He says, for the positive conception 'freedom is not the freedom to do what is irrational, or stupid, or wrong'.[8] If this were correct, then it would imply that a person who commits a morally wrong action is not free, but since freedom is the precondition for moral responsibility, we would get the absurd consequence that people are not responsible for their evil acts. Does Kant's view really lead to such a paradoxical conclusion? Let me show that it doesn't.

There are two alternative ways to interpret Kant's identification of being rational with being moral, based on two different senses of morality and rationality. The inclusive sense contrasts rational with non-rational and moral with non-moral. All people are rational and moral in the sense that they can act for reasons and they can evaluate their actions with respect to moral principles. In contrast, animals and machines are non-rational and non-moral because they do not have a free will and their behaviour is causally determined.

The second sense of rationality and morality is the narrow sense that applies not to agents, but to actions. Accordingly, rational action is contrasted with irrational action and moral action is the opposite of immoral action. For Kant, the degree of morality and immorality of an action depends on the way the underlying will is determined. If the will is completely determined by inclinations, then the action is irrational (since it is not based on reasons) and immoral (since it is not guided by moral principles). If the will is determined completely by respect for the moral law, which amounts to acting from duty, then the action is moral, hence rational. Kant admits that in most particular cases, the will is determined by both inclinations and moral principles. Furthermore, the real motives of action may be hidden from the person.[9] Hence, we cannot classify all actions into two pigeonholes of moral and immoral actions; they are the two ends of a spectrum and most real actions fall somewhere in between.

Let us have a closer look at Kant's classification of actions with respect to the narrow sense of morality. Kant classifies actions according to their motivations (source of determination of the will) as right or wrong. Acting from duty is right and acting from inclination is wrong. He also classifies actions with respect to their consequences as good or bad. Acting in conformity to duty is good, whereas acting contrary to duty is bad. As a result, actions are classified into four groups: moral, not immoral, not moral and immoral. Moral and not immoral actions are autonomous since they stem from duty; not moral and immoral actions are heteronomous since they are externally determined by the inclinations. We can schematise Kant's classification of actions as follows:

---

[8] Berlin (1969), p. 148.
[9] Kant (1949), *Fundamental Principles of the Metaphysics of Morals*, The Liberal Arts Press, p. 24.

Consequences Motivations	Good	Bad
Right	Acting from duty Acting in conformity to duty ∴ Moral / Rational (Doing the right thing, for the right reason)	Acting from duty Acting contrary to duty ∴ Not immoral / Not irrational (Doing the wrong thing, for the right reason or with good will)
Wrong	Acting from inclination Acting in conformity to duty ∴ Not moral / Not rational (Doing the right thing, for the wrong reason)	Acting from inclination Acting contrary to duty ∴ Immoral / Irrational (Doing the wrong thing, for the wrong reason)

Berlin interprets Kant's views on the inseparability of freedom, rationality and morality with respect to the narrow sense, whereas I will argue that the inclusive sense is the correct interpretation. In other words, Kant does not argue that the irrational and immoral actions are not free, but rather he asserts that non-rational and non-moral creatures are not free. If we express this in Hegelian terminology, animal behaviour is non-moral since it is the non-mediated satisfaction of impulses and instincts; human action is moral in so far as satisfaction of desires is mediated through reason. Since people can choose their ends through critical reflection, moral and rational human action that is based on reasons is categorically different from impulsive behaviour. Hence, a rational being is identical with a moral being in the inclusive sense.

This interpretation seems to have a very thin content; it states that morality, rationality and freedom are exclusive features of humans. Nevertheless, this underlines an important distinction between negative and positive conceptions of freedom. For the defenders of a negative conception of freedom, human freedom is not different from the freedom of animals, or even rivers. Freedom is a natural property of all things capable of movement. In Hobbes' words,

> Liberty, or freedom, signifies the absence of opposition; (by opposition I mean external impediments of motion) and may be applied no less to irrational and inanimate creatures, than to rational...And so of all living creatures, whilst they are imprisoned or restrained, with walls, or chains; and of the water whilst it is kept in by banks, or vessels, that otherwise would spread itself into a larger space, we use to say, they are not at liberty.[10]

In contrast, for the advocates of a positive conception of freedom, freedom is not naturalistic; it belongs exclusively to humans, and it stems from the faculty of reason. For Kant, since freedom is based on our moral capacities, cultivation of freedom is linked with the exercise of these moral capacities and faculties.

---

[10] Hobbes (1996), p. 204.

Otherwise, even if we are independent to satisfy our desires (similar to animals) this independence does not imply freedom. Freedom is due to reason and it transcends nature.

O'Neill and Rawls interpret Kant's views with respect to the inclusive sense of rationality and morality. O'Neill remarks that the moral will should not be associated with a virtuous person because Kant only claims that 'a free will is a will capable of moral action, and not that all free action is actually morally acceptable: a will capable of moral action is also capable of immoral action.'[11] So, freedom implies the freedom to make mistakes or even to choose evil. Indeed, Kant argues that people are always responsible for their wrong deeds, no matter what social and environmental factors have motivated them to commit crimes.

> For whatever his previous deportment may have been, whatever natural causes may have been influencing him, and whether these causes were to be found within him or outside him, his action is yet free and determined by none of these causes; hence it can and must always be judged as an *original* use of his will. He should have refrained from that action, whatever his temporal circumstances and entanglements; for through no cause in the world can he cease to be a freely acting being.[12]

Rawls shows us the roots of the narrow and inclusive interpretations of Kant, in two different theories about human nature. He claims that Kant's moral theory is ambiguous. One can find enough evidence to interpret it in accordance with the 'Manichean moral psychology' or the 'Augustinian moral psychology'.

In Manichean moral psychology, a person is made up of the good self (as a rational being) that has a 'predisposition…to act from moral law' and a bad self (as a natural being) that is guided towards the goal of happiness. Rawls claims that interpreting Kant in this way may lead to 'moral fatalism'.[13] It faces the difficulty of linking freedom and responsibility because our good deeds naturally stem from the 'good self' and the bad deeds are a result of the 'bad self'. This leaves no place for the idea of an agent who is above those two selves and actively chooses which path to take. Dismissing the idea of a free chooser, who can also make errors, results in the denial of the link between freedom and responsibility.[14] Moreover, if

---

[11] O'Neill, O. (2000), *Bounds of Justice*, Cambridge University Press, p. 44.

[12] Kant, I. (1960), *Religion Within the Limits of Reason Alone*, Harper & Row, p. 36.

[13] Rawls, J. (2000), *Lectures on the History of Moral Philosophy*, Harvard University Press, pp. 303-5. I am grateful to my supervisor Prof Sean Sayers for calling my attention to Rawls' interesting interpretation of Kant.

[14] It should be remarked that the link between freedom and responsibility is controversial. For example, the ancient Greek conception of freedom was not related to individual responsibility. Also in modern times, Nietzsche has argued that the link between freedom and responsibility is valid only for a particular theory of action. According to Nietzsche, free will is a myth invented to make men accountable, punishable for their actions. 'Men were thought of as free so that they could become guilty; consequently, every action had to be thought of as willed, the origin of every action as lying in consciousness'. He draws the radical conclusion that since no one gives a person his qualities (neither his environment,

the 'true self' is taken as equivalent to the 'good self', then this would open the way towards Berlin's criticism that advocates of positive freedom legitimize the repression of the empirical bad self, by the rational good self in the name of freedom.[15]

On the other hand, 'Augustinian moral psychology' does not posit a divided self and thereby 'overcomes these defects by attributing to the self a free power of choice and enough complexity for a satisfactory account of responsibility...The origin of moral evil, then, lies not in a bad self with its natural desires but solely in the free power of choice'.[16] According to this view, both moral and immoral actions are freely chosen as opposed to non-moral actions, which are not chosen. So, in contrast to what Berlin attributes to Kant, non-virtuous actions are also free actions, provided that they are not purely impulsive.

> That choice which can be determined by pure reason is called *free choice*. That which can be determined only by inclination...would be *animal choice*. *Human choice*, however, is a choice that can indeed be affected but not determined by impulses...*Freedom of choice* is this independence from being determined by sensible impulses; this is the *negative concept of freedom*. The *positive concept of freedom* is that of the ability of pure reason to be of itself practical.[17]

So far, we have dealt mainly with Kant's negative concept of freedom based on the free will. We have also demonstrated that Kant equates freedom with rationality and morality in their inclusive senses. But does Kant also use rationality and morality in their narrow senses? In order to answer this question, we should focus on how Kant relates freedom with autonomy, which would also highlight his positive concept of freedom.

3. Autonomy, Virtue and Rational Self-Determination as an Ideal

Kant first shows the possibility of rational self-determination, by associating it with the free will and secondly, he asserts rational self-determination as an ideal, by linking it with the autonomous will. With these arguments, he shows that rational self-determination is not a natural given but something to be achieved. Nevertheless, he cannot establish under which social conditions rational self-determination becomes actualised; this task is left to Hegel.

Kant defines autonomy positively in a three-fold way. Firstly, 'autonomy of the will is that property of it by which it is a law to itself (independently of any

---

nor himself), there is no accountability. Nietzsche, F. (1990), *Twilight of the Idols/ The Anti-Christ*, Penguin Books, pp. 64-5.

[15] Berlin (1969), p. 132.

[16] Rawls (2000), p. 305.

[17] Kant, I. (1996), 'Metaphysics of Morals', *Practical Philosophy*, Cambridge University Press, p. 375. Elsewhere, Kant expresses the positive concept of freedom as the 'consciousness of the freedom of the will'. Kant (2001), p. 37.

property of the objects of volition)'.[18] In other words, any will that completely determines itself by rational/moral principles is an autonomous will. Secondly, autonomy is the only thing we know about the absolutely good will; the objects of an absolutely good will are indeterminate but its form is autonomy.[19] Thirdly, the moral law (categorical imperative) commands autonomy, as well as presupposing autonomy.[20]

He also defines autonomy negatively, by contrasting it with the 'heteronomous will', which is either determined by *external causes* (contingent desires and inclinations), or by *external purposes* (when a person wills something not because it has an intrinsic worth, but as a means to happiness, or perfection), or by the *external authorities* (when one submits to religious, political or legal authorities).[21] In short, when characterized negatively, an autonomous will is independent from external causes, purposes and authorities.

The positive content of autonomy is obeying only those moral laws that one has prescribed to himself, or being self-directing. In other words, freedom of the will lies in its autonomy.[22] The will is free because its object is not causally determined by the external world; but the will *becomes* autonomous when its object is internally determined.

Autonomy is the same as the ideal of rational self-determination, where rationality is taken in its narrow sense.[23] This is an ideal to which all moral agents should aspire, but none can fully achieve. Partaking in both the realm of nature and the realm of reason, all moral agents are imperfect since they are not guided by moral principles in all their actions. In Kant's words,

> All my actions as only a member of the world of understanding [the intelligible world] would therefore conform perfectly with the principle of autonomy of the pure will. As only a part of the world of sense they would have to be taken to conform wholly to the natural law of desires and inclinations, hence to the heteronomy of nature.[24]

Hence, if people were purely autonomous they would always act in accordance with the moral law; it would be like their second nature rather than an imperative. Since people have an internally complex self with conflicting motivations, following the moral law is an imperative and autonomy is the aspired destination. This reveals three senses of autonomy. Autonomy as an ideal corresponds to virtuous people; the capacity for autonomy is common to all moral agents, and autonomy is a predicate that applies to actions in greater or lesser degree. The more we can determine our actions on the basis of objective principles that we impose on ourselves, the more autonomous our actions become.

---

[18] Kant (1949), p. 57.

[19] *Ibid*, p. 61.

[20] *Ibid*, p. 57.

[21] Kant (2001), p. xxvi.

[22] Kant (1997), para. 447.

[23] People with autonomous and those with heteronomous will are both moral in the inclusive sense, but a heteronomous will is not moral in the narrow sense.

[24] *Ibid*, para. 453.

The inclusive and narrow senses of rationality and morality are related in the following way. When rationality and morality in the inclusive sense are fully developed (which is an individual achievement through using one's theoretical and practical reason), then they converge into rationality and morality in the narrow senses, i.e. the virtuous individuals of the 'kingdom of ends'.[25] Kant posits virtue as an ideal that we should always aspire to, although we can never practically achieve. 'Virtue is always in progress...it is an ideal and unattainable, while yet constant approximation to it is a duty.' Since human nature is always affected by inclinations, 'virtue can never settle down in peace and quiet with its maxims adopted once and for all, but if it is not rising, is unavoidably sinking'.[26]

Kant's 'negative concept of freedom' refers to morality in the inclusive sense, and the 'positive concept of freedom' refers to morality in the narrow sense or to virtue. Since humans are rational and moral beings, they have dignity, which refers to their intrinsic value. Their rationality imposes on them a universal duty to seek their own 'perfection' by cultivating their faculties. Virtue is an important component of this ideal, 'human morality in its highest stage'.[27] In Kant's words, virtue is 'a self-constraint in accordance with a principle of inner freedom'; 'virtue is the moral strength of a human being's will in fulfilling his duty, a moral constraint through his own lawgiving reason'.[28]

The link between inclusive and narrow senses of rationality and morality can also be explained as analogous to the relationship between *is* and *ought*. The inclusive sense explains what it *is* to be a human, and the narrow sense deduces moral obligations and duties that every rational being *ought* to conform, to be 'worthy of humanity'. In Kant's words, since moral laws hold for every rational being, 'we must derive them from the general concept of a rational being'.[29] This is an instance of 'ethical naturalism', where an idea of human good is deduced from an idea of human nature. In Kant's words,

> A human being has a duty to raise himself from the crude state of his nature, from his animality, more and more toward humanity, by which alone he is capable of setting himself ends; he has a duty to diminish his ignorance by instruction and to correct his errors...The capacity to set oneself an end –any end whatsoever– is what characterizes humanity (as distinguished from animality). Hence, there is also bound up with the end of humanity in our own person the rational will, and so the duty, to make ourselves worthy of humanity by culture.[30]

Nevertheless, this interpretation (the link between is and ought) faces two problems. Firstly, it is controversial whether one can deduce concrete moral obligations and duties from the purely formal criteria of universalizibility and what

---

[25] Kant defines 'kingdom of ends' as the union of rational beings by common laws and says that it is only an ideal. Kant (1949), p. 49.

[26] Kant (1996), p. 537.

[27] *Ibid*, pp. 515-7.

[28] *Ibid*, pp. 525, 533.

[29] Kant (1949), p. 29.

[30] Kant (1996), pp. 518, 522.

it means to be a human. As we shall see in the next chapter (chapter 8, section 2), this is one of Hegel's criticisms of Kant's moral theory, as lacking any content. Secondly, it is not clear whether Kant's system would allow deducing 'ought' from 'is', since morality is an autonomous domain for Kant. The distinctness of facts and values corresponds to the separateness of phenomena and noumena. As long as Kant cannot establish a relation between these two domains, he cannot adequately bridge the inclusive and narrow senses of morality.

4. Conditions for Actualising Rational Self-Determination

The ideal of autonomy puts forward certain preconditions for people to achieve rational self-determination, in greater degree. Firstly, all moral actions are grounded in subjective principles that mediate desires and the agent should have a strong will so that he would act in conformity to those principles. Secondly, those subjective principles of action (or what Kant calls the 'maxims') should be universalizable in a consistent way. In Kant's words 'we must be able to will that a maxim of our action should be a universal law'.[31] This gives us the first formulation of the moral law, the 'categorical imperative'. If an action is moral then one must will its maxim to be a universal law for everyone. Thirdly, the moral action should be such that it respects the inherent dignity of all people that are affected by the action. This means not treating people merely as a means, but always as ends-in-themselves, which is the second formulation of the moral law.[32]

The first formulation of the moral law (universality of the maxim) shows us the universal form of an autonomous will, whereas the second formulation of the moral law (treating people as ends in themselves) gives autonomy a positive and pluralistic content.[33] It puts forward a criterion that justifies some restriction of everyone's freedom of action so that everyone can have an autonomous will. If a person treats others merely as an instrument (as in the case when he is part of a relation of domination) then he cannot have an autonomous will even when he has a strong will and acts morally.

This can be the basis of a critique of exchange relations of market economy, where everyone treats each other merely as a means to advance his self-interest. Liberals answer this objection as follows: since nobody violates the legal rights of each other in market relations, everyone's dignity is respected. Kant would not fully endorse this answer since he argues that the principle of respect requires not only the 'maintenance' of humanity as an end-in-itself, but also the 'advancement' of humanity as an end-in-itself.[34] The latter goal requires the development of people's talents and capacities. But since Kant calls these 'imperfect duties' and claims that external law cannot enforce imperfect duties, it seems that we can neither impose any positive duties to the state, nor expand the scope of human

---

[31] Kant (1949), p. 41.

[32] *Ibid*, p. 45.

[33] *Ibid*, p. 53.

[34] *Ibid*, p. 47.

rights on the basis of these imperfect duties. Alternatively, we may argue that Kant's respect principle extends the notion of harm by including cases of degradation, exploitation and degrading work conditions as instances of harm.

Although Kant links freedom with morality, he divorces morality and politics in two ways. Firstly, the source of ethical obligations is the identification with a non-historical, imaginary community of rational men, which he calls 'the kingdom of ends', rather than through identification with the institutions of one's actual community as Hegel claims. Secondly, moral norms cannot provide an agenda for reform in politics. Kant argues that we cannot guarantee the existence of a real 'kingdom of ends', where everyone would have an autonomous will. The kingdom of ends is not a political ideal; 'the moral condition of men is beyond the scope of politics. Political society cannot take as one of its goals of making men become moral beings'.[35] For these reasons, Kant's political theory converges to the utilitarian political theory, where the problem of politics is considered as limiting the negative freedom of people so that they can peacefully coexist.[36]

The separation of morality from politics makes Kant's theory of freedom immune to the liberal charge that any positive conception of freedom would involve a 'paternalistic' state. Since, politics can neither be organised towards making people virtuous, nor towards making them happy (by favouring a particular conception of the good life above others) the totalitarianism charge does not apply to Kant.[37]

Kant's theory of freedom is unaffected by the paternalism objection only at the cost of making autonomy an abstract, universal capacity on the one hand, and a non-historical ideal on the other hand. In the former sense all people are autonomous agents and in the latter sense no one can be fully autonomous (since virtue is always beyond our reach).[38]

In the previous chapter we have seen that, in contrast to Kant, Green points out the social preconditions and duties of the state so that it would 'hinder hindrances to moral autonomy'. In this way, autonomy is transferred from a transcendent ideal to a feasible political achievement. Green's account of freedom is largely influenced by Hegel's views. In the next chapter we will explore how Hegel remedies the defects of Kant's theory through his notion of 'concrete freedom'.

---

[35] Taylor, C. (1985), 'Kant's Theory of Freedom', *Philosophy and the Human Sciences: Philosophical Papers*, vol. 2, Cambridge University Press, pp. 326-7.
[36] Taylor, C. (1996), *Hegel and Modern Society*, Cambridge University Press, p. 78.
[37] Taylor (1985), p. 332.
[38] If Kant had emphasized the need for moral education and some positive duties of the state as preconditions for the actualization of autonomy, this would have made autonomy dependent on contingent social requirements. It would then conflict with Kant's argument that any human being can aspire to the ideal of autonomy, merely because he is a rational/moral being.

Chapter 8

Hegel on Concrete Freedom

In *Philosophy of Right* Hegel uses the dialectical method in order to make an exposition of the conceptual development of the idea of freedom. Accordingly, the idea of free will determines itself by passing from more abstract to more concrete moments or stages. The first stage includes the 'immediate or natural will' determined as 'abstract personality' within the sphere of 'formal right'. In the next stage, the 'self-reflective or moral will' is determined as 'subjective individuality' in the sphere of morality. This process culminates in the unity of these two moments in the 'free will in itself and for itself' determined as 'concrete individuality' within the sphere of the 'ethical life' (*Sittlichkeit*). Hegel remarks that this conceptual sequence may be different from the 'temporal sequence of their actual appearance'.[1] Hence, the above sequence does not directly correspond to the historical evolution of different forms of freedom. Hegel passes from one stage to another claiming that being one-sided, it necessarily gives way to the other stage, which negates it, and this process ends in the 'negation of the negation' that gives us both the totality and the most adequate notion of freedom.

In my exploration of Hegel's theory of freedom I will interpret him as arguing against two rival positions. The first stage of 'natural will' corresponds to the purely negative aspect of freedom, which is mistakenly identified with the whole of freedom by the liberal position. Hegel argues that this standpoint captures an important aspect of modern freedom, but by itself it is not enough to give an adequate account of what freedom involves. In Hegel's words it implicates particularity without universality. The second stage of 'moral will' corresponds to the purely positive aspect of freedom, which is exemplified by Kant. Although this viewpoint grasps another dimension of freedom, it is also abstract and inadequate since it involves subjectivity without objectivity. As we shall see in this chapter, Hegel tries to do justice to those standpoints whilst avoiding their abstract understanding of freedom, through his notion of 'concrete freedom', which is 'being with oneself in an other' or self-realization in and through relations with others.

---

[1] Hegel, G. W. F. (1995), *Elements of the Philosophy of Right*, Cambridge University Press, para. 32A, 33A.

1. The Negative Aspect of Freedom

Hegel describes the negative aspect of freedom as independence from immediate determination by natural factors, which resides in the 'indeterminacy' of the will. He argues that the 'pure indeterminacy' of the will is based on the 'absolute possibility of abstracting from every determination...the flight from every content as a limitation'.[2] In other words, freedom from natural determination is the negative aspect of freedom, which stems from the will.

Having a will is something more than having the capacity for intentional action. An intentional action can be immediate and impulsive (as in the case of animals) or mediated through subjective reasons. Although animals can act intentionally, they cannot have a will because having a will implies not only the capacity for intentional action but also the possibility of *not* being able to translate intentions into action due to internal factors, as in the case when someone has a weak will.

Whereas animals are immediately motivated by their desires, humans mediate these through the faculty of will. This enables not only a choice of which desire to act upon, based on a comparison of the strength and consequences of various desires, but also a second-order evaluation of the value and significance of particular desires. As a result, humans are free from natural determination since they can choose to act against even their strongest desires. Suicide is an example of a person's overcoming his strongest natural impulse for survival.

In this way, having a will opens up both the possibility of freedom and unfreedom (due to internal constraints such as the lack of self-mastery). The power to mediate desires makes a person rational (and moral) in the inclusive sense, as opposed to animals and machines. As we have seen in the previous chapter, Kant has a similar understanding of the negative aspect of freedom.

An important difference between Kant's and Hegel's understanding of the negative aspect of freedom stems from their different understandings of the function of the will. Whereas Kant uses the will to reinforce a duality within the self (between reason and desires) Hegel conceives the will as the key to reuniting the internally complex self. For Kant, when an action is motivated by desires, rather than by pure respect for the moral law then it is irrational or not rational.[3] In contrast, Hegel thinks that desires as such are not irrational. Since every action is mediated by the will, even a person whose actions are motivated only by desires is 'rational in-itself'.

> The immediate or natural will is only free in itself, i.e. the naturally determined drives, desires, inclinations are its immediately present content, which originates in the will's rationality and it is thus rational in itself, but expressed in so immediate a form, it does not yet have the form of rationality...The animal, too, has drives, desires and inclinations, but it has no will and must obey its drive if nothing external prevents it. But the human being, as wholly indeterminate, stands above his drives and can determine

---

[2] *Ibid*, para. 5.
[3] See the schema in chapter 7, section 2.

and posit them as his own. The drive is part of nature, but to posit it in this 'I' depends upon my will.[4]

How does Hegel's description of the negative aspect of freedom apply to the liberal understanding of freedom? Both social contract theory and the utilitarian version of liberalism take people as naturally free and consider social relations and the state as imposing external constraints on this natural freedom.[5] Hegel refers to this aspect of freedom when he says that we are free simply in virtue of having a will. Nevertheless, the liberal view is mistaken in taking this negative aspect as the whole of freedom. Freedom also has a positive aspect (rational self-determination) and social institutions form the necessary context for this aspect of freedom.

Whereas liberals assume a fundamental conflict between the self and others, Kant and Hegel see the fundamental division as being between nature and the self. According to the latter, a person can, does and ought to transcend his natural existence. Consequently, for the liberal defenders of negative freedom natural factors do not constrain freedom, whereas for the defenders of positive freedom determination by natural factors prevents one from becoming free. Freedom is something that has to be achieved through a development of certain capacities, in particular the capacity for rationality and morality.

Another pitfall of identifying freedom with the merely negative aspect is that freedom then gets reduced to arbitrary action. This is what Hegel calls freedom as indeterminacy, which is expressed by the liberal view as the possibility to act as one pleases. However, for Hegel concrete freedom is not merely the possibility of arbitrary action but a 'determinate way of acting'.[6]

> Since I have the possibility of determining myself in this or that direction –that is, since I am able to choose– I possess an arbitrary will, and this is what is usually called freedom... The common man thinks that he is free when he is allowed to act arbitrarily, but this very arbitrariness implies that he is not free.[7]

When I arbitrarily choose some content to my will, it then determines me by leading to the subordination and sacrifice of other desires that also demand satisfaction. The problem is that the arbitrary will has no objective yardstick to decide which object to choose, which course of action to take. But freedom of choice requires the existence of a specific criterion to evaluate various options and desires. This is why liberals are mistaken in taking freedom of choice as identical with the freedom to refuse. Being not completely determined by natural and social factors, the will is free to refuse any particular content. Freedom of choice requires not only the freedom to refuse but also the existence of a particular kind of self-reflective action.

---

[4] *Ibid*, para. 11, A.
[5] Hegel, G. W. F. (1988), *Introduction to the Philosophy of History*, Hackett Publishing Company, p. 43.
[6] Wood, A. (1990), *Hegel's Ethical Thought*, Cambridge University Press, p. 39.
[7] Hegel (1995), para. 15A.

Hegel means two things when he talks about the arbitrary will. The will is arbitrary when it has an immediate *form*, and a particular, contingent *content*.[8] Let us apply these criteria to the natural will. Firstly, the natural will immediately translate the most pressing desire into action. The goal of happiness imposes 'abstract universality' on the content of the will by providing some criterion to compare desires, but it is still purely subjective. Secondly, the object of desire has no essential relation to the self. The self could have chosen some other desire, and other objects could well have satisfied the same desire. Hegel calls this the 'double indeterminacy' of the arbitrary, natural will.[9] In the final analysis, freedom of the will as arbitrariness stems from 'reflection which abstracts from everything, and the dependence on an inwardly or externally given content'.[10] The natural will is dependent on an externally given content whereas the purely 'moral will' (which will be explained when considering the positive aspect of freedom) has an internally given content. They constitute two different cases of the arbitrary will for Hegel.

Identifying freedom only with its negative aspect makes freedom something that is shared by everybody, stemming from the free will. It disregards that liberation is a process that requires the development of self-consciousness and the projection of the self towards a direction that he chooses, which is also open to further revisions.

> In order to be ourselves we must be always becoming something which we are not, in other words, we must always recognize that we are something more than we have become; liberty, as the condition of our being ourselves, cannot simply be something which we have, still less something which we always had –a *status quo* to be maintained. It must be a condition relevant to our continued struggle to assert the control of something in us, which we recognize as imperative upon us or as our real self, but which we only obey in a very imperfect degree.[11]

Bosanquet's reference to the 'real self' is similar to Kant's idea of the 'moral will' (who acts only from moral duty) that refers to the positive aspect of freedom. Bosanquet emphasizes that the self should not be taken as static, in the moment of choice, as determined by his choice, but rather within a continuous process of becoming. This makes freedom an achievement that requires rational self-control.

The purely negative aspect of freedom refers firstly to the faculty of the will that transcends natural determination, and secondly to a specific way of exercising the will in arbitrary action (without a universal goal that integrates various desires and where the subject is not really self-conscious of the significance of his action). The negative view is mistaken in identifying freedom with only the negative aspect of freedom, which leads it to conceive freedom as being lawless. This view thereby fails to recognise how freedom is intimately related with abiding laws. Hegel calls

---

[8] *Ibid*, para. 19.
[9] *Ibid*, para. 12.
[10] *Ibid*, para. 15.
[11] Bosanquet, B. (1955), *The Philosophical Theory of the State*, Macmillan, p. 118.

the purely negative aspect of freedom particularity without universality. We will now consider how the purely positive aspect of freedom complements these defects, but is inadequate in other respects.

2. The Positive Aspect of Freedom

The positive aspect of freedom is the power of self-determination; it is the ability of the will to determine itself, which requires both the development of self-consciousness and the achievement of rational self-control. These positive abilities can only develop through social life. Hegel charges Kant with failing to acknowledge this necessary social context of the positive aspect of freedom and thereby arriving at another abstract notion of freedom.

Hegel relates the purely positive aspect of freedom with the 'moral will' that has a positive power for self-determination. Self-consciousness is the basis of subjective freedom; it involves acting on the basis of one's own reasons. Hegel exemplifies this purely positive aspect of freedom with Kant's moral theory because Kant has grasped that freedom is not a state of lawlessness, but rather the self-imposition of laws.

Both Kant and Hegel agree the consciousness of freedom emerges through moral consciousness, or through the recognition of the moral will. Hegel expresses the difference between the purely negative and the purely positive aspects of freedom by emphasizing the role of self-consciousness, by distinguishing between the 'freedom in itself' (freedom as a capacity) and the 'freedom for itself' (the subjective consciousness of freedom).

> The child is *in itself* a human being, it has reason only *in itself*, it is only the potentiality of reason and freedom...The human being who is rational *in himself* must work through the process of self-production by going out of himself and by educating himself inwardly, in order that he may also become rational *for himself*.[12]

In the above quotation, 'inward education' refers both to the will's taking itself as an object, conceiving itself as a raw material to be shaped and also a person's awareness that self-discipline is required for self-creation. In the Hegelian terminology, it corresponds to the development of subjectivity, the development of the moral will through culture and education. What Hegel means by 'going out of himself' is the transcendence of merely particular existence towards universality.

We had characterised the negative view as particularity without universality. Now, let us see how the positive view incorporates universality. For Kant, the natural will is shaped by particular inclinations, whereas the moral will obeys universal moral duties imposed by transcendent reason. Kant assumes a duality between transcendent, universal reason and particular, contingent desires. The moral will is universal because it acts on the basis of universal duties.

---

[12] Hegel (1995), para. 10A.

Like Kant, Hegel associates particularity with the immediate existence of the natural will, and links universality with the moral will. In contrast to Kant, Hegel argues that there is continuity between the natural will and the moral will. Through the process of socialization the former is transformed into the latter. Rational self-determination does not mean escaping from desires, or repressing them by reason, but rather mediating, integrating and sublimating desires through reason (embodied in social norms). This is the first difference between Kant's and Hegel's notion of the self. Whereas Kant assumes a divided self, Hegel takes the self as internally complex.

Hegel also emphasizes self-consciousness as another source of the universality of the will. In his words, it is *'particularity* reflected *into itself* and thereby restored to *universality'*.[13] Self-consciousness is not merely a relation of the self with himself, but it is mediated through relations with others. In other words, self-consciousness develops through the recognition that one is a social being whose identity is shaped within concrete social relations, institutions and practices. As a result, for both Kant and Hegel moral will is universal, a feature that was absent in the natural will assumed by the purely negative conception of freedom.

Hegel appreciates the merit of Kant's moral theory in emphasizing the relationship between freedom and duty. For both thinkers, 'in doing my duty, I am with myself and free'. However, for Hegel, Kant's notion of duty is 'indeterminate', 'abstract universality' and 'empty formalism'. Hegel says 'the point of view of Kant's philosophy is sublime inasmuch as it asserts the conformity of duty and reason, but...is defective in that it lacks all articulation'.[14]

Hegel's best known criticism of Kantian morality is the above-mentioned charge of its emptiness. According to one interpretation, Hegel criticises Kant's categorical imperative for being incapable of providing a criterion to separate morally right and wrong actions; according to another interpretation, which I will assume, Kant's moral law cannot generate concrete moral duties.[15]

Kant considers moral duties as devoid of any empirical content; they are supposed to be generated only through the principle of non-contradiction, according to the first formulation of the moral law (i.e. 'So act that you can will the maxim of your action be a universal law'.) If this is the case, then we cannot deduce any specific duties from such a formal principle. Otherwise, if it can generate specific duties, then this is only because Kant implicitly assumes the legitimacy of some social institutions, and thereby introduces an empirical content.

Another way to express the emptiness charge is that, the moral law is empty because the moral will is empty.[16] For Kant, good will is the will that acts from duty for duty's sake; acting from other empirical motives and interests are ruled out as being against the moral disposition. In contrast, for Hegel moral actions stem from the responsibilities associated with concrete social roles. For example, a mother's caring behaviour to her child is the manifestation of a moral disposition,

---

[13] *Ibid*, para. 7.
[14] *Ibid*, para. 135A.
[15] Wood (1990), p. 154.
[16] *Ibid*, p. 168.

although it is not done merely for the sake of an abstract duty. As a result, Kant has failed to see that empirical interests, needs and social relations are the real basis of moral actions. Our moral duties are not abstract and universal but concrete and specific to the socio-historical context. This defect is based on Kant's assuming an abstract individual rather than a socially embedded individual.

Hegel considers this deficiency as not specific to Kant but as an inherent feature of the standpoint of morality (*Moralität*), which he contrasts with the standpoint of the 'ethical life' (*Sittlichkeit*). Morality denotes the domain of formal, universal principles that are supposed to apply throughout history in all societies, whereas ethical life refers to specific duties defined within actual social institutions and practices.[17]

The moral standpoint in fact reflects the self-consciousness of the modern bourgeoisie whose dominant mode of action is private self-seeking. 'It fails to appreciate the specificity of the social relationships because private individuals see these relationships only as a natural expression of their contingent, particular volition.'[18] The duties and virtues of the bourgeois are taken to be universally binding and they are identified with the moral will.

On the other hand, ethical life has both an objective and a subjective aspect. The objective side refers to concrete social institutions – in particular the family, civil society and the modern political state – whereas the subjective aspect denotes the self-consciousness of individuals as shaped by participating in these institutions.[19]

Hegel's point is that unless we take the individual as socially embedded within specific social institutions and relations, we cannot reach concrete moral duties that would liberate us. Thereby, Hegel challenges all individualistic accounts of morality that take moral principles as either products of a priori reason or of pure individual deliberation, regardless of one's social context.

Replacing the point of view of morality with that of ethics implies that reason is not transcendent but is immanent within the real world, concretely embodied in social institutions.

> It was Hegel's great achievement to see human consciousness, will and reason in concrete and dialectical, social, historical and developmental terms. Practical – moral and political – ideals, he insists, are not the product of a transcendent reason operating *a priori*, nor are they purely subjective. On the contrary they are historical products and arise out of and reflect 'the ethical world' (that is to say social institutions and relations). He rejects the dualism which is presupposed by the Kantian philosophy. 'Reason is in the world', says Hegel, it is a social product and does not need to be brought from outside by the 'critical' philosopher.[20]

In the previous chapter, we have seen that Kant has defined freedom as rational self-determination. By changing the meaning of rationality Hegel also brings new

[17] Hegel (1995), para. 33.
[18] Wood (1990), p. 132.
[19] *Ibid*, p. 196.
[20] Sayers, S. (1998), *Marxism and Human Nature*, Routledge, p. 97.

insights into the meaning of freedom. Subjectively, rational self-determination denotes the process in which self-consciousness evolves in parallel with one's changing relations with others. Objectively, it denotes a free society, in which the subjective and objective aspects of the ethical life correspond to each other. In other words, a free or rational society is a place in which the social institutions do fulfil individual aspirations and needs. This is not self-evident because on the one hand, any social order may produce some needs that it fails to satisfy. On the other hand, being a moral agent and having subjective freedom, the individual does not completely internalise social norms and values; he can also develop a critical attitude.

3. Concrete Freedom

Hegel defines the concrete concept of freedom as self-realization in and through relations with others, which he formulates as 'being with oneself in the other.' Humans are socially embedded beings; one's identity and self-consciousness are constituted through his specific social relations. To put it differently, individuality is achieved and extended through relating with others. As these social relations become more universal, comprehensive and various, the boundaries of the self are extended. Freedom as rational self-determination involves self-consciousness of oneself as part of a larger whole, which is united around common rational interests. This means abandoning the perspective of the isolated, abstract self and embracing a notion of self-in-relations.

The first examples Hegel gives of 'being with oneself in the other' are friendship and love, in which 'we willingly limit ourselves with reference to an other' and thereby achieve the consciousness of ourselves as 'we'. 'Freedom is to will something determinate, yet to be with oneself in this determinacy and to return once more to the universal'.[21] Friendship involves a 'limitation' from the point of view of the private self, because being a true friendship requires an integration of the interests of two persons, and a giving up of selfishness. But this limitation is identical with the liberation of a universal and social self. A similar point applies to a love relationship, which is possible only by mutual surrender. In Hegel's words, 'Love means in general the consciousness of my unity with another, so that I am not isolated on my own, but gain my self-consciousness only through the renunciation of my independent existence and through knowing myself as the unity of myself with another and of the other with me'.[22]

Social relations transform us from natural into moral beings. 'We' is something more than 'me' plus 'you'; it denotes a common standpoint, or direction. In other words, in such relationships there is an increase in self-consciousness through incorporating the interests of another as inseparable from one's own. This is why we can achieve self-realization only through fulfilling social relations in an ethical life.

---

[21] Hegel (1995), para. 7A.

[22] *Ibid*, para. 158.

Hegel emphasizes three components of the modern ethical life: the family, civil society and the state.[23] On the one hand, he argues that participation in all these institutions shapes our identity and self-consciousness in different ways; they are complementary. On the other hand, he claims the highest, most important form of ethical life to be the modern state. Let us briefly consider Hegel's argument to understand why he describes the state as 'the actuality of concrete freedom'.[24]

The family is the place where we first recognize our immanent unity with others in the level of feeling; we become individualized gradually through our membership in the family. When considered historically, the family becomes fragmented due to the pressures of individualism inherent in civil society.[25] The household as a productive unit, in which people were internally related has given way to civil society that includes external relations between people, mediated through the 'system of needs'.

Civil society consists of market relations between individuals who consider themselves as self-sufficient, as an end-in-itself, and others as merely means, without recognizing their universal interdependence. It is a social form in which people satisfy the needs of each other without intending to do so, not on the basis of rational decisions. Furthermore, people conceive their public duties (such as the payment of taxes) as external impositions that restrict their subjective freedom. They fail to recognise that the social and political institutions are the concrete embodiments of universal ends, which are the necessary background of individual well-being and self-realization. Nevertheless, civil society contributes to liberation because in the realm of work, people transcend their selfishness by becoming aware that they contribute the satisfaction of the needs of others. Getting satisfaction from the knowledge that one is performing socially useful labour is an important component of freedom.[26] But in the final analysis, civil society is not adequate to reconcile individuality and sociality on a rational basis, which is the task of the state.

The state is a combination of various political institutions, which embodies the common interests of all citizens. Whereas liberals conceive the state merely as an external means to satisfy individual interests, Hegel carries Rousseau's idea of the 'general will' to a new level, by divorcing it from the social contract theory and introducing an organic conception of the state which is not a product of contract but rather exists internally in the self-consciousness of the citizens and externally in social institutions. The state is valuable in itself because it is the unity of the 'subjective will' and the universal, 'rational will'. 'It is in the State that freedom attains its objectivity... Only the will that is obedient to the law is free, for it obeys itself'.[27]

Now, let us consider the sense in which Hegel thinks that social duties liberate us. Firstly, fulfilling our social duties gradually transforms the natural will into the

---

[23] *Ibid*, para. 33.

[24] *Ibid*, para. 260.

[25] *Ibid*, para. 33A.

[26] *Ibid*, para. 199.

[27] Hegel (1988), pp. 40-41.

moral will and thereby replaces our natural egoism with communal feelings. Secondly, through the performance of our social duties we contribute to sustaining the concrete social institutions that are the necessary background for individual freedom and self-realization.

Historically, in pre-modern forms of ethical life, there seems to be an immediate unity of the person with the society because laws and institutions are habitually accepted; 'the habit of the ethical appears as a second nature which takes the place of the original and purely natural will... in habit the opposition between the natural and the subjective will disappears'.[28] Although these social institutions *are* the absolute authority, the subject does not consider them as alien and external since his self-awareness is mediated through them.[29]

However, modern individuals have also a need for subjective freedom and this is why they can attain full freedom not merely by obeying laws and performing social duties; they further have to be self-conscious of the social significance of their law-abiding actions. In other words, one can achieve real freedom only if the social institutions really correspond to individual aspirations and needs and if the people are self-conscious of this correspondence. This is what Hegel means by 'feeling at home in one's society', that is in contrast with an alienated social existence, in which the state is conceived as an external authority that frustrates individuality and subjective freedom.

Liberals are mistaken in assuming that the common interest and self-interest are always in an antagonistic relation; this involves generalizing an alienated social life and identifying it with the universal feature of any social order. In contrast, Hegel argues that the self can fulfil itself only within society, by also serving others. Even when the individual is thinking that he is pursuing his self-interest, he is also unconsciously promoting the common interest by helping others satisfy their needs through the work he performs.[30]

Our concrete moral duties arise from the requirements of specific social roles and identities. As Hegel has challenged the common understanding of freedom as arbitrariness when discussing the limitations of the purely negative aspect of freedom, now he questions the related widespread belief that duties restrict freedom.

A binding duty can appear as a *limitation* only in relation to indeterminate subjectivity or abstract freedom, and to the drives of the natural will or of the moral will which arbitrarily determines its own indeterminate good. The individual, however, finds his *liberation* in duty. On the one hand, he is liberated from his dependence on mere natural drives...and on the other hand, he is liberated from that indeterminate subjectivity which does not attain existence... To this extent, duty is not a limitation of freedom, but only of freedom in the abstract, that is, of unfreedom: it is the attainment of essential being, the acquisition of affirmative freedom.[31]

---

[28] Hegel (1995), para. 151A.
[29] *Ibid*, para. 146-7.
[30] Hegel (1977), para. 351.
[31] Hegel (1995), para. 149, A.

Every social role that is a component of one's identity is intimately related with certain obligations towards others. Not fulfilling those obligations amounts to the impairment of the basis of that relationship. For example, being a parent requires providing the conditions for the well being of a child voluntarily, sometimes even at the price of limiting one's self-interest. This is why a parent who does not contribute in this way (who does not fulfil the obligations related to his social role of being a parent) is not a 'true' parent, although he may still be the biological parent. The particular duties of a parent may change from society to society and these form the yardstick of making a moral evaluation of individual actions.

Let us challenge this argument by imagining a society in which the socially expected duty of a mother is not to work, and be completely engaged in looking after her children. Are mothers liberated if they fulfil such duties, even if it implies a restricted mode of life, which seems to be in contrast with self-realization, when understood as the overall development of various capacities? To put it differently, are there universally valid conditions for women's liberation, independent of particular social conditions? Hegel claims that the correspondence of individual aspirations to the immanent rationality of social institutions is necessary for concrete freedom. But is it also a sufficient condition? What about the cases, in which individuals identify with 'oppressive' social institutions? Can the contented slave be free?

Here we see a fundamental difference between the liberal and the Hegelian positions. Liberals propose the model of a liberal society as the universal model for a free society; they claim that illiberal societies are less free than the liberal ones, regardless of considering whether the institutions of these societies correspond to the aspirations of people. In contrast, Hegelians argue that there are no universal, trans-historical criteria of a free society independent of the concrete perceived needs of the people.

Since the hallmark of a free society is the correspondence of individual aspirations and social institutions, if the social institutions and practices frustrate the needs and expectations of most women, then it is a society in which women have limited freedom. However, if it is a society in which women are reconciled with their maternal roles, being housewives, etc.; then it would be hard to condemn such a society as restricting the freedom of women. As a result, there are no universally valid conditions for women's liberation, independent of particular social conditions, according to Hegel's understanding of the ethical life.

What is missing from such a perspective is that people are not always conscious of their unfreedom, especially if they do not know the existence of alternatives. Furthermore, even if they feel oppressed, they may be afraid of expressing their feelings in the face of the repressive authorities. For example, people living in extremely repressive societies (such as under the Islamic law) may be afraid to voice their frustrations, because of the heavy legal sanctions imposed on dissidents, in a society where people have minimum civil rights. In such a case, we cannot claim that it is a free society, just because there seem to be no protesters in public spaces.

As a result, both liberals and Hegelians are right in different respects. Hegelians are right in claiming that a society in which people's needs are unfilled and their aspirations are frustrated is not a free society. The liberals are also right in arguing that a society without civil and political liberties is not a free society. These views reveal two different necessary conditions for a free society.

Which methods are appropriate for achieving a harmony between individual needs and social institutions? Hegelian political theory does not have a clear answer on how social institutions and individual aspirations can be reconciled in such a way that would enhance freedom. The progressive version (such as that of the left-Hegelians) argues that it is the social institutions that should be transformed to match individual aspirations, whereas the conservative version claims that the individuals should change their minds to reconcile with the existing social order, which is arbitrarily taken to be rational.

The progressive version is in line with Hegel's view that subjective freedom is a criterion for the legitimacy of any modern political order. In other words, a modern state that violates the subjective freedom of citizens is not legitimate. 'The right of the subject's *particularity*, to find satisfaction –to put it differently– *subjective freedom*, is the pivotal and focal point in the difference between *antiquity* and the *modern* age'.[32]

On the other hand, we can also find conservative elements in Hegel's theory of the state. When he argues that rationality is immanent in every social order to some degree, it seems to imply a justification of the status quo. Nevertheless, as the left Hegelians point out, since the actual world contains both elements of rationality and irrationality, there is still some scope for critical analysis and transformation of society.[33] Sayers sets out the reasoning behind this conclusion as follows:

> The existing social order contains not only forces which support and sustain it, but also forces which oppose and negate it. The established order is itself contradictory. Negative aspects and critical tendencies arise *within* it. For this reason, there is no reason to look for a 'transcendent' basis for critical and negative ideas, an absolute moral standard outside existing conditions.[34]

Consequently, there is no fixed yardstick to measure the extent to which a social order is rational. According to the Hegelian-Marxist conception of historical progress, every society creates some new aspirations in people, some of which it fails to satisfy. When the society is transformed so that these aspirations can be realized through concrete social institutions, it becomes more rational. This is the core of the Hegelian immanent critical method.

For Hegel, humans can be fully free only in a free/rational society. It is not some universal ideal to be constructed from scratch and imposed upon people regardless of their customs and practices. 'We must search for what is rational in the existing world and allow that rational element to have its fullest expression. In

---

[32] *Ibid*, para. 124.
[33] Sayers (1998), p. 103.
[34] *Ibid*, p. 117.

this manner we can build on the reason and virtue that already exists in a community.'[35]

The purely negative conception of freedom is wrong in assuming a permanent conflict between the individual and society, whereas the purely positive conception of freedom is mistaken in imposing a necessary conflict within the self. By rejecting these divisions Hegel reconciles negative and positive aspects of freedom, through his notion of concrete freedom. As a result, achieving concrete freedom requires neither the sacrifice of individual self-interests to promote the common interest, nor the repression of one part of the self by another.

Hegel accepts that in alienated historical periods when the ethical life starts to disintegrate, the actual social order and customs may fail to satisfy individual aspirations.[36] It is Marx who emphasizes that alienated historical periods are not exceptional cases but features of all class societies where interests of one class are promoted at the expense of the needs of another class. So, individual failure to identify with the social order is neither a matter of an inevitable conflict between society and the individual (as the liberals assume), nor a sign of 'false consciousness' (as the conservative version presumes). It is a sign of real alienation and unfreedom that can ultimately be transcended through radical social changes, such as the abolition of classes.

Hegel's point is that 'we have a fundamental need for rational, reflective identification with a social role, and that modern individuals cannot be truly free until they create a social order in which this is possible.'[37] He thereby draws our attention to the objective and subjective preconditions for a harmonious modern ethical life. What is missing in Hegel's theory is an account of economic equality and democracy as the objective conditions for such a free society, which will be discussed in chapters 10 and 11.

Hegel illuminates the social and historical dimension of freedom with his distinction between morality and ethical life, which shows that freedom is not a natural given arising merely from our inherent rationality and moral agency, but a social achievement since the capacities for morality and rationality can only develop and have a specific content in an actual society, through relations with others. Moreover, he draws our attention to the modern need for both subjective freedom and for belonging to a community, and having fulfilling social roles and relations.

In the next chapter, I will explore how the communitarians develop Hegelian ideas on the necessary socio-historical context of freedom, by arguing that the value of community should be taken seriously in order to create and sustain a free society in which people would 'feel at home'.

---

[35] Singer, P. (1983), *Hegel*, Oxford University Press, p. 36.
[36] Hegel (1995), para. 138.
[37] Wood (1990), p. 51.

Chapter 9

Communitarians on
the Social Context of Freedom

Liberalism as a political doctrine is difficult to characterise accurately because of the immense variety within the tradition. Historical changes in the meaning of the term 'liberalism' from the opposite of conservatism to the defence of individualism and free markets make it hard to draw the boundaries of liberalism. The same difficulty applies to the term 'communitarianism'. In a wider sense, it refers to a long tradition of social philosophy from Plato, Aristotle to Hegel and Green; in its contemporary sense, it includes thinkers such as Taylor, Sandel, and MacIntyre. Some of these thinkers accept conservative political theories that defend traditional forms of communities, whereas others embrace radical political views. Most of them do not even classify themselves as communitarians. What unites them is the defence of an essentially social conception of the self, an emphasis on the intrinsic value of community and conceiving freedom as a social achievement that requires specific social institutions and practices. Contemporary communitarians formulate their views in opposition to the individualistic theory of liberalism, and they target in particular the Kantian liberalism of Rawls.

Recent communitarian thought has reawakened in the 1980s USA, as a response to the revival of excessive free-market liberalism (of the Reagan and Thatcher governments) that triggered social crises with symptoms such as the disintegration of local communities, the increase in violence, and distrust in governments. Communitarians assert the value of community, the importance of solidarity and point out the negative effects of individualism on the social order.

In this chapter, I will first contrast the liberal conception of the naturally autonomous self (assumed by Rawls) with the communitarian account of the socially embedded self, as defended by Bradley (conservative version) and Taylor (progressive version) in different ways. This will show the advantages of the communitarian understanding of the self.

Secondly, we will see that both the liberal picture of a society as a collection of autonomous individuals and the communitarian notion of a society as based on shared values are problematic. The former can describe the reality of the modern capitalist society to some extent, but the latter portrays neither the past, nor the present societies.

Thirdly, I will argue that both the liberal and the conservative communitarian positions are inadequate and one-sided in so far as they treat autonomy and community as antagonistic and universal values. This reveals their lack of a historical understanding of freedom.

Lastly, I will explore the concrete historical basis on which the value of autonomy emerged in parallel with the new social institutions and social relations through which people have become relatively autonomous. We will see that although communitarianism explains the social context of freedom, which is overlooked by the liberals, it cannot propose a concrete vision of a free society.

1. The Socially Embedded Self versus the Naturally Autonomous Self

In the first part on the negative conception of freedom, we haven't touched upon the underlying notion of the individual and society, partly because these thinkers deny that their theory is based on a specific conception of human nature. They claim to present a universal account of freedom that applies to all, regardless of people's particular socio-historical settings. Communitarians disclose the individualistic assumptions underlying liberalism and argue that it cannot give a satisfactory account of the person, the society and social conditions of freedom.

We can distinguish between utilitarian and deontological (Kantian) liberalism with respect to their metaphysical basis. Although the former takes happiness and the latter considers autonomy as the most fundamental value to be promoted, they share similar individualistic presuppositions. Both of these traditions conceive freedom as choosing one's own conception of the good and acting upon it without intervention by others.

If Kantian liberals have such a negative conception of freedom, then why have we analysed Kant as a part of the positive conception of freedom? As we have noted before, Kant's theory involves a gap between morality and politics; his moral theory supports a positive conception of freedom, whereas his political theory is compatible with a negative conception of freedom. This is partly due to the ambivalent notion of autonomy. If we take autonomy as an ideal related with moral actions then it is about the positive aspect of freedom that requires the development of certain capacities for rationality and morality. On the other hand, if we take autonomy as a capacity that everybody has, as the presupposition behind any action, then it converges to the liberal notion of freedom of choice, or negative freedom.

Rawls grounds his theory of justice on the presupposition that people are naturally autonomous, in the sense that they have 'a higher-order interest in the capacity to frame, revise and rationally pursue their own conceptions of the good'.[1] The essential feature of humans is being an autonomous chooser of ends; it makes them moral subjects with dignity as well as justifying why autonomy is a fundamental value to be preserved. Thereby, autonomy is raised to the status of a natural human right that is valid for all people in all historical periods.

---

[1] Mulhall, S. and Swift, A. (1997), *Liberals and Communitarians*, Blackwell, p. 11.

According to Sandel, such views imply that the subject is prior to and detached from its ends. It presupposes what Sandel calls an 'unencumbered self'. Since no end or value is integral to the identity of a person, the 'antecedently individuated' self can have no 'constitutive attachments'. All of one's goals and values are based on deliberate choice rather than on non-reflective emotional ties and engagements with others.

Are these fair charges on Kantian liberals? In other words, does claiming autonomy to be a natural given and the ultimate value imply neglecting the significance of the social matrix in shaping one's identity and his conception of the good? If this charge were correct, then liberals would have an unrealistic, non-satisfactory account of the person, failing to account for the construction of the self through relations with others.

Rawls argues that it is not a fair charge because his conception of the person is limited in scope; it only describes how people ought to deliberate about justice, within the framework of a social contract theory. Communitarian criticisms are based on Rawls' description of the 'original position', where people are behind a 'veil of ignorance', detached from their particular conceptions of the good. In this context, Rawls does not claim that one's identity *is* actually formed by pure individual choice, but rather his theory is about how a just political society *ought* to be constructed. Consequently, Rawls does not deny that the *moral self* is socially embedded and has a particular conception of the good that might originate from his social identity. Rawls emphasizes that people have a capacity to critically evaluate and revise their attachments, which does not imply that they can 'detach themselves from all values at the same time'.[2] He argues only that as a *political self*, he should bracket his particular interests and values when deciding about which principles of justice are reasonable.[3] However, this modification gives us a divided self, with the possibility of incompatible moral and political identities.[4]

It is not clear why the self should detach from his particular values and goals when deliberating about justice. For liberals, this is the only way to secure a 'neutral' state, based on a neutral conception of justice, valid for everyone regardless of their private interests. Communitarians challenge this project by arguing against the liberal assumption that right is prior to good. This issue, though central to the liberalism versus communitarian debate, is beyond the scope of this chapter. What is relevant for our purposes is that just like Kant's account of freedom, Rawls' theory is either based on an unencumbered self or a divided self, and both are unsatisfactory accounts of the person. It gives us good reasons to raise doubts on the validity of Rawls' initial assumption that the self is naturally autonomous.

---

[2] *Ibid*, pp. 195-6.
[3] Such reasoning is common among social contract theories, for which in order to reach a consensus on the principles of a just society, people should decide not with respect to their private wills, following their desires but by using disembodied public reason. I think the communitarian argument against Rawls is more illuminating when directed against the pitfalls of social contract theories, from a Hegelian perspective.
[4] *Ibid*, pp. 195, 197.

Now let us compare two accounts of the socially embedded self, as given by Bradley and Taylor. Bradley exemplifies the conservative version of communitarianism, since he defends the value of community at the price of neglecting the importance of autonomy and individual freedom. On the other hand, Taylor represents the progressive version because he acknowledges autonomy and community to be mutually supportive values. He argues that the modern individual has both the need for autonomy and a need for fulfilling social relations.

Individualism takes society as a collection of individuals 'held together by force, illusion or contract'.[5] In contrast, Bradley argues that the individual apart from the community is merely an empty abstraction. One achieves his identity, values and self-knowledge only through social relations. As Bradley says in his famous passage,

> The child does not even think of his separate self, he grows with his world, his mind fills and orders itself; and when he can separate himself from that world, and know himself apart from it, then by that time his self, the object of his self-consciousness, is penetrated, infected, characterised by the existence of others. Its content implies in every fibre relations of community...his life widens out from one little world to other and higher worlds, and he apprehends through successive stations the whole in which he lives.[6]

Following Hegel's views on the 'ethical life', Bradley emphasizes three social roles in the construction of the self's identity: as a family-member, within one's profession and as a citizen. He further derives the conservative conclusion that 'to be moral is to live in accordance with the moral tradition in one's country' and that 'in my station my particular duties are prescribed to me, and I have them whether I wish to or not'.[7] Although he acknowledges a possible criticism of his views that 'the community in which he is a member may be in a confused or rotten condition'[8] he cannot provide an answer to this objection. In the end, in his battle against the 'worship of the individual'[9], he puts forward a worship of the community by defending the absolute value of any community, which is also a one-sided and unsatisfactory position. This gives rise to a well-known liberal charge against communitarianism that it may justify repression of individual freedoms in the name of the common good.

Norman provides us with valuable insights on the pros and cons of Bradley's position. Bradley 'succeeds in showing the ethical importance of the social relations which serve to define the individual' and emphasizes how our social relations and emotional commitments impose on us certain concerns and specific duties, which are necessary to sustain these relationships. Nevertheless, Bradley's focus on institutionalised relationships, and in particular our role as a citizen is too

---

[5] Bradley, F. H. (1972), 'My Station and Its Duties', *Ethical Studies*, Oxford University Press, p. 164.

[6] *Ibid*, p. 172.

[7] *Ibid*, pp. 173, 176.

[8] *Ibid*, p. 203.

[9] *Ibid*, p. 201.

narrow; 'small-scale and short-term social relations' also have an ethical significance and they come prior to the institutionalised forms. Norman gives the example of promising that creates and presupposes a relationship of trust; breaking a promise is wrong precisely because it violates the relationship of trust.[10]

The emphasis on the self as a social being shows that society and social relations have an intrinsic value for the pursuit of a fulfilling life. Since social relations are the building blocks of our identity, the value of society cannot be reduced to a mere means to the satisfaction of individual interests and desires.[11] However, accepting the intrinsic value of society does not imply that all societies can provide the necessary conditions for the self-realization of people, in contrast to what Bradley and other right Hegelians presume.

Taylor's account of the socially embedded self preserves the useful insights of Bradley's theory whilst avoiding the repression of individuality under the strict confines of particular social duties. It thereby exemplifies the progressive version of communitarianism.

For Taylor, humans are self-interpreting animals who can articulate their self-understanding, goals and values only through a linguistic community, with shared meanings.[12] Every choice is made on the basis of a background, an indispensable horizon of 'strong evaluations'[13] that is not purely a product of choice. This does not mean that one cannot revise any element that makes up his identity. It rather means that he cannot detach from all his 'constitutive attachments' and choose with a disinterested attitude, as presupposed by Rawls' social contract theory. Taylor considers the capacity for attachment with others, commitments towards certain conceptions of the good (which are formulated from the specific viewpoint of one's linguistic community) as the central features of a person.

 We should be careful in not interpreting Taylor's emphasis on the linguistic community as solely referring to a trait shared by members of the same nation. People speaking the same mother tongue do not form a homogenous linguistic community. Taylor emphasizes that our experiences are partly shaped by our interpretations. A person who interprets his experience in terms of sophisticated adjectives such as 'shameful', 'humiliating' and 'courageous' would belong to a different linguistic community from another person who does not have these notions in his vocabulary, but who describes his experience simply in terms of pleasure and pain. How we interpret our experience is partly constitutive of the experience itself.[14]

As a result, if we become more articulate about our experiences and emotions, we can then live more fulfilling and self-conscious lives. This requires living in a community with a rich, expressive language embodied in common institutions and

---

[10] Norman, R. (1998), *The Moral Philosophers: An Introduction to Ethics*, Oxford University Press, pp. 114-5.

[11] *Ibid*, p. 117.

[12] Taylor (1986), p. 63.

[13] See chapter 5, section 2 for a further discussion of Taylor's notion of 'strong evaluations'.

[14] Taylor (1986a), p. 101.

practices.[15] Another conclusion is that not only the origins but also the content of particular conceptions of the good are communal.

Having established that our conception of the good is not purely individualistic, but based on social values and options, we can no longer consider individual visions of the good as necessarily separate, and the overlapping of them as mere coincidences. In contrast to what the liberals suppose, 'we are neither as transparent to ourselves nor as opaque to others'[16]; we learn what we value through interaction with others.

2. Different Visions of Society: Based on Shared Understandings versus as an Aggregate of Autonomous Individuals

Whereas the liberals conceive society as an aggregate of naturally autonomous individuals, communitarians argue that society exists prior to the autonomous individual. Society is the necessary medium for the development of various human capacities, values and identities. So, autonomy should be taken as a particular socio-historical product, rather than as the natural starting point for all. Although communitarians give a historical account of autonomy as a historically specific, rather than a universal value, we cannot see a similar historical approach in their understanding of the community as a harmonious unity, based on shared values. Let us consider the merits and defects of those two visions of the society.

The liberal picture is right in seeing the modern society as an aggregate of autonomous individuals, but wrong in presupposing autonomy to be a universal value, a trans-historical yardstick with which we can make moral evaluations of various societies. For example, it is not valid to argue that autonomy is sacrificed and repressed in favour of some collective good in a pre-capitalist society. Since the necessary economic and institutional conditions for the emergence of autonomous individuals were absent in such societies, we cannot talk about the repression of something that was almost non-existent. This is why it is anachronistic to talk about the value of autonomy about times when individual identities were predetermined by their social roles and when there was little scope for personal choice of one's life style. In other words, a society of autonomous individuals is a relatively new phenomenon, rather than the universal norm.

Communitarians consider a community of shared values and understandings as the paradigm society, as an ideal to be aspired to. But where does this ideal belong? Does it describe pre-capitalist societies or the present ones? Neither is the case. It is a romantic idealisation, which disregards the immanent conflict of interests that prevail in all class societies. Even in pre-modern times, societies were largely hierarchical and there were sharp divisions between classes and sexes. These conflicts of interests were reflected in different values and norms. As

---

[15] Taylor, C. (1986b), 'Hegel's Philosophy of Mind', *Philosophical Papers: Human Agency and Language*, vol. 1, Cambridge University Press, p. 87.

[16] Sandel, M. (1987), 'Justice and the Good', *Liberalism and Its Critics* (ed. Sandel, M.), Basil Blackwell, p. 166.

Kymlicka remarks, such communitarians fail to acknowledge that these 'shared understandings and ends' are based on historical practices which are 'gender-coded, race-coded and class-coded, even when women, blacks, and workers are legally allowed to participate in them'.[17]

Secondly, the scope of the communitarian ideal community is not clear. If it refers to citizens of a nation state then even when these people do have common tastes, beliefs, habits as shaped by the same cultural environment, these are still too vague and minimal, inadequate to generate distinctively communitarian policies based around the notion of a common good. On the other hand, if it refers to self-governing local communities then it would be hard to understand how adequate this would be as the model of a free society, in the present age of complex and interdependent national states and regional unions.

Thirdly, people do have shared interests and common goals as members of the same class if this membership is also supplemented by class-consciousness, but communitarians fail to give due attention to the notion of class. Because of these reasons, the communitarian picture of the community as a harmonious whole is the weakest part of their theory, which can portray neither the past nor the present societies.

3. The Value of Community and the Value of Autonomy

Communitarians charge liberals with exaggerating the capacity of individuals to distance themselves from social relationships, and overemphasizing their capacity for autonomy. Presented this way, it seems that being socially embedded we are less autonomous than we think we are. In other words, autonomy and community are antagonistic; the more of one means the less of the other. Is this true? This interpretation is based on taking autonomy and community as extreme forms, in a one-sided and abstract way. Autonomy does not mean complete detachment from one's particular social identity, nor does being a member of community deprive one of the power to criticise its values and traditions.

The conservative version of communitarianism commits the above fallacy of taking autonomy and community as antagonistic. For instance, MacIntyre argues that the emergence of autonomous individuals in modern society is partially responsible for the disintegration of communities. The increase in divorce rates is presented as a particular example of this phenomenon.[18]

As Sayers clarifies, the above argument is incoherent because it conflicts with the fundamental communitarian premise that all persons are essentially social. If the premise is true, then it is meaningless to talk about the dissolution of communities, which amounts to saying that there can be individuals who are not embedded in any social relations. Modernity has not destroyed community as such

---

[17] Kymlicka, W. (1997), *Contemporary Political Philosophy: An Introduction*, Oxford University Press, p. 227.
[18] Bell, D. (1993), *Communitarianism and Its Critics*, Clarendon Press.

but has transformed communities.[19] For example, the change from pre-arranged marriages to the free choice of partners, the shift from big families to small families, the emergence of the option of cohabiting without marriage have transformed the institution of marriage into a new type of association that allows more scope for free choice.[20]

Interpreting these changes as the shattering of family ties expresses a nostalgia for traditional families, as the paradigm for the institution of family and a failure to conceive the evolution of social institutions. The conservative version sees only the negative effects of modernity, disregarding its positive contributions to relative autonomy and human fulfilment.[21] This is partly because it operates with a romantic idea of community as a harmonious whole formed by shared understandings and values, as we have explored in the previous section.

Which type of community is necessary for the development of autonomous persons? As Sayers argues, 'the growth of autonomy does not involve an escape from all frameworks, it is a *relative* autonomy, achieved only in and through identifications with a diversity of frameworks'.[22] Belonging to various communities, sometimes with conflicting values and demands, compels a person to exercise critical thinking and conscious choice and thereby develops his capacity for autonomy.

The fact of relative autonomy and the value of autonomy have emerged with modernity and the development of capitalist social relations. As can be seen, putting autonomy in a socio-historical context and showing its relative and gradational aspects, when compared with the liberal version of autonomy as a universal value indicates two different perspectives on individual and society.

The modern social institutions of wage labour, consumer freedom, freedom of contract, and the possibility of social mobility have increased the relative autonomy of people. Since this is the framework in which we all live, it is hard to realise the historical specificity of the social institutions that embody and enable autonomy. Elster reminds us of the following example that Marx gives. When a worker starts receiving wages rather than being 'paid in kind', he achieves the freedom to spend it on alcohol rather than meat for his children. Thereby, he has more personal freedom and becomes responsible for his choices on how to spend his money.[23] This is an example of relative individual autonomy in the private sphere. Meszaros questions the limits of the value of autonomy as follows:

> To seek remedy in 'autonomy' is to be on the wrong track. Our troubles are not due to a lack of autonomy, but on the contrary, to a social structure –a mode of production– that forces on men a cult of it, isolating them from each other. The vital question that must be asked about autonomy is: what can one do with it? If one just 'has' it as a

---

[19] Sayers, S. (1999a), 'Identity and Community', *Journal of Social Philosophy*, vol. 30, p. 149.

[20] Raz (1988), p. 392.

[21] Sayers, S. (1995), 'The Value of Community', *Radical Philosophy*, no. 69, p. 3.

[22] Sayers (1999a), p. 155.

[23] Elster, J. (1998), *Making Sense of Marx*, Cambridge University Press, p. 207.

'psychological faculty', a feature of 'character structure', or as a hollow right confined to 'privacy', for all practical purposes this comes to the same thing as *not* to have it at all.[24]

These words emphasize that autonomy is not the utmost value; it is not a magical wand that would by itself ensure happiness and well-being. Autonomy in the private sphere may coexist with alienation and disempowerment in the economic and public spheres. The gradual achievement of the all-embracing right to vote is an example of autonomy in the public sphere. Nevertheless, as voting has become a universal right, it also has become practically less meaningful. People start to question the legitimacy of representative democracy as a vehicle for social decision making after realising that voting once in a few years is neither sufficient to make the governments accountable to people, nor for real political participation.[25]

The above discussion reveals the complex and historically evolving forms of autonomy. As seen in the case of representative democracy, social institutions that once have increased autonomy may later turn into inadequate vehicles to achieve further autonomy. Another example is the institution of wage labour that first increases autonomy through introducing job mobility, but after being transformed into alienated work and wage-slavery, it prevents further kinds of autonomy, as we shall discuss in chapter 11.

Having relative autonomy in one sphere of life is not sufficient to assure coherent, fulfilling identities that also require living in a non-alienated society. The above considerations reveal that the value of autonomy and that of community are complementary and both are necessary to achieve positive freedom.

Liberals conceive society as a voluntaristic organisation for mutual co-operation, having only instrumental value, whereas the conservative/romantic version of communitarians think of community as a coherent ethical whole, where individual differences are mostly insignificant. Both are one-sided and deficient because they take community as a fixed, non-historical form rather than an evolving body of concrete social institutions. The progressive version sees community as both shaping human nature and transformed through collective actions. Community is valuable because only in a suitable social medium we can develop and exercise our capacities for autonomous choice and can have coherent and fulfilling identities.

---

[24] Meszaros, I. (1986), *Marx's Theory of Alienation*, Merlin Press, p. 267.

[25] Taylor, C. (1984), 'Hegel: History and Politics', *Liberalism and Its Critics* (ed. Sandel, M.), Blackwell, p. 186.

4. Freedom as a Social Achievement

Taylor makes an immanent critique of liberalism arguing that although liberalism aims to promote freedom it also undermines the preconditions for the achievement of freedom.

Firstly, he emphasizes that liberals are mistaken in their assumption that all humans 'possess the full capacity of choice as a given rather than as a potential which has to be developed'.[26] In contrast, for Taylor, the capacity for autonomous choice depends on the capability of conceiving alternatives and evaluating what one really wants. These capacities can only develop within the context of a social matrix and require certain social institutions that we often take for granted, such as museums, universities, laboratories, political parties and law courts.[27] 'In short, even someone committed to values or goods that are essentially individual in content must also be committed to defending the communal structures underpinning those individualist values'.[28]

Secondly, people have an obligation to actively sustain this social framework; merely not-violating each other's rights is not enough to maintain a free society. As long as people value freedom and autonomy they have positive duties and responsibilities to maintain the background social conditions of their individual freedoms.[29]

Nevertheless, liberal ideology encourages people to have an atomistic self-understanding. People become primarily concerned with their individual choices in the private sphere, conceive others as a means for their self-interests and get detached from political institutions. All these factors become barriers to further freedom, which can be achieved by extending the scope of autonomy from private to public sphere, through collective action, as we shall see more in the next two chapters.

Taylor emphasizes the importance of political participation in democratic institutions for the preservation and enhancement of our freedom. 'If realizing our freedom partly depends on the society and culture in which we live, then we exercise a fuller freedom if we can help determine the shape of our society and culture'.[30] Sandel's critique of liberalism is also along similar lines. He says, 'The procedural republic cannot secure the liberty it promises, because it cannot sustain the kind of political community and civic engagement that liberty requires.'[31]

Do Taylor and Sandel put the whole blame on the liberal ideology? It seems that they are against both uncontrolled market economy and the welfare state, on

---

[26] Taylor, C. (1985a), 'Atomism', *Philosophy and the Human Sciences*, vol. 2, Cambridge University Press, p. 197.

[27] *Ibid*, p. 204.

[28] Mulhall and Swift (1997), p. 126.

[29] *Ibid*, p. 207.

[30] *Ibid*, p. 208.

[31] Sandel, M. (1998), *Democracy's Discontent: America in Search of a Public Philosophy*, The Belknap Press of Harvard University Press, p. 24.

the same grounds that they do not allow scope for democratic self-government. In Sandel's words,

> Where libertarian liberals defend the private economy and egalitarian liberals defend the welfare state, communitarians worry about the concentration of power in both the corporate economy and the bureaucratic state, and the erosion of those intermediate forms of community that have at times sustained a more vital public life. [32]

Such anxieties about the welfare state illustrate that communitarians are not much concerned with the equality related criticism of liberalism. This leads them to underestimate the effects of private property and power relations on freedom and individual identity. As a result, they conceive the established identities in abstraction from their material and economic basis, which partly explains their emphasis on 'shared values' or the common good. In contrast to Green, communitarians fail to give an adequate content to the notion of common good because they refrain from associating it with the welfare state or with any other concrete embodiment.

In capitalism, people's identities are primarily shaped by the material conditions in the production process. For example, as employees in unfulfilling jobs, serving their employer and customers, as well as competing with fellow workers, threatened by the fear of unemployment leave little scope for genuine, non-instrumental, enduring social relations and community ties. As Sayers argues, alienation is rooted in objective conditions and is not due to people's erroneous self-interpretations.[33] The way to overcome alienation is not only by emancipating people from the liberal ideology, but also through modifying the social order so that the economic basis of the fundamental antagonisms within society would be eliminated.

Following Hegel, Taylor argues that people become alienated when 'the public experience of their society ceases to have any meaning for them'; to fill this gap they may turn to other local communities such as religious communities or it may lead to a rise of nationalism, both of which are inadequate ways to achieve freedom, since they do not give adequate scope for subjective freedom and autonomy.[34]

Nevertheless, other communitarians embrace some conservative political policies, as Gutman remarks below, in her comparison of the different paradigms of the earlier critics of liberalism in 1960s, which are inspired by Marx and the later communitarian critics of liberalism in 1980s, which are inspired by Aristotle and Hegel.

> The political implications of the new communitarian criticism are correspondingly more conservative. Whereas the good society of the old critics was one of collective property

---

[32] Sandel, M. (1987a), 'Introduction', *Liberalism and Its Critics* (ed. Sandel, M.), Basil Blackwell, p. 6.
[33] Sayers (1999a), p. 153.
[34] Taylor (1984), p. 186.

ownership and equal political power, the good society of the new critics is one of settled traditions and established identities. For many of the old critics, the role of women within the family was symptomatic of their social and economic oppression; for Sandel, the family serves as a model of community and evidence of a good greater than justice. For the old critics, patriotism was an irrational sentiment that stood in the way of world peace; for MacIntyre, the particularistic demands of patriotism are no less rational than the universalistic demands of justice. The old critics were inclined to defend deviations from majoritarian morality in the name of non-repression; the new critics are inclined to defend the efforts of local majorities to ban offensive activities in the name of preserving their communities way of life and the values that sustain it. [35]

In summary, liberals criticise communitarians on the grounds that individuals come prior to society. They argue that either giving priority to, or emphasizing community would legitimise the repression of individual liberties in the name of community values or solidarity. As we have seen above, this criticism applies only to the conservative version, but not to the progressive version of communitarianism.

On the other hand, as can be seen from Gutman's quote, Marxists criticise communitarians from a different perspective. The Marxist account of class implies that community is fundamentally divided; the communitarian ideal of a harmonious and unified community does not lie in the past, but rather in the future. So, a romantic idealisation of the pre-capitalist communities should be replaced with the positive project of overcoming class divisions so that people could have shared values and organise around a common good. [36]

Communitarians explore the social context of freedom, which was ignored by the liberals. However, as the Marxist critique reveals, they fail to provide a concrete vision of the free society, in which everyone can have the social opportunities for self-realization. In the next chapter, I will explore the objective social conditions of freedom, which is the missing link in the communitarian account of freedom.

---

[35] Gutman, A. (1994), 'Communitarian Critics of Liberalism', *Communitarianism: A New Public Ethics* (ed. Daly, M.), Wadsworth Publishing Company, pp. 89-90.

[36] Freedoms could be enlarged through the establishment of collective ownership of means of production in the strategic sectors of economy, and a working participatory democracy where the decision-making processes start from the bottom of the society and are transmitted to the administrative units.

Chapter 10

Freedom as the Power for Self-Determination

In his characterization of positive freedom, Berlin overemphasizes one aspect of freedom (rational self-determination) but neglects the other essential component of positive freedom, namely the power to achieve self-determination. This misrepresentation helps Berlin in depriving positive freedom of its concrete content.[1]

In this chapter, I will reveal two fundamental flaws of the negative view and discuss how they are remedied by the positive view. Firstly, assuming a sharp distinction between unfreedom and inability (or having freedom versus being able to use freedom) leads the negative view to disregard social and economic constraints on freedom, and identify freedom merely with the non-violation of civil rights. However, positive freedom as the power for self-determination has both political conditions (the protection of civil liberties against external interventions) and economic conditions (having access to conditions of life and labour).

Secondly, concentrating exclusively on freedom of action, without acknowledging that some actions are more significant than others, the negative view fails to explain the overall freedom of a person. Whilst trying to be neutral between different conceptions of the good, it robs freedom of its concrete content and neglects the normative aspect of freedom. This defect is remedied by the positive view's emphasis on the essential normative aspect of freedom, which is explained through specifying the universal goal of freedom as self-realization, and proposing freedom as an 'exercise-concept'. The link between positive freedom and 'ethical naturalism' will also be used to highlight the normative aspect of freedom.

Thirdly, I will focus on the internal debate between three versions of the positive view, as defended by Norman, Gould and Macpherson. Whereas Norman takes the goal of freedom as meaningful and effective choice, the latter thinkers emphasize self-development. Lastly, I will draw attention to the consensus between these three thinkers about the social conditions of positive freedom, in so far as they emphasize the link between freedom, equality and democracy.

---

[1] It also enables Berlin to identify positive freedom with 'value monism' and 'metaphysical rationalism', which is unfair. Macpherson (1973), p. 117.

1. Negative Freedom as a Necessary Condition for Positive Freedom

Although Berlin is considered as the founder of the distinction between negative and positive conceptions of freedom, his views are ambiguous on how these two conceptions of freedom are related. At times, he claims that they present two different accounts of self-mastery that have historically diverged.[2] Other times, he posits them not as rivals, but as dealing with distinct questions.[3] But most of the time, he argues that negative freedom is the only coherent account of freedom, and positive freedom is merely a confusion of freedom with other values such as equality, social justice, democracy and self-realization.[4] He expresses the difference between negative and positive freedom as follows:

> Emphasis on negative liberty, as a rule, leaves more paths for individuals or groups to pursue; positive liberty, as a rule, opens fewer paths, but with better reasons or greater resources for moving along them; the two may or may not clash.[5]

As seen from the above quotation, a person having various options would be negatively free even if he is not competent to assess these alternatives or cannot pursue the option he values due to lack of material means. It is in this sense that Taylor claims negative freedom to be an 'opportunity-concept', whereas positive freedom is an 'exercise-concept', which requires one to effectively control and shape his life.[6]

The main difference between the negative and positive conceptions of freedom lies in the opposite accounts of the relation between freedom and power (or abilities). Berlin and Hayek agree that the lack of power or inability does not imply a lack of liberty.[7] A person's freedom is constrained only if another agent can be held directly responsible for restraining him. Consequently, for Hayek, social factors such as poverty and lack of education can limit people's actual choices but cannot thereby make them unfree, since nobody is directly responsible for them.[8] This distinction between human and non-human obstacles and the assumption that only human obstacles constrain freedom is common to all versions of the negative view.[9]

---

[2] Berlin (1969), p. 132.

[3] *Ibid*, p. 122.

[4] *Ibid*, p. 155.

[5] *Ibid*, p. lvii.

[6] Taylor (1991), pp. 143-4.

[7] Berlin (1969), p. 122.

[8] Hayek (1991), p. 85.

[9] Berlin accuses the positive view of failing to acknowledge this distinction and thereby confusing freedom with the 'conditions of freedom'. Berlin (1969), p. xlviii. Nevertheless, there is not a direct link between these two distinctions; one may accept the former and reject the latter. As we have seen before, Miller (chapter 2) and Cohen (chapter 4) revise the negative conception of freedom so that they keep the distinction between human and non-human constraints, but reject the distinction between freedom and conditions of freedom, without falling into any contradictions.

Milder versions of the negative view define human constraints as those that are either caused or can be remedied by human arrangements, rather than identifying human constraints with personal interventions. In this sense, poverty is a human constraint if the action or inaction of certain social institutions necessarily produces poverty, and if modifying or abandoning these institutions can remedy poverty. In contrast, the mainstream liberal ideology asserts that poverty is an inevitable fact arising from 'natural' factors such as the disproportion between scarce resources and infinite desires and through mechanisms of the 'impersonal market forces'. Granting this framework as inevitable, they further argue that poverty is a matter of individual responsibility; some people are poor because they are lazy, or lack the necessary talents to succeed. As a result, the notion of social and economic constraints becomes invisible for the negative view. Issues such as poverty and exploitation are claimed to be matters of social justice rather than as also intimately related with freedom.

Based on the unwarranted assumption that individual freedom can be constrained only by the intervention of others and state coercion, having civil liberties is taken as a sufficient condition to have freedom. Freedom is reduced to the legal permission to act as one pleases (as long as one does not violate similar rights of others) regardless of whether one can actually use his civil liberties to shape the course of his life.

Berlin accepts that one might have civil liberties, yet lack the material resources to exercise these. 'If a man is too poor or too ignorant or too feeble to make use of his legal rights, the liberty that these rights confer upon him is nothing to him, but it is not thereby annihilated.'[10] Defenders of positive freedom agree with Berlin that having civil liberties (or formal freedoms) is a necessary condition of freedom but it is not sufficient to be a free person, which also requires being able to exercise one's formal freedoms, the presence of significant options and the cultivation of the capacity to make informed choices. Berlin disagrees, 'freedom without sufficient material security, health, knowledge, in a society that lacks equality, justice, mutual confidence may be virtually useless...but improving such conditions does not always imply an expansion of liberty...paternalism can provide the conditions of freedom, yet withhold freedom itself'.[11]

After all, there is not a real disagreement between two sides of the debate. Berlin claims that providing enabling conditions for freedom is not sufficient to guarantee freedom, if it also involves a restriction of civil liberties by the state. The advocates of positive freedom formulate it the other way around; the existence of civil liberties is not sufficient to guarantee the existence of enabling conditions for freedom. In the end, both civil liberties and material resources to exercise them effectively are necessary conditions for freedom, and neither is sufficient by itself.

The positive view remarks how economic inequalities prevent the effective exercise of civil liberties. For example, like every citizen, a poor person has a right to get a lawyer when accused but he cannot exercise this right unless he has enough money to hire a lawyer. Another example is that, everyone has a right to

---

[10] *Ibid*, p. liii.
[11] *Ibid*, p. liv-lv.

live in a healthy environment but these rights can be violated as a result of the 'freedom of enterprise' of a factory that spoils the environment.

A person living in a society where civil liberties are ensured by law is a person who is negatively free. If he further has the material means to exercise these liberties, he is able to transform his formal freedom into effective freedom, and can satisfy his arbitrary desires. But are these sufficient to make him positively free? In other words, can positive freedom be reduced to effective negative freedom?

Firstly, as Wood argues, the gradual expansion of civil liberties were designed to remove feudal privileges and to protect the individual from the state, but these rights do not remove class inequalities and are useless in 'dealing with the wholly new disposition of social power that emerged with modern capitalism.'[12] Secondly, as I will argue in the next section, reducing positive freedom to effective negative freedom would amount to striping the positive view of its essential normative aspect. The extent of our positive freedom is proportional to the extent in which we are able to shape our lives (both in private and public domains) in accordance with our values. This brings us to the question of why we value freedom, or the goal of freedom.

2. The Normative Aspect of Positive Freedom

The negative view tries to find universal constraints on freedom without specifying the goal of freedom, because it assumes that spelling out an objective goal of freedom would be incompatible with freedom itself. From their perspective, whether a person has or lacks freedom is something that is empirically verifiable, and purely descriptive; it is related neither with the various subjective uses of that freedom, nor with the issue of whether a person values that freedom or not. If we remember MacCallum's formula (x is free from y to do z), then the goal of freedom (or z) is anything that the person might desire to do, according to the negative view.

There are at least two problems with this account. Firstly, it is impossible to find universal constraints on freedom without specifying the goal of freedom. For example, a rock blocking a path (for simplicity, let us assume that it is the result of a human arrangement and not just a natural obstacle) might constrain the freedom of a mountain climber (assuming his goal is to reach the peak), but it does not affect the freedom of a wandering photographer, who uses the rock as a suitable background for his photographs. Only after we decide what we want to do with our freedom, can we classify things as constraints or as useful means to achieve our purposes.

Secondly, if we take the goal of freedom as the satisfaction of arbitrary desires, then we face the paradox of the contented slave (as discussed in the first section of chapter 5). Modifying the goal of freedom as doing what one values or as the non-

---

[12] Wood, E. M. (2000), *Democracy Against Capitalism: Renewing Historical Materialism*, Cambridge University Press, p. 230. I will expand on this issue in chapter 11, while discussing 'market imperatives'.

restriction of 'significant' options is also useless as seen when discussing the hybrid theories of freedom. Even though these hybrid theories reduce freedom to freedom of choice and procedural autonomy, which falls short of positive freedom, their remarkable contribution is pointing towards the possibility of an 'illusion of freedom'. It is astonishing to discover that a person is not always the best judge of his freedom. We might be unaware of other significant options, as well as fail to perceive some of the constraints on our freedom. Freedom cannot be reduced to a subjective feeling of contentment and we cannot be introspectively aware of our freedom (or unfreedom), similar to our immediate awareness of pain or sorrow. Even when a person does what one values, there is still a possibility of error as Taylor remarks (chapter 5, section 2). The notion of internal constraints on freedom is useful in explaining how one can restrict his freedom, consciously or unconsciously. Furthermore, a person may fail to appreciate the value of freedom and voluntarily choose to give up her freedom, as in the case of the submissive wife.

The objective goal of freedom (that one may fail to perceive, or appreciate) is self-realization. Taylor is right in arguing that only a person who has achieved self-realization to some extent can be aware of the internal constraints to his self-development. Similarly, for Mill, only those who have experienced 'higher pleasures' would be able to see why the satisfaction of merely 'lower pleasures' could never make a person free. Freedom is related with self-realization, rather than with any subjective feeling of contentment. This is the gist of his famous words, 'better to be Socrates dissatisfied, than a pig satisfied'. Taylor illuminates that relating freedom with self-realization implies an exercise concept of freedom; the actual exercising of control over one's life and the achievement of some self-development is necessary to be able to remove internal barriers and become more free.[13]

The above discussion reveals the essential normative aspect of positive freedom. A person has positive freedom to the extent that he actively develops himself, makes qualitative distinctions between his various desires and goals, and integrates his various desires in accordance with his fundamental commitments. These are the necessary (but not sufficient) conditions for rational self-determination. These capacities can be cultivated only when one has access to material and intellectual resources, and has the means of life and labour. It is in this sense that having the power for self-determination and rational self-determination are two sides of the same coin.

What are the possible challenges and objections to our view that relates positive freedom with self-realization? Some might say we are identifying freedom arbitrarily with a specific preferred use of freedom. Yes, this is indeed what is being done, but there is nothing to be ashamed of. If freedom is an exercise concept, then it should have a specific direction and a concrete content, rather than be a merely formal notion that implies the license to travel in one way or the other at

---

[13] Taylor (1991), p. 144.

random. An adequate conception of freedom should be able to explain why freedom is valuable.

The second objection would follow up a theme of the first objection. If only a person who pursues self-realization is free, then a person who commits a crime would not be free. Since freedom is the necessary precondition for moral responsibility, he would not be responsible for his crime. This *reductio ad absurdum* argument is not valid because it involves fallacious reasoning; it confuses two senses of freedom (positive freedom and freedom of action). A criminal is not positively free,[14] even though he acts freely (voluntarily, without external coercion) when committing the crime.

It is important to clarify the distinction between positive freedom and freedom of action. A person who has positive freedom might have unfree actions (when he is threatened by another person, for example) and a person who lacks positive freedom might be enjoying full freedom of action. Nevertheless, freedom of action to pursue 'significant' options is necessary (but not sufficient) to have positive freedom.

Here is a third objection: If only a person who pursues self-realization is positively free, then someone who lives from day to day, merely pursuing indiscriminate pleasures would not be positively free (even if he feels free). If so, then someone (or the state) who claims to be a better judge of his freedom might 'force him to be free'. This argument (which we have referred as the totalitarianism charge in chapter 6) is also an invalid argument; although the premise is true, the conclusion does not follow from the premise. A person might be wrong about whether he is a positively free person, but this does not imply that others can decide better on behalf of him. Since positive freedom requires self-activity and self-government, it does not allow a person to be liberated against his will. A society in which all people have positive freedom can be utopian, but still it is a worthwhile ideal to strive for. Even in a free society that provides all the background conditions for self-realization, some people may prefer not to develop themselves, but rather kill their times with various diversions, without any fundamental goals (unless we allow 'killing time' to be considered as a fundamental goal). So, a free society is not necessarily a place where all people have positive freedom, since eradicating social and economic constraints can be compatible with the existence of internal constraints on self-realization.

The last objection might argue that it is unacceptable to associate freedom with making 'right' choices. What makes a choice right would depend on one's conception of human good and it would change arbitrarily from one person to

---

[14] This statement is based on the implicit assumption that one has positive freedom only if he develops himself in ways that would not harm others. Based on this assumption, we can also argue that positive freedoms of people would not conflict. Alternatively, one may argue that the notion of self-realization is compatible with harming others. In that case, it is possible for a criminal to be positively free if he has developed himself in some way. But then positive freedom would not always be socially valuable. I am in favour of the former route of stipulating the definition of positive freedom by combining self-realization with the harm principle.

another. But what is wrong with claiming that only people who can make 'right' choices have positive freedom? This is what Green believes (as we have seen in the first section of chapter 6), since he relates freedom with willing the right objects that means being motivated towards self-perfection. Also Kant argues that a person, whose actions follow from respect for the moral law, would be approaching the ideal of autonomy. Even for Hegel and communitarians, it is the self-conscious identification with one's community that gives a concrete content to freedom. All of these accounts are based on the implicit assumption that becoming a free person means the development of distinctively human capacities and the satisfaction of distinctively human needs. The distinctively human capacity for being rational is linked with the motive for self-perfection by Green, and with the respect for the moral law by Kant. Hegel's account of concrete freedom follows from taking the need for mutual recognition and the socially embedded capacity for rational self-determination as a fundamental component for both human nature and individual fulfilment.

Baldwin rightly argues that ethical naturalism (as opposed to moral scepticism) lies at the basis of all positive conceptions of freedom. According to this view, it is in our interest to be moral because we are essentially moral beings; the essence of human nature involves commitment to some moral ideals. Moral freedom (which is common to Kant, Green, Hegel and the communitarians) is the attainment of that condition in which 'we are what we should be'. To put it simply, 'positive freedom is living in accordance with the human essence'.[15]

The difference between various versions of positive freedom is ultimately grounded on different notions of the human nature. For almost all versions of the positive view, moral freedom cannot be achieved in private, since it requires an active commitment to the welfare of others (either in the form of respecting the inherent dignity of humankind, or as contributing to a society of mutual recognition, or in other forms). So, when moral ideals include political ideals, positive freedom requires political activity as a means of liberation.[16]

As a result, a genuine defender of positive freedom should have an implicit or explicit theory of human nature underlying his account of freedom. One cannot give a concrete content to freedom while trying to remain morally neutral between different conceptions of human nature and human good. This is the essential normative aspect of freedom, which forces social scientists to take a side, and decide which account of human nature is more satisfactory than others.[17]

---

[15] Baldwin, T. (1984), 'MacCallum and the Two Concepts of Freedom', *Ratio*, vol. 26, issue 2, pp. 139-40.

[16] *Ibid*, p. 142.

[17] As we shall explain in the next section, when discussing Macpherson's account of freedom, even the negative view is not morally neutral, and is based on a specific account of human nature, which it fails to acknowledge.

3. The Goal of Positive Freedom: Meaningful and Effective Choice versus Self-Development

Norman on Meaningful and Effective Choice

Norman argues that the debate between negative and positive conceptions of freedom is not an insoluble ideological debate, in so far as freedom has an objective content based on our common understanding of why freedom is valuable.[18] The reason why we value negative freedom is because we want to make our own choices; the ability to make choices is central for both conceptions of freedom. The extent of one's freedom depends both on the range of 'meaningful' choices and also on his subjective ability to evaluate these options.[19] In short, freedom is the 'availability of and the capacity to exercise meaningful and effective choice'.[20]

By formulating freedom in terms of individual choice, Norman wants to allow a great scope for various subjective uses of freedom, without identifying freedom with a particular 'right' way of using it. On the other hand, the notion of 'meaningful' choice introduces an objective normative criterion, with a dual critical function. This notion is designed firstly to distinguish 'genuine choices' from 'passing whims' of an individual,[21] and secondly to evaluate which social order opens up more significant choices.

The former aspect can be captured with the idea of a competent chooser, which requires one to develop his capacities for critical thought. In this sense it embodies a developmental account for which the development of certain capacities is crucial to become positively free. The notion of a competent chooser is discussed by the first version of the hybrid view but ignored by the negative view.

The latter aspect is based on the possibility of a social consensus about which options are more significant. For example, if one can choose between forty kinds of cheese but cannot effectively choose his job, then it is a sign that the scope of meaningful choices is limited. To take a less trivial example, if we compare a country where there is wide scope for 'consumer freedom' but high levels of unemployment with another country in which there is job security for all citizens but very limited consumer freedom, then which country provides more 'meaningful choices' to its citizens?

Norman claims that the notion of coercion presupposes that we have a shared idea of meaningful choices.[22] I am sympathetic to the idea of distinguishing meaningful choices as a critical tool to evaluate choices available in a particular social system, but I have doubts on whether we can derive the content of

---

[18] Norman, R. (1987), *Free and Equal: A Philosophical Examination of Political Values*, Oxford University Press, pp. 6-7.

[19] *Ibid*, pp. 35, 37, 41.

[20] *Ibid*, p. 90.

[21] Norman, R. (1989), 'Book Review of Gould's *Rethinking Democracy*', *Journal of Applied Philosophy*, vol. 6, no. 2, p. 236.

[22] Norman (1987), p. 40.

meaningful choices merely from the notion of coercion since there is an ongoing debate between the negative and positive views about the scope, content of coercion and constraints. We cannot assume that there is a consensus on the content of 'meaningful choice' for people with different conceptions of good. We need a more comprehensive notion of individual fulfillment or self-development as the reference point that would give a concrete content to the idea of meaningful choice.

When it comes to the notion of 'effective choice', it is a crucial component for any version of the positive view and it implies more than having autonomy in the private sphere. As Norman argues, 'Autonomy…is too circumscribed if it is confined to the private activities of individuals, to their choice of life-style or even to their economic activities. Political life too must be a sphere for the exercise of autonomy'. This is why we need a broader notion of 'shared or collective autonomy' that is absent in individualistic liberalism.[23] Democracy understood as 'citizenship of active participation' broadens the scope of autonomy through increasing control over one's life.[24] The core of positive freedom is self-activity and self-government that requires both freedom of choice and autonomy in a broader sense.

Gould on Self-Development

Gould starts her analysis by pointing out three defects of the negative conception of freedom. Firstly, it ignores the social and economic means for pursuing one's goals because it takes freedom as an abstract capacity for choice rather than the actual exercise of that capacity in specific choices.[25] Absence of constraints gives only 'abstract freedom' but 'concrete freedom' also requires availability of enabling conditions. Gould thereby agrees with Norman that effective choice is an essential component of positive freedom.

For example, although there may be no legal or discriminatory barriers to prevent someone from entering a given profession or trade, one cannot make such a choice effectively if there are no jobs available. Thus the availability of jobs is an enabling condition for making one's choice effective or for realizing one's purposes.[26]

Gould's second critique of the negative conception of freedom is that it focuses on isolated actions and overlooks freedom as the process of development of an agent through time, by engaging in long-term projects.[27] In other words, a positively free agent cannot be reduced to somebody who is negatively free in most of his actions.

---

[23] Norman, R. (1995), *Studies in Equality*, Avebury Series in Philosophy, pp. 87-8.

[24] Norman (1982), p. 91. The link between freedom and democracy goes beyond the scope of my book.

[25] Gould, C. (1988), *Rethinking Democracy: Freedom and Social Cooperation in Politics, Economy and Society*, Cambridge University Press, pp. 35-6.

[26] *Ibid*, p. 38.

[27] *Ibid*, p. 35.

Maybe we can extend this critique to apply to positive freedom as effective choice by imagining a person who has the material means and intellectual abilities for effective choice, but who does not have long-term plans or any fundamental commitments. In this sense, having effective choice is not sufficient to be a self-developing person.

Thirdly, the purely negative conception of freedom cannot account for 'social and economic domination' as a constraint on freedom because it conceives coercion as a causal relationship between two agents. Domination cannot be represented as a causal relationship; it involves control over the conditions that are necessary to carry out actions towards self-development. Economic domination involves control over the means of production and means of political expression, whereas racism involves control over the access to means of education and earning a living.[28] As a result, any adequate account of positive freedom should be able to explain in what sense exploitation and social domination constrain freedom.

Is the notion of meaningful and effective choice sufficient to account for such domination? In other words, is it true that a person with effective choice does not suffer from exploitation or racial oppression? This can only be established by assuming that social, racial and class domination decreases 'meaningful' options, or impedes one's capacity to become a competent chooser. But this is not a sufficient argument to convince those who deny the existence of exploitation, and define it solely in terms of a 'freedom of contract' between free and equal exchangers. What we consider as the abolition of exploitation and the resulting increase in 'meaningful' choices, they will consider as the closing of 'meaningful' options. For example, introducing land reform policies in a country where landlessness is high and there is a concentration of land in the hands of a few landowners will increase the 'meaningful' options for the majority of agricultural producers who were previously landless. However, the big landowners would consider such policies as restricting their wealth and reducing their 'meaningful' choices.[29]

Gould's interpretation of positive freedom would be an adequate account of freedom only if she could show in what sense relations of domination and exploitation constrain positive freedom as self-development. She wants to establish that domination prevents exercising choice towards self-development, which she defines as follows.

> The courses of action that would count as self-developmental are only those that express the agents' own purposes and are not imposed on them by others; that involve the growth of capacities or the enrichment of the individual's range of activity; and that

---

[28] *Ibid*, p. 42.

[29] According to the landowners, land reform policies would not increase the 'meaningful choices' for the poor either, since they consider landless people as lazy, ignorant and incapable of cultivating land efficiently. From the point of view of the landowners, the 'new' peasants would not even be able to earn subsistence income. Hence, this policy would lead to a waste of a valuable resource (land) and would not increase the meaningful options for anybody.

serve to realize long-range projects, consciously undertaken. Such courses of action may also contribute to the development of an integrated character over time.[30]

The first problem with Gould's definition of self-development is its ambiguity; it refers to distinct criteria, which might give opposite results. For example, if choosing one's own purpose is enough for self-development then it can be reduced to the notion of effective choice. On the other hand, if the growth of capacities is sufficient then one can develop himself even when his ends are imposed from outside. Another example is the oppressed housewife who is unfree in so far as she cannot develop her capacities, but free since she acts with respect to her self-imposed and long-term plans of being a 'good' wife and mother. On the other hand, if all those conditions were necessary for an activity to be self-developmental, then only few people would count as positively free, but Gould would not be willing to accept this conclusion for the reasons we will specify soon.

Norman emphasizes two possible objections to identifying freedom with self-development; it is either arbitrary or empty. Firstly, it 'is too vulnerable to the objection that freedom is being identified with a particular preferred use to which freedom might be put.'[31] Norman asks whether the person who lives from day to day is unfree because his activity does not fit into Gould's criteria for self-development. If so, then self-development is too determinate because it assumes that unless people make the 'right' choices they are not free.[32]

Gould argues that her notion of self-development is not too determinate and it does not identify freedom with an arbitrarily preferred use of freedom because it does not assume an essentialist conception of the self; which capacities are to be developed is chosen by the individual. Then Norman is right in asking that if self-development is so relative to individual choice, then in what sense is it different from effective choice? Gould answers that since effective choice refers to a particular moment of choice, whereas self-development describes a process, it is hard to link 'unconnected episodes of individual free choice' into an overall freedom of the agent.[33]

One might further ask why should everyone take self-development as the goal of his activity? Gould says that people need not choose self-improvement as a conscious goal; it is not an alternative to other goals such as pleasure and virtue; all of these values require self-development one way or another.[34] It is within daily activities that people achieve self-development, without explicitly choosing self-improvement as a goal.[35] Strangely enough, she argues that self-development is the 'norm rather than the exception in ordinary life'.[36] But then self-development becomes natural and includes almost all activities. Elster challenges this claim by

---

[30] *Ibid*, p. 51.
[31] Norman (1989), p. 235.
[32] I have already answered this criticism in the previous section.
[33] Gould (1988), pp. 36, 58.
[34] *Ibid*, p. 58.
[35] *Ibid*, p. 48.
[36] *Ibid*, p. 55.

noting the objective constraints and subjective motivational barriers that lead people to prefer passive enjoyment rather than self-developmental activities, which are often hard and painful in the beginnings of the learning and deepening process.[37] Gould seems to disregard the internal constraints on positive freedom.

In the final analysis, being either ambiguous or empty, Gould's notion of self-development is not adequate to show in what sense domination and exploitation are barriers to positive freedom. One can develop his capacities through work even when he is being exploited, provided that the job is complex enough. Even though Gould argues that self-development excludes 'assembly-line work or household drudgery or dead-end jobs such as secretarial work', she also acknowledges that these activities may contribute to self-development in other ways, such as social relations with co-workers and earning a living to become independent.[38] Hence, Gould fails to construct a concrete notion of self-development that is antagonistic to exploitation and domination. As we shall see now, Macpherson's account of self-development has more to offer in this respect.

Macpherson on Extractive and Developmental Powers

Macpherson begins his account by distinguishing between two types of power: 'extractive power' is the ability to use other men's capacities, whereas 'developmental power' refers to a man's ability to use and develop his capacities.[39] He also distinguishes between the 'descriptive concept' of power underlying the liberal individualist tradition and the 'ethical concept' of power, which is the basis of the 'democratic humanist ideal'. The former view considers man's power as his present ability to achieve satisfaction with any means, based on a conception of humans essentially as 'consumers'. Extractive power is considered as a legitimate and a necessary means to increase one's developmental power. Since the only way one can increase his extractive power is through domination, which decreases other people's extractive power, the competition for power is conceived as a zero-sum game. It is argued to be impossible to increase the extractive (or developmental) powers of everyone in a society.[40]

In contrast, the 'democratic humanist' view considers man's power as his ability to use and develop the 'essential human capacities', which is based on a different conception of human nature as active and productive beings, who can mutually flourish.   Consequently, it becomes possible to increase the developmental powers of all people through the minimization or the abolition of

---

[37] Elster, J. (1990), 'Self-Realization in Work and Politics: The Marxist Conception of the Good Life', *Alternatives to Capitalism*, Cambridge University Press, p. 138.

[38] Gould (1988), p. 51.

[39] Macpherson, C. B. (1973a), 'Problems of a Non-Market Society', *Democratic Theory: Essays in Retrieval*, Oxford University Press, p. 43.

[40] *Ibid*, pp. 47-8. This is very similar to Steiner's view that the total amount of freedom in a society is always constant because the gain of freedom by anyone necessarily implies its loss by another. Steiner (1994), p. 52.

extractive power. Macpherson situates himself as an advocate of this view.[41] Since 'economic and social domination' are instances of extractive power, this argument would be enough to show the sense in which relations of domination are impediments on positive freedom as self-development. Let us now concentrate on each step of this argument.

Macpherson argues that the identification of power with extractive power is not a theoretical mistake of individualist liberalism; it reflects the real situation in capitalism where the whole power of each individual is almost equivalent to his extractive power. In a competitive capitalist economy, in the relation between owners and non-owners of capital, all power is reduced to extractive power. Non-owners have no extractive power, whereas owners have all the extractive power. Non-owners have to sell continuously their productive capacity to the owners of means of production for a wage.[42]

Moreover, individualist liberalism fails to link the economic extractive power with the political power of the state. This view identifies political power with 'state's monopoly of physical coercive power'. Although it conceives political power as power over others, it does not relate it to extractive power and thereby fails to see that political power is the means of consolidating the extractive power of the owners of capital. Focusing only on the source of the political power, the liberal individualist view fails to perceive the 'purpose of political power in any unequal society, which is to maintain the extractive power' of the ruling classes.[43] By ignoring concrete relations between the economic extractive power and political power, liberals overlook the possibility that a fully democratic and egalitarian state can eliminate extractive power in order to increase developmental powers of all people. In order to challenge the above-mentioned liberal view, we need a different conception of human nature as active and productive, and should acknowledge the possibility of an alternative society in which people can develop their 'essentially human capacities' without hindering the development of similar capacities of others.

Macpherson argues that the notion of 'essentially human capacities' (as opposed to those shared with animals) is a crucial starting point for any ethical theory, as a postulate from which rights and obligations can be derived without any additional value premise. Norman is right in objecting that referring to distinctively human potentialities is not helpful as the basis of rights because this notion is too indeterminate. Furthermore, it is not clear why we should value all distinctively human capacities when we recall that the capacity for mass destruction is also a distinctively human capacity.[44]

Macpherson's next move is stipulating the 'essentially human capacities' so that it would include only those capacities, the exercise and the development of which does not hinder other people's using and developing their capacities. He admits this is an 'optimistic view' that considers all destructiveness as arising from

---

[41] Macpherson (1973a), pp. 40-41.

[42] *Ibid*, pp. 43, 45.

[43] *Ibid*, pp. 46-7.

[44] Norman (1998), p. 122.

'intellectual error and scarcity' both of which are removable in another kind of society where 'potential substantial harmony' can be reached.[45] In other words, it is based on the assumption that the 'rights or freedoms men need in order to be fully human are not mutually destructive'. Some of these non-conflicting, essential human capacities are, the capacities for rational understanding, moral judgment and action, aesthetic creation and transforming nature (which includes the capacity for materially productive labour).[46] The fully human capacities can be summarized as the 'rational, moral, aesthetic, emotional and productive' capacities.[47]

There is much to be criticized about the 'optimistic view'. We cannot specify any non-conflicting capacities because it is possible to use any capacity in harmful ways. Norman gives the following example. 'The nimble-fingered person who decides to go in for the life of a pick-pocket rather than a concert pianist is just as certainly realizing his potentialities.'[48]

The best way to understand Macpherson's account of the non-conflicting positive freedoms is to remark the similarities between his project and Green's idea of a 'non-competitive common good' as discussed in chapter 6. Like Green, Macpherson argues that social conflict arises when people pursue competitive goods and social harmony can be established if people are interested in achieving a common good above particular ends.

Every social order is based on restricting some freedoms of all, to enhance other freedoms that are taken to be more significant, based on the specific hierarchy of freedoms one assumes. The negative view reconciles freedoms through the harm principle, whereas Macpherson and Green use the notion of common good as a broader principle (that includes but goes beyond the harm principle) to reconcile individual freedoms. As a result, a person is free to act in ways that would not exploit and dominate others as well as not harm others. Since this criterion establishes the legitimate limits of positive freedom, by definition it implies a society in which there is a harmony between people exercising their positive freedoms. For Macpherson, a free society where everyone has equal positive freedom is 'a society of non-conflicting but non-prescribed ends', which is yet different from a 'preordained harmonious pattern'. This ideal can only be actualized if scarcity and class conflicts are over.[49]

It is important to remark that negative and positive views operate at different levels; whereas the former tries to reconcile conflicting freedoms in personal relations, the latter does it in more comprehensive grounds by focusing on the social and economic factors that underlie the conflicting interests of individuals, as members of various groups and classes.

The negative view claims that a formal system of civil liberties is sufficient to guarantee the mutual freedom of all. In contrast, for many defenders of the positive

---

[45] 'That view has always been at the root of the democratic vision, and indeed of the liberal vision: one has only to think of the Encyclopaedists'. Macpherson (1973a), p. 54.
[46] *Ibid*, pp. 53-5.
[47] *Ibid*, p. 61.
[48] Norman (1998), p. 122.
[49] Macpherson (1973), p. 102.

view, the freedom of each is not compatible with the freedom of all under capitalism due to the existence of economic inequalities. They can be made compatible only in a free society, in which everyone has equal positive freedom. This has objective social conditions, such as equal access to material resources and education, so that everyone has actual opportunities to develop himself.

In the final analysis, an advantage of the notion of self-development is its critical power in evaluating the effects of a specific social system on the positive freedoms of people. Whereas the notion of meaningful and effective choice concentrates on the negative *effects* of capitalism on disadvantaged people who cannot use their freedoms effectively, the notion of self-development also draws attention to the structural *causes* of oppressive relations in capitalism that stem from the unequal extractive power of classes, and which allows some people to benefit at the cost of restricting the developmental power of others.[50]

4. Social Conditions of Positive Freedom

Society is the medium through which some capacities of some people are developed and some others are impeded. We should concentrate on 'hindrances in modern market societies' as a guide to what should be done to pass from liberal market society to a fully democratic society.[51] Whereas other normative political philosophers try to find universal conditions of freedom for any abstract person, Macpherson draws attention to concrete historical impediments that restrict the freedom of non-owners and shifts the focus to 'unfreedom due to capitalist property institutions'.[52]

He makes an immanent critique of capitalism by analysing the disparity between the possibilities of extending developmental power opened up by technological advancements in capitalism, with the new impediments to freedom due to exploitation. A man's developmental power should be measured in terms of the absence of external impediments, with respect to a maximum level of self-development affordable in a particular society, depending on its level of command over nature and productivity.[53] According to him, the aim of a fully democratic society is to maximize the 'aggregate developmental powers of people'. This does not have the problem of increasing some men's power at the cost of reducing others' because by definition people's developmental powers do not conflict.

---

[50] For Macpherson, the 'human powers of the non-owners are diminished by their lack of conscious control over their productive and other activities' in three ways. Firstly, there is a continuous net transfer of surplus value from non-owner to owners. Secondly, non-owners lose the satisfaction they would have achieved if they were controlling the use of their own productive capacities. Thirdly, they have a diminished control over the extra-productive use of their capacities in their leisure time since doing 'mindless' work increases the possibility of 'mindless' activities in leisure. Macpherson (1973a), pp. 67-70.

[51] *Ibid*, p. 57.

[52] Macpherson (1973), pp. 98, 99, 102.

[53] *Ibid*, pp. 58, 68.

Macpherson's agenda to achieve a free society is minimizing or abolishing the extractive powers of people by subordinating the economic domain to the political authority of a democratic state.

Although Gould cannot show why the absence of domination is necessary for positive freedom, she is right in pointing out that the absence of domination or exploitation is not sufficient for positive freedom as self-development.[54] For example, a self-sufficient farmer who lacks education and who lives in poverty is not exploited but also does not have much scope for self-development. This shows that Macpherson is mistaken in so far as he thinks 'the measure of liberty is the absence of extractive power'.[55] Now, let us have a brief look at the concrete policies that are necessary to enhance positive freedoms.

Norman, Gould and Macpherson agree that a free society is an egalitarian and a fully democratic society. It should be egalitarian in the sense that there is an 'equal distribution of positive conditions of freedom',[56] or people should have 'equal rights to the conditions of self-development',[57] It should be fully democratic because the power for self-determination is enhanced by collective self-determination through participatory democracy in various levels of social life.

According to Norman's classification, the social conditions that are required to broaden the scope of effective choice are political, material and cultural conditions.[58] The extent of one's positive freedom is directly proportional to these factors. The political condition refers to political participation or democracy. The scope of one's freedom can be 'limited both by the interference of those who hold political power, and by my own lack of political power'.[59] The material conditions include a decent income, satisfaction of basic needs, technical progress and increase in leisure time, whereas the cultural conditions involve education, knowledge and the development of critical reasoning which enhance the subjective ability to make choices.[60] As a result, political power, economic well-being and equal opportunity for education, as well as negative freedom are necessary to be positively free.

Norman effectively argues that liberty and equality are not only compatible, but also interdependent; the ideals of a free society and an equal society coincide.[61] His vision of a free society is in which there is a 'radical participatory democracy, the common ownership and democratic control of economic institutions, the communal provision of welfare services, parity of incomes, and a common

---

[54] *Ibid*, p. 39.

[55] Macpherson (1973a), p. 51.

[56] Norman (1987), p. 133.

[57] Gould (1988), p. 80; Macpherson (1973a), p. 51.

[58] Norman (1987), p. 41.

[59] *Ibid*, p. 42.

[60] *Ibid*, pp. 44, 48, 49.

[61] Norman (1982), p. 85. There is a huge literature on whether freedom and equality are compatible which is beyond the scope of this book. The typical libertarian who argues freedom and equality to be incompatible is Nozick, whereas Norman convincingly defends the compatibility of freedom and equality.

educational system giving everyone the opportunity of developing his or her abilities to the full'.[62]

Although both Gould and Macpherson consider positive freedom as self-development, they propose different social conditions for positive freedom. Gould's ideal is workers' self-management whereas Macpherson defends increased political participation in order to control and regulate the economic activities.[63] Macpherson's critical analysis of the objective and subjective constraints on self-development in capitalism is in sharp contrast with Gould's view that self-development is an ordinary feature of our daily lives. This difference is reproduced in what they propose as models for a free society. Whereas Gould thinks capitalism with more worker participation and control in workplace is sufficient, Macpherson recognises how the exploitation immanent in capitalism severely limits positive freedom of the majority.

In the next chapter, I will explore how the Marxist historical account of concrete freedom illuminates freedoms and unfreedoms that are specific to capitalism, by making an immanent critique of capitalism.

---

[62] Norman (1987), p. 126.
[63] Gould (1988), p. 20.

Chapter 11

The Historical Account:
Freedoms and Unfreedoms in Capitalism

In this final chapter, I will analyse how the Hegelian-Marxist historical account of freedom can reveal some important aspects of freedom that are ignored by the negative and positive conceptions of freedom. To put it briefly, like the negative conception, it emphasizes individuality, and like the positive conception, it draws attention to the social context of freedom; it further conceives the emergence of new freedoms and unfreedoms within a historical perspective. In so far as the historical account defines freedom as linked with self-realization, it can be considered as a version of the positive view, rather than as going beyond both negative and positive conceptions of freedom.

For the historical account, the conditions of freedom change through history, in parallel with the historical development of human nature, and as a result of the changing forms of domination and exploitation. This is why instead of searching for universal conditions of abstract freedom we should rather focus on the concrete forms of freedom and unfreedom in capitalism, and further distinguish those unfreedoms that are shared by all and those that affect only a certain class.

Firstly, I will explore the enhancements of everyone's freedom in capitalism through the emergence of economic and political freedoms for all. Freedom of enterprise and free labour are the two sides of economic freedom. In the achievement of freedom of enterprise, free labour was coercively created. Although the introduction of free labour was not subjectively perceived as a form of liberation, objectively it liberated people from the narrow, local relations and made them freer through producing more universal beings.

Secondly, in contrast to the negative view, I will argue that capitalism is not a system where everyone is equally free, by comparing the equal formal freedom in the realm of exchange with the unequal substantive freedom in the realm of production. As we concentrate on the new relations of domination in production, it will be seen that in capitalism, workers and capitalists have necessarily antagonistic interests (improvement of capital through maximizing profits versus improvement of labour as self-development). This is why freedom of the few is at the expense of the unfreedom of the many, making capitalism a society of unequal positive freedom.

Thirdly, I will focus on the limitations of everyone's freedom in capitalism through being subject to the impersonal laws of the market. I will use E. M.

Wood's notion of 'market imperatives' as well as Marx's notion of alienation to explain this new form of unfreedom specific to capitalism, which refers to the situation in which people are ruled by alien market laws that they cannot control. Capitalism hinders positive freedom as self-development in so far it leads to people's having a one-sided relationship with the world.

Lastly, I will focus on the relationship between work, leisure and self-development. According to Marx, the unfreedom in work is the main form of unfreedom in capitalism. Whereas the mainstream liberal view considers work as necessarily toil, and equates the domain of freedom with leisure, Marx emphasizes the intrinsic need for work as a component of self-development. I will follow Sayers' argument, which establishes that both work and leisure contribute to individual freedom, in different ways. Marx's idea of a free society (where everyone has equal positive freedom) is a system where freedom in work (through socialized production and appropriation, and democratic control over economic activities) is combined with freedom in leisure. I will emphasize that this is not a transcendent critique based on a universal ideal, but rather an immanent critique of capitalism. Although capitalism creates both the objective possibility and the subjective need for non-alienated work and extended leisure, it fails to actualize these essential components of positive freedom. Hence, a society where everyone is positively free is a real historical possibility both created and hindered by capitalism.

1. The Historical Account of Freedom

The historical account argues that the conditions of freedom changes through history, in relation to particular forms of domination. We can find the roots of the historical account of freedom in Hegel's account of concrete freedom. As we have seen in chapter 9, Hegel defines concrete freedom as opposed to two versions of abstract freedom. These are the purely negative conception of freedom, which ignores that the fact that sociality is essential for freedom, and Kant's positive account of freedom, which reduces freedom to a subjective, moral act.

On the one hand, communitarians develop Hegel's view that sociality (or identification with one's society) is essential for moral agency, which is the foundation of freedom. On the other hand, Norman, Gould and Macpherson embrace Hegel's view that being a free individual requires being a member of a free society, and elaborate the meaning of a free society by linking freedom with equality and democracy, that was missing in Hegel's account.

There is still an important aspect of Hegel's concrete freedom, which is absent in all other versions of positive freedom that we have discussed. This is the historical and progressive dimension of freedom. There can be universal social conditions for freedom only if we assume that constraints on freedom do not change through history and that there is a universal human nature. However, if both of these factors change historically then the conditions of freedom would likewise change. But then how can we talk about the historical progress of freedom? This is possible in so far as the goal of freedom is taken as self-development and if we can discuss which social system is more conducive to self-development.

Marx can be taken as a key figure, representing the historical account as based on historical materialism rather than on Hegel's idealism. Marx explains the historical progression of freedoms and unfreedoms through the conflicts between forces and relations of production rather than as a consequence of the self-expansion of the Spirit. However, the dialectical method that Marx has adopted from Hegel, and their similar themes (such as the link between freedom, self-realization and work) enable us to talk of a Hegelian-Marxist historical account of freedom.

We can understand the significance of the historical account by showing how it illuminates and solves the defects of the other conceptions of freedom. Whereas the negative view defines freedom as the as the absence of universal constraints, the abstract positive view identifies freedom with the presence of universal conditions. In short, they take freedom as a *situation*, rather than as a *process* of overcoming particular obstacles through developing new powers.[1] We can observe this process both in the maturation of an individual and in the historical development of mankind. What were once the conditions, in which an individual fulfils himself, may later start to be conceived as obstacles when one has acquired new powers, demands and values. This is why we cannot list the conditions, which would make people free once and for all, without focusing on the specific form of domination they suffer.

The negative and positive views ignore this historical dimension of concrete freedom, in their own ways. On the one hand, the negative conception of freedom starts from the assumption of a universal human nature, the content of which is abstracted from the competitive individuals in capitalism. On the basis of equating individual freedom with free competition, it puts forward personal coercion and state's intervention in economic relations as the universal constraints on individual freedom. However, these 'universal constraints' were the basis of the social relations in pre-capitalist societies, where economic and political powers were intertwined. As a result, in order to put forward capitalism as the model of the 'free society', the negative view wrongly generalizes the individual in capitalism as representing universal human nature, and hides the historical specificity of a certain mode of production by defining individual freedom in terms of freedom of exchange.

Within the framework of negative freedom, we cannot even ask the questions 'which freedoms?' and 'for whom?' As we shall see in this chapter, the historical account corrects this distorted picture of reality, by arguing that we should interpret the negative view as revealing which new freedoms are introduced by capitalism (relative to feudalism), but at the same time hiding (through an individualist methodology and non-historical, universalist approach) which new unfreedoms are sustained in and through capitalism.

---

[1] Gould, C. (1978), *Marx's Social Ontology: Individuality and Community in Marx's Theory of Social Reality*, MIT Press, p. 101.

On the other hand, Norman, Gould and Macpherson are right in arguing that freedom positively requires equal access to resources and democracy, and negatively requires the absence of relations of domination. However, this view is too abstract without a discussion of the modes of domination specific to capitalism, and their sources.

Marx defines freedom as liberation, as the 'power, domination over the circumstances and conditions in which an individual lives'.[2] The arguments pertaining to the historical progress of freedom depends on the following claims. Firstly, through history humankind has achieved 'mastery over nature' through technological developments, which enabled us to overcome scarcity of means of subsistence. Secondly, we have become more 'universal beings', with wider needs, expectations and social relations. Thirdly, the gradual achievement of civil rights has contributed to the quality of life. As a result, it can be argued that the possibilities for self-development have increased historically. However, there is another side of the same coin. Mastery over nature has resulted in severe environmental crisis. Furthermore, there emerged the new problem of mass poverty amidst abundance. Although humans now have wider social relationships, most of them are alienated relationships since people who are forced to compete conceive each other as mere means to their own self-interest. And lastly, the extension of the scope of civil rights did not help removing class inequalities. The historical account reveals such contradictions of capitalism through making an immanent critique, by comparing what is the case with what else could have been.

2. Enhancements of Everyone's Freedom in Capitalism

In capitalism, there emerge two new freedoms for all: economic and political freedoms. The economic freedom refers to the individual freedom to do whatever one wants (buy, sell and improve) with what one owns. On the one hand, economic freedom implies 'freedom of enterprise' that is achieved through the dissolution of the economic, legal and political privileges of the feudal aristocracy and the guild restrictions. On the other hand, economic freedom involves the creation of 'free labour' as opposed to being bonded to the land and the lords in feudalism.

In contrast to Marxists, liberals take freedom of enterprise and free labour as universal features of human nature, as parts of the 'natural' freedom we have, which only wait for the overcoming of legal and political constraints to develop fully. This point can be seen in Macpherson's analysis of the 'possessive individualist' assumptions underlying liberalism, from Hobbes and Locke to the neo-liberals. Their main assumption is that humans are essentially self-owners in two senses. Firstly, they owe nothing to society for what they have, and secondly they are free to do anything with what they own, which implies that they are free to dispose their labour power in the market. As a result, freedom is defined as the absence of dependence on the wills of others and human society is taken as

---

[2] Marx, K. (1976), 'The German Ideology', Marx, K. and Engels, F., *Collected Works*, vol. 5, Progress Publishers, p. 301.

consisting of a series of market exchange relations, which are presented as the only model of freedom preserving social relations. As Macpherson argues, this picture projects the 'competitive, possessive individuals' in capitalism as a natural state, characterising universal human nature.[3]

The assumption that humans have a natural inclination for the 'competitive pursuit of economic goals in the market', leads to a purely negative definition of freedom as the removal of social and political restrictions on the freedom of enterprise.[4] However, it is neglected that what they consider as universal restraints on individual freedom, such as bonds of serfdom and guild restrictions were progressive factors when they first emerged, and served as the necessary framework of social action for many decades. They started to be perceived as constraints for specific groups only after the development of new power relations, with the rising economic power of the bourgeoisie.[5]

As Marx argues, the primary component of freedom is not the 'removal of restrictions' but rather it is a 'consequence of the new creation of power…The actual tearing down of restrictions…is at the same time an extremely positive development of the productive forces, real energy, and satisfaction of urgent requirements, and an expansion of the power of individuals'.[6] What we have once considered as the 'natural' limits of action, turn into 'restrictions' only after we gain the capacity to overcome them.

Whilst the bourgeoisie emancipated itself from the all-encompassing political authority of the aristocracy and achieved freedom of enterprise, as a by-product it also liberated others by promoting the emergence of free labour and the establishment of political freedom for all, in the sense of the equality of all citizens before the law, having equal rights. Throughout this chapter we will keep the following question in mind. Is such a political emancipation (having equal rights as citizens) enough for human liberation, for people to have equal positive freedoms?

Marx analyses the emergence of free labour as specific to a new mode of production, which is oriented towards the production of commodities and where the labour-power of the producers also become commodities. This discloses two faces of free labour. Free labour can positively be characterised as the achievement of self-ownership (as ownership of one's labour-power as a commodity) and negatively as a loss, as the separation of labour-power from the objective conditions of its existence.

> For the conversion of his money into capital, therefore, the owner of money must meet in the market with the free labourer, free in the double sense, that as a free man he can dispose of his labour-power as his own commodity, and that on the other hand he has no

---

[3] Macpherson, C. B. (1962), *The Political Theory of Possessive Individualism: Hobbes to Locke*, Oxford University Press, pp. 263-9.

[4] Sayers (1992), p. 121.

[5] Marx, K. (1971), *The Grundrisse* (ed. McLellan, D.), Harper & Row Publishers, pp. 128-9.

[6] Marx (1976), pp. 304-5.

other commodity for sale, is short of everything necessary for the realisation of his labour-power.[7]

The transformation of masses into free labourers was neither voluntary, nor perceived by them as liberation. Marx gives an illuminating account of the forcible creation of free labour, in the transformation from feudalism to capitalism.

> Hence, the historical movement, which changes the producers into wage-workers, appears on the one hand, as their emancipation from serfdom and from the fetters of the guilds, and this side alone exists for our bourgeois historians. But, on the other hand, these new freedmen became sellers of themselves only after they had been robbed of all their own means of production, and of all the guarantees of existence afforded by the old feudal arrangements...The expropriation of the agricultural producer, of the peasant, from the soil, is the basis of the whole process.[8]

Making their previous life form impossible was not sufficient to transform producers into industrial workers. This was achieved by disciplining them through new institutions such as factories, prisons and schools. 'Thus were the agricultural people, first forcibly expropriated from the soil, driven from their homes, turned into vagabonds, and then whipped, branded, tortured by laws grotesquely terrible, into the discipline necessary for the wage system'.[9]

We should also remark that capitalism does not have a uniform effect on all parts of the world. As the history of colonialism makes it clear, capitalism has not only introduced wage labour in the home countries where industry develops, but also introduced slavery in the colonies. 'In fact, the veiled slavery of the wage-workers in Europe needed, for its pedestal, slavery pure and simple in the new world'.[10]

Marx does not describe the transformation from feudalism to capitalism in purely negative terms. He also refers to the 'civilising' effects of capitalism by transforming individuals submerged within narrow social relations into more 'universal' human beings, who are part of wider social relations and have extended horizons and self-consciousness.[11]

On the one hand, capitalism transforms the 'submerged' individuals in feudalism (as part of self-sufficient households, having fixed social roles and

---

[7] Marx (1947), p. 147.

[8] *Ibid*, pp. 738-9.

[9] *Ibid*, p. 761.

[10] *Ibid*, p. 785.

[11] 'Hence, the great civilizing influence of capital...Nature becomes for the first time simply an object for mankind, purely a matter of utility; it ceases to be recognized as a power in its own right...capital has pushed beyond national boundaries and prejudices, beyond the deification of nature and the inherited, self-sufficient satisfaction of existing needs, confined within well-defined bounds, and the reproduction of the traditional way of life. It is destructive of all this, and permanently revolutionary, tearing down all obstacles that impede the development of productive forces, the expansion of needs, the diversity of production and the exploitation and exchange of natural and intellectual forces'. Marx (1971), pp. 94-5.

status) into 'detached' individuals (as self-owners, having a wider scope of choice in how to lead their lives). In this respect, they are individualized.[12] On the other hand, these seemingly isolated individuals are brought together in new social relations, institutions and become more interdependent than ever in the satisfaction of their needs. In this respect, it is a process of socialization. As a result, in contrast to what the liberal view presumes, the extension of individuality and sociality are not antagonistic but are parallel processes. Marx expresses this phenomenon as follows.

> But the period in which the isolated individual becomes prevalent is the very one in which the interrelations of society...have reached the highest state of development. Man is in the most literal sense of the word a *zoon politikon*, not only a social animal, but an animal which can develop into an individual only in society.[13]

As a system based on universal commodity production, capitalism dissolves relations of personal dependence that characterized feudal societies and links individuals through exchange relations, which gives rise to alienation since social relations are not personal relations but rather what Marx calls 'social relations between things'.[14]

Capitalism increases individual freedom through introducing political and economic freedoms as well as triggering a process of individualization and universalization. As we shall see now, this is not a linear progression of freedoms but rather a dialectical process, in which people have achieved equal political freedom on the basis of unequal economic freedom, and they can achieve only one-sided individuality without genuine social relations in which individuals can exist in their particularity.

3. The Unequal Positive Freedoms in Capitalism

Liberals refer to capitalism as a free market society. Voluntary relations in the realm of exchange are put forward as the basis of individual freedom. Starting from this claim and the fact that people have equal rights as citizens, the negative view argues that capitalism is a society in which everyone is equally free. In contrast, I will argue that people have unequal positive freedom in capitalism because of the relations of domination in the realm of production. Marx agrees that there is formal freedom in the realm of exchange. In his words,

> This sphere...within whose boundaries the sale and purchase of labour-power goes on is in fact a very Eden of the innate rights of man. There alone rule Freedom, Equality, Property and Bentham. Freedom, because both buyer and seller of a commodity, say of labour-power, are constrained only by their own free will. They contract as free agents,

---

[12] For an illuminating discussion of 'freedom of detachment', see Cohen, G. A. (1974), 'Marx's Dialectic of Labor', *Philosophy and Public Affairs*, vol. 3, no. 3, pp. 239-43.

[13] Marx (1971), p. 17.

[14] Marx (1947), pp. 41-56.

and the agreement they come to, is but the form in which they give legal expression to their common will. Equality, because each enters into relation with the other, as with a simple owner of commodities, and they exchange equivalent for equivalent. Property, because each disposes only of what is his own. And Bentham, because each looks only to himself. The only force that brings them together and puts them in relation with each other is the selfishness, the gain and the private interests of each.[15]

At this level, it seems that individuals have equal freedom of using whatever they own for self-betterment according to what they conceive to be in their self-interests. But if we classify people with respect to what they own (land, capital and labour-power), then individuals can be taken as members of the landowners, capitalists or workers, with respect to their specific ownerships, rather than as abstract individuals.

The basis of exchange between these three classes is the realm of production. We should remark that in liberal theory, the realm of production disappears partly because it conceives capitalism as evolving out of the development of exchange relations between individuals, the extension of markets and the advance in technology, rather than as based on radical changes in the domain of production through the power struggles between various classes. In contrast, for historical materialism, capitalism refers to a specific mode of production involving a distinctive mode of economic appropriation.[16]

We start to perceive a new mode of domination, when we shift our attention from the realm of exchange to the realm of production, in which a new mode of appropriation operates. Capitalists dominate the workers through purely economic ways, in contrast to feudalism, where there is direct appropriation from producers through the use of legal, political or military coercion. In capitalism,

The appropriation of surplus takes place in the 'economic' sphere by 'economic' means... Although the coercive force of the 'political' sphere is ultimately necessary to sustain private property and the power of appropriation, economic need supplies the immediate compulsion forcing the worker to transfer surplus labour to the capitalist in order to gain access to the means of production.[17]

Wood illuminates how the political freedom of individuals (as equal citizens) is at the price of their disempowerment in the realm of production. Capital owners have transferred their coercive authority to the state (having a monopoly of coercive force), and in return they have achieved a new kind of authority over the

---

[15] *Ibid*, p. 155.
[16] 'The historical conditions for the existence of capital are by no means given with the mere circulation of money and commodities. It can spring into life, only when the owner of the means of production and subsistence meets in the market with the free labourer selling his labour power...The capitalist epoch is therefore characterized by this, that labour-power takes in the eyes of the labourer the form of a commodity which is his property; his labour consequently becomes wage-labour. On the other hand, it is only from this moment that the produce of labour becomes a commodity'. *Ibid*, p. 149.
[17] Wood, E. M. (2000), pp. 28-9.

producers, in the sense of the direct control and organization of production.[18] As a result, capital has full authority in the domain of production through exercising its power to control and organize the production process. On the other hand, the labourer merely disposes his labour-power for a wage and has no control over the organization of the production and the work conditions.[19] This description applies to all cases of wage labour, not only to unskilled but also to skilled labour, and both to low-wage and high-wage jobs. The relations of domination/exploitation in work have negative affects on the scope of workers' positive freedom.

In a competitive market economy, the interest of the capitalist is to extract the maximum surplus product, that is to produce with minimum costs and maximum profits. To achieve this goal, either he employs cheap labour, or extends the workday, or introduces more machinery and less labour, thereby increasing the level of unemployment. The worker's interest is antagonistic to the capitalist's since the worker wants to increase his wages and his leisure time so that he will have the means for self-development. In other words, the improvement of capital for maximizing profits restricts the improvement of labour as self-development. Since we define positive freedom as self-development, the worker is in this sense less free than the capitalist.

It should be remarked that Marx does not aim for an increase in wages, but the abolition of the wage system, which is necessary to transform the relation of the worker to his alienated labour, and to others. 'Wages are a direct consequence of estranged labour, and estranged labour is the direct consequence of private property. The downfall of one aspect must therefore mean the downfall of the other'.[20] I will analyse alienation, which affects not only workers but everyone else, in the next section.

Changing our perspective from an individualistic analysis, to a class perspective reveals that free labour (enhancement of negative freedom) is identical with 'wage slavery' (limitation of positive freedom). Although the individualistic perspective when taken in its historical specificity is helpful in showing how capitalism has enhanced individual freedoms with respect to feudalism, it is not adequate to capture the new forms of unfreedom created by capitalism, because it conceals exploitation in the realm of production.

> Capitalist exploitation, far from being more transparent than other forms, is more opaque than any other, as Marx pointed out, masked by the obscurity of the relation between capital and labour in which the unpaid portion of labour is completely disguised in the exchange of labour power for a wage, where the capital pays the worker in contrast, for example, to the peasant who pays rent to a lord...the juridical equality,

---

[18] For an inspiring discussion of the changing relations between the economic and political powers, in terms of the formal separation of the economic and the political spheres in capitalism, see Wood, E. M. (2000), Chapter 1.

[19] *Ibid*, pp. 30-31.

[20] Marx, K. (1967), *Economic and Philosophic Manuscripts of 1844*, Progress Publishers, p. 77.

contractual freedom, and citizenship of the worker in a capitalist democracy are likely to obscure the underlying relations of economic inequality, unfreedom and exploitation.[21]

An important consequence of the above analysis is that, as Marx claims, 'political emancipation' is necessary but not sufficient for 'human emancipation'.[22]

Even when the state treats all citizens as equal, regardless of distinctions of wealth, education and occupation if these distinctions still operate in people's lives and determine the level of their economic freedom, then equal political freedom coexists with unequal economic freedom. Wood illuminates the inadequacy of political freedom in capitalism with the following example. If the slave or the serf had political freedom (equal rights), this would have terminated their economic oppression because surplus-extraction was done by extra-economic means before capitalism. However, although the worker has equal political status as the capitalist, this is not sufficient to terminate the economic domination.[23]

Hence, the equal formal freedom in the realm of exchange coexists with the substantive unfreedom of workers in the realm of production. In so far as exploitation of workers is immanent to capitalism, it cannot be a society where everyone is equally free.

4. Limitations of Everyone's Freedom in Capitalism

Whereas the common form of unfreedom in feudalism is the relations of personal dependence, capitalism introduces a new mode of unfreedom (market-dependence) by making everyone equally subject to the 'impersonal laws of the market'. Liberals argue that market forces do not restrict freedom because they are impersonal, as we have discussed in chapter 3. This argument is based on the mistaken assumption that laws of the market are like natural laws, something we should accept as given. In contrast, the so-called market laws are the outcome of specific human arrangements and can be changed through political action. Hence, we cannot dismiss the possibility that they are a form of unfreedom, merely from the fact that no particular person is responsible for them.

In this section, I will evaluate E. M. Wood's argument that emphasizes 'market imperatives' as opposed the liberal focus on 'market opportunities', in comparison with Marx's discussion of alienation as a form of unfreedom that applies to all, both the worker and the capitalist.[24] My aim is to show in what sense market imperatives are a new form of unfreedom that applies to all people.

---

[21] Wood, E. M. (2000), p. 282.

[22] Marx, K. (1996), 'On the Jewish Question', in *Modern Political Thought: Readings from Machiavelli to Nietzsche* (ed. Wootton, D.), Hackett Publishing Company, p. 769.

[23] Wood, E. M. (1999), 'An Interview with E. M. Wood', *Monthly Review*, vol. 51, no, 1, p. 90.

[24] Although some thinkers like Althusser argue that the notion of alienation is specific to early Marx, I will side with other thinkers such as Avineri, and will hold that alienation (early-Marx) and 'commodity fetishism' (late-Marx) denote similar phenomena. It should be

We should start by noting that market imperatives are not identical with class oppression and exploitation. Firstly, market-dependence is not specific to all class societies. It does not exist in pre-capitalist societies in which 'the market was not the medium of self-reproduction, for either direct producers or exploiters. Direct producers were generally in possession of the means of production...and exploitation took the form of direct surplus extraction by coercive force'.[25] Furthermore, market-imperatives such as the economic pressures to compete, accumulate, profit-maximization and increasing labour productivity can persist even after the abolition of classes, as in the case of market socialism. In short, there would be market-dependence in all cases where the majority of people do not have 'non-market access to the means of subsistence'.[26]

The impersonal laws of the market rather than any form of collective decision making and planning shape how resources will be allocated for production, and forces *all* individuals to compete for maximum material gains.[27] On the one hand, the competition between capitalists is guided by the imperative of reducing costs, increasing profits and market shares. On the other hand, the competition between workers, especially in a context of large unemployment, reduces their wages further, as well as preventing class solidarity and organization.

In the previous section, I have argued that the capitalists are more free when compared to workers. Now, I would like to argue that both classes are unfree when compared to another system in which the market imperatives are abolished.

The universal dependence on market imperatives makes exchange relations appear as the primary social relations. Marx argues that the reduction of all social relations to exchange relations is the result of alienation, whereas the liberals claim this to be the essence of all social relations.[28] This is why alienation and the new unfreedom it signifies become invisible in liberal theory. Marx reveals the central contradiction at the heart of capitalism, starting from his early works.

> The worker becomes all the poorer the more wealth he produces, the more his production increases in power and range. The worker becomes an ever cheaper commodity the more commodities he creates. With the *increasing value* of the world of things proceeds in direct proportion the *devaluation* of the world of men. Labour produces not only commodities; it produces itself and the worker as a *commodity*.[29]

---

remarked that Marx uses alienation in an ambiguous way: sometimes in a general way, to refer to the dullness of work, whereas other times as an attribute of the commodity production system that is specific to capitalism. When I refer to alienation, I will use it in the latter sense.

[25] Wood, E. M. (1999a), 'The Politics of Capitalism', *Monthly Review*, vol. 51, no. 4, p. 13.

[26] *Ibid*, p. 22.

[27] Marx (1976), p. 48.

[28] 'We see then how economics *establishes* the *estranged* form of social commerce as the *essential* and *fundamental* form appropriate to the vocation of man'. Marx, K. (1975), 'Excerpts from James Mill's *Elements of Political Economy*', *Early Writings*, Vintage Books, p. 266.

[29] Marx (1967), p. 66.

From the above quotation it seems that the root of the problem with capitalism is in the concentration of wealth and capital and the increasing poverty of the masses. Nevertheless, Marx's critique goes beyond that; he does not merely want a society in which everyone can satisfy their basic needs, but also imagines the possibility of a society where everyone can develop their capacities and talents in an all-rounded way, and thereby can achieve positive freedom.

The satisfaction of basic needs is the first condition of freedom, which requires the development of the productive forces, so that people can be equal in wealth rather than equal in poverty.

> People cannot be liberated as long as they are unable to obtain food and drink, housing and clothing in adequate quality and quantity. 'Liberation' is a historical act and not a mental act, and it is brought about by historical conditions, the level of industry, commerce, agriculture, intercourse...men must be in a position to live in order to make history.[30]

More than that, people should be able to live a human life, in which they have a multiplicity of needs including needs for aesthetic appreciation, creative activity, and personal relationships that cannot be reduced to exchange relations. It is at this point that Marx sees a wide gap between the possibilities created within capitalism and how the private property system that commodifies everything and forces people to compete (where one person's gain is another's loss) is a barrier to anyone's becoming fully free.

> Every new product represents a new potency of mutual swindling and mutual plundering. Man becomes poorer as man; his need for money becomes ever greater if he wants to overpower hostile beings. The need for money is therefore the true need produced by the modern economic system, and it is the only need which the latter produces...Private property does not know how to change crude need into human need.[31]

Marx thinks that in a better future society, people will have not only the material means to satisfy their needs as they perceive them; but they will also have a variety of irreducible needs, which are ends in themselves. This requires the 'emancipation of the senses', refinement of sensibilities, and a richer way of relating with the world, not reducible to mere utility. We should note that the ability for aesthetic appreciation and artistic creativity are crucial for Marx, because in art we relate with objects as ends in themselves, rather than in terms of utility.

If we interpret Marx's notion of positive freedom as the all-rounded development of capacities, senses and a richer way of relating to nature and others, then we can understand how market imperatives, and a system of private property are barriers to such freedom. Freedom is a function of the quality of one's relations with the world, rather than a matter of possessing things. Marx's following

---

[30] Marx (1976), pp. 38, 41.
[31] Marx (1967), pp. 107-8.

example illuminates the restricted way of being, shared by both the rich and the poor, because of the one-dimensional way in which they relate with the world.

> The sense caught up in crude practical need has only a *restricted* sense. For the starving man, it is not the human form of food that exists, but only its abstract being as food; it could just as well be there in its crudest form, and it would be impossible to say wherein this feeding-activity differs from that of *animals*. The care-burdened man in need has no sense for the finest play; the dealer in minerals sees only the mercantile value but not the beauty and the unique material of the mineral: he has no mineralogical sense. Thus, the objectification of human essence both in its theoretical and practical aspects is required to make man's *sense human*, as well as to create the *human sense* corresponding to the entire wealth of human and natural substance.[32]

We can use the above quote as a starting point to understand Marx's argument that both the worker and the capitalist are alienated in different ways. Although the part where he discusses the alienation of the 'non-worker' breaks off unfinished, he still gives us the clues of why the capitalist is also alienated.

> Everything which appears in the worker as an *activity of alienation*... appears in the non-worker as a *state of alienation*...Secondly, that the worker's *real, practical attitude* in production and to the product (as a state of mind) appears in the non-worker confronting him as a *theoretical* attitude.[33]

On the one hand, both the capitalist and the worker have a disinterested attitude to the nature of the work done, they are detached from their activity (whether it be practical through manual labour, or theoretical through mental labour) and conceive it only as a means to earn money. On the other hand, they do not care about what they produce and why they produce; whether it will satisfy the needs of others or not does not matter to them. Although capitalism makes everyone interdependent in the satisfaction of their needs, people conceive each other externally as rivals rather than as internally contributing to their own self-development. In *Grundrisse*, Marx extends the same theme in his description of the new form of unfreedom that applies to all individuals.

> The mutual and universal dependence of individuals who remain indifferent to one another constitutes the social network that bonds them together...The social character of activity, and the social form of the product...are here opposed to individuals as something alien and material; this consists...in their subordination to relations that exist independently of them and arise from the collision of indifferent individuals with one another.[34]

So, the market imperative for competition creates a society where everyone is at war with each other. It seems that Hobbes' description of the state of nature is well suited as a description of the market society. Exploitation makes some people

---

[32] *Ibid*, p. 101.

[33] *Ibid*, p. 78.

[34] Marx (1971), p. 66.

more unfree than others whereas the free market society hinders the positive freedom of all people. The abolition of classes is necessary to terminate exploitation, and the subordination of economic activities to collective, democratic control is necessary to overcome the market imperatives.

5. Work, Leisure and Self-Development

As Marx claims, unfreedom in the realm of production, or unfreedom in work is a central component of unfreedom in capitalism. However, this does not mean that freedoms can flourish only beyond work. In contrast, the key to achieve further freedom is to overcome the unfreedom in work.

Mainstream views (both in the right and the left) present work as the opposite of freedom; it is claimed to be toil, or an essentially alienating activity, whereas leisure is presented as the realm of freedom. The demand for freedom is then reduced to the demand for freedom from work. This argument is presented also as in line with the new phenomenon of mass unemployment that accompanies 'flexible' production, which makes it difficult for everyone to have the opportunity to work. Sayers effectively opposes such arguments by re-interpreting Marx, and showing that work and leisure are complementary avenues for the self-development of the modern individual.[35]

Work is a liberating activity in three respects. First of all, if we take work as a practical activity in which one intentionally transforms nature, then it involves an activity of overcoming obstacles through the development of new capacities and the extension of human nature. This opens up new mediated ways of relating with the world (as opposed to animals who have a direct, unmediated relationship with nature through the activity of consumption) and thereby extends our freedom by achieving control over the natural forces. Secondly, it enhances self-mastery, self-consciousness and self-esteem through the recognition of our capacities in an objectified form in the product; this sense of achievement is an important source of satisfaction. Thirdly, in so far as it is a social, co-operative activity, the recognition that we are performing a socially useful service, by contributing to the satisfaction of the needs of others, is itself a source of satisfaction, constituting an important part of the 'meaning of life'. We feel that we belong to a larger whole, through recognising that our work is appreciated and needed by others.

There is an important difference between those three features of work. The first two belong to any productive activity (practical and theoretical); they are attributes of labour in general. Someone who builds a cottage and another person who solves a difficult problem in mathematics can be given as examples. In other words, it does not matter whether these activities are part of work or leisure activities. Any creative activity that involves a challenge would fit into this category. The third feature applies not to any form of labour, but to work defined as socially necessary

---

[35] Sayers, S. (1989), 'Work, Leisure and Human Needs', *The Philosophy of Leisure* (ed. Winnifrith, T. and Barret, C.), Macmillan Press, pp. 34-5. I am greatly indebted to this brilliant article, which reveals the need for work and leisure as specific historical needs.

productive activity. Work in this sense is a subset of labour, just as rest is a subset of leisure.

In order to understand the difference between work and labour, let us compare a retired person who goes fishing as a hobby (what I will call a fishing-man), with a fisherman. Although their fishing activities (as labour) are the same, the fishing-man performs it as part of his 'leisure',[36] whereas the fisherman performs it as his 'work'. Both men can develop their capacities and have a sense of achievement in their labour, but only the fisherman can have the feeling that he is performing socially useful labour, contributing to the needs of others. To put it differently, for the fishing-man his activity is only an end in itself, whereas for the fisherman it is related with his social role.

If we accept Hegel's argument that the need for recognition is a fundamental need, then we can understand why the fisherman is more free than the retired fishing-man. Even if we assume that those two men spend their day in a similar way, still the fisherman knows that he is performing socially useful labour whereas the other man might think that he is of no use to anyone. A life of pure leisure would lack this third aspect of freedom through work. It is in this sense that work and leisure are complementary activities and both of them are necessary for freedom and self-development. As Sayers argues,

> What may be enjoyable and rewarding as a hobby or a spare time activity is insufficient as the central activity of life. For such pursuits have value primarily in contrast to work –and precisely because they are not work, not necessary activities, but engaged in simply for the pleasure they bring.[37]

On the other hand, even a monotonous, repetitive work may involve some fulfillment in so far as the worker knows that he is performing socially useful labour. Work is essential to have self-esteem based firstly on the awareness that he is competent in dealing with the objects of his work, and secondly as the acknowledgement that he is satisfying needs of others by producing useful products.[38]

It is this fulfillment, which is lacking for most wage-labourers in capitalism. They are unfree partly because they do not feel that they are performing a socially useful labour. They know that their work directly creates wealth for the capitalist, and only indirectly satisfies the desires of consumers, if the demand and supply meet in the market. In other words, wage-labourers work at the service of the capitalists, rather than at the service of the society as a whole. Let us now try to understand how this unfreedom of wage-labour can be overcome within a different mode of production.

Every mode of production can be taken as involving a particular organisation of time. In capitalism, the working day of a wage-labourer consists of three

---

[36] We should note that leisure is defined only in contrast to work. When one is retired, we cannot specify the limits of his leisure activity.

[37] *Ibid*, p. 49.

[38] Sayers (1998), p. 41.

components: the necessary labour time, the surplus labour time and the disposable time (or leisure). As we have seen in the third section of this chapter, the capitalist has full control over the organization of the production process. In order to increase his profits (which are directly proportional to the surplus labour time), he either increases surplus labour time by extending the workday or reduces the necessary labour time through the introduction of machinery (thereby replacing some workers by machines and creating unemployment). In the former case, the extension of the workday leaves little time for self-developmental leisure activities; leisure is used only for resting and the satisfaction of basic needs. In the latter case, the unemployed neither has enough money to engage in self-developmental activities, nor has motivation (since life often seems to be more meaningless after the loss of self-esteem accompanying the dismissal from work).

The increased productivity in capitalism leads to a decrease in the necessary labour-time. 'But although its tendency is always to create disposable time, it also converts it into surplus labour...the masses of workers must appropriate their own surplus labour'.[39] This is the way production could and should be organized so that unfreedom in work due to exploitation may disappear.

> Individuals are then in a position to develop freely. It is no longer a question of reducing the necessary labour time in order to create surplus labour, but of reducing the necessary labour of society to a minimum. The counterpart of this reduction is that all members of society can develop their education in the arts, sciences, etc. thanks to the free time and means available to all.[40]

This is the basis of Marx's immanent critique of capitalism. Capitalism cannot meet the needs for fulfilling work and leisure that it has created. Sayers spells out this point in a striking way.

> What socialism demands, therefore is not the liberation of people from work-capitalism is already doing that all too successfully by throwing millions onto the dole - but rather the liberation of work...The *subjective* conditions for a more satisfactory and rational organization of work of society are developing here and now. What is lacking is the *objective* framework of economic and social relations, and the objective organization of work, which would allow this need to be satisfied.[41]

Sayers' approach is in sharp contrast with Elster's view, which takes the need for work and self-realization as universal, absolute values and argues that most people fail to perceive these as needs due to the lack of appropriate motivations. Within Elster's framework, it becomes almost impossible to claim that wage-labour involves a form of unfreedom that is distinctive to capitalism. Furthermore, it is strange to insist that work is a real need whilst claiming that most people do not prefer to work if asked. Most of the responsibility in the 'lack of self-realization' is shifted from the objective system, to the people who do not develop

---

[39] Marx (1971), p. 144.
[40] *Ibid*, p. 142.
[41] Sayers (1998), pp. 57, 59.

themselves because of their 'risk-aversion, or myopia'.[42] Elster emphasizes the internal constraints on freedom over and above the economic constraints.

In the final analysis, both work and leisure can be made more free in a socialist society where the production process is controlled rationally and democratically by the 'associated producers'. When economic activities are shaped through the democratic decision making of people rather than by alien market imperatives, as a result of which both people's workdays and their leisure time are liberated. Socialised production and socialised appropriation might overcome the divorce between labour and capital and enable the flourishing of many-sided activities and social relations. Probably this is what Marx had in mind, when he imagined a society in which 'the free development of each is the condition for the free development of all'.[43]

---

[42] Elster (1990), pp. 138-47.
[43] Marx (1962), p. 54.

Conclusion

To live! Like a tree alone and free
Like a forest in brotherhood
This yearning is ours.

Nazim Hikmet
(Turkish poet, 1902-63)

Liberals claim that we are living in a free world. With the downfall of the actually existing socialist regimes, and the pressures to dismantle the welfare states, globalisation is taken to be another name for the final victory of capitalism. Each individual has total freedom to buy, sell, invest and improve himself in proportion to his natural talents, individual efforts and the resources he owns. Everyone is on his own and responsible for his choices and his social condition. People's destinies are no longer determined by distinctions of status at birth as it was before capitalism. Classes are not rigid categories since each individual can rise above his class by being successful in the competitive market society, using 'market opportunities' for his self-interest. If there is still poverty, then it is either because the poor are lazy, untalented and thereby deserve their condition, or nobody is responsible for their deprivation. The distribution of wealth is due to the 'unintended consequences' of individual transactions in the market. After all, the poor, the ignorant and the disabled are as free as all others since people have equal legal rights and freedom is not related with the scope of choices one has. So the story goes. We learn that although capitalism may include great inequalities of wealth and income, increasing crime rates and other misfortunes it is still the best model of a free society where there is an equal distribution of individual freedom.

This approach takes as its starting point the assumption that the competitive and acquisitive self in capitalism represents universal human nature, and concludes that capitalism is the model of a free society. This view is based on taking voluntary consent as the sign of freedom and 'freedom of contract' as the social basis of freedom. However, when the parties of the contract are conceived as abstract individuals, who are equal in terms of self-ownership, some crucial factors are overlooked. Voluntary consent is not identical with free choice. There can be 'coercive offers', or offers one cannot refuse. When there are immense disparities of power between the two parties of the contract, the strong may abuse the vulnerable position of the weak. For example, in periods when there is mass unemployment, the poor may voluntarily accept low-paid and dangerous jobs without this being a product of genuinely free choice.

Another version of the negative view, which claims to give a purely descriptive theory of freedom, takes voluntary consent as one of the criterion to distinguish free from unfree actions. These thinkers (such as Oppenheim, Steiner and Miller) choose 'free action' as the main unit of analysis (chapter 2). In fact, they first dwell upon the meaning of unfree action so that they can define freedom negatively, as the opposite of unfree action. Nevertheless, this starting point leads to a very narrow set of constraints on freedom according to which, only personal constraints (direct interventions and threats by others) limit freedom. It follows that most of us are free in most of our actions when freedom is taken as the norm and unfreedom is considered as exceptional, as something to be explained. It is not a coincidence that, like the liberals, this version of the negative view also assumes that we are naturally free.

The main difference between the negative and positive conceptions of freedom is whether they take freedom as the starting point or as a goal. Whereas the negative view takes freedom as natural, as something to be protected against intervention by others, the positive view considers freedom as a social and historical achievement. We can see the origins of the former view in Hobbes' mechanistic theory of human action as not different in kind from animal behaviour (since both humans and animals are natural beings, just matter in motion, free to move unless restricted by external impediments) and in Locke's view that life, liberty and property are *natural* rights and the basic goal of the political union is to preserve them. On the other hand, the roots of the positive conception of freedom can be extended back to the ancient Greek philosophers like Aristotle who conceive humans as 'political animals', requiring a fulfilling social environment to realize their potentialities and become full human beings. The modern roots of the positive conception of freedom lie in Kant's notion of autonomy that emphasizes the distinctively human capacity for rational self-determination.

The assumption that humans are naturally free makes and focusing exclusively on freedom of action makes it difficult to give an adequate account of personal freedom. It is the hybrid view, which starts to challenge this framework by focusing on 'free choice' and free agency. Hybrid theories define freedom of choice negatively, by specifying the conditions that restrict free choice. Forms of insanity, deliberate manipulation of one's choices by others (e.g. being hypnotised, but not being persuaded through advertisements), compulsions and the weakness of the will can constrain freedom of choice. With this move the constraints on freedom are extended to include internal constraints.

The hybrid view focuses in particular on how one's freedom can be restricted by the weakness of will. When a person cannot resist compulsive desires, his action is still free and voluntary; but it does not follow that he is a free agent. One is a free agent to the extent that he can achieve some detachment from his immediate desires, reflect upon them, choose the more significant ones, and act upon these 'second order' choices. This is why the advocates of the hybrid view define freedom as doing what one values, which requires self-consciousness (to articulate what one values) and self- discipline (to overcome internal and external obstacles so that he can act on the basis of his values).

As a result, freedom is not the natural starting point for all, but increases in proportion to self-discipline and self-development. If people were only natural beings (acting according to a pleasure-pain calculus) then they could not be free. We are free and can be more free because of being moral agents who can achieve self-determination. With these themes, the hybrid view gets closer to the positive view, in terms of the internally complex self and moral agency underlying freedom. However, it falls short of the positive conception of freedom because of its essentially individualist framework, which overlooks that humans are socially embedded beings.

Surprisingly, the hybrid view ignores two fundamental factors that can limit freedom of choice; poverty restricts the scope of choice and ignorance is a barrier to informed choice. This is a crucial difference between the hybrid view and the positive conception of freedom. The former takes freedom as an individual achievement (through self-consciousness and self-discipline) and therefore considers only the subjective aspect of freedom, whereas the latter conceives freedom as a social achievement, which has both subjective and objective components.

According to Hegel and Green, humans become moral agents through participating in various social institutions and having concrete social roles and obligations. The development of free agency requires both the existence of material resources to exercise free choice (i.e. the objective component of freedom), and the cultivation of subjective abilities to assess alternatives (i.e. the subjective component of freedom). Poverty and ignorance can make people less free by not providing them the enabling social conditions for free agency.

The positive view implies an amendment of the relationship between freedom and individual responsibility. It is meaningless to claim that a person is responsible for things that are beyond his individual control. Impersonal market forces do restrict the scope for individual freedom and responsibility. If widespread poverty and ignorance are the result of human arrangements, then they can be and should be remedied by adopting different policies. For example, the state should have a positive duty to provide public education and other welfare services, so that people can have more control over their lives.

The strictly individualistic understanding of freedom shared by the negative and the hybrid views makes it impossible to talk about the objective social conditions for freedom. They take the existing social order as given, with no influence on the extent of individual freedom. In contrast, for the positive conception of freedom, individual freedom ultimately requires a free society, in which everyone has equal access to resources. This shows another crucial difference between the negative and positive conceptions of freedom; only the latter takes freedom as inseparable from equality and democracy.

As a result, the negative aspect of freedom (absence of external and internal constraints) is not the whole of freedom. Freedom also has a positive aspect (having power for self-determination). This opens up the possibility of extending freedom from the non-violation of civil rights, and consumer freedom to the real opportunities for self-development.

What is missing in both the negative and positive conceptions of freedom is the historical dimension of freedom. The negative and positive views propose universal conditions of freedom. However, their theories reflect specific historical demands of certain groups against different forms of domination. In order to understand which theory of freedom has more explanatory power in today's world, we should reveal their particular socio-historical contexts and compare these with the socio-economic conditions of the present times.

The negative conception of freedom emerged in 17th-19th century Britain and Europe. It reflected the rising bourgeoisie's demand for equality before the law and civil liberties (against feudal privileges) and freedom of enterprise (against the extra-economic, direct appropriation of the surplus product). With the new mode of production and new political institutions that transformed feudal society into the capitalist society, gradually everyone had negative freedom. As a result, the negative view explains the senses in which individuals are more free in capitalism when compared with pre-capitalist societies.

Freedom of contract was crucial as a non-coercive, purely economic mode of relation between equal citizens until the 19th century. Thereafter, with the increase in oligopolistic enterprises, an individual worker was no longer confronted with an individual capitalist, but in general with a big corporation. This was the historical context when voluntary consent started to diverge from free choice, because of the increasing inequalities of wealth that transformed free competition into a myth.

In late 19th century Europe, the demands of the working classes for social reform, the reduction of the work day and universal suffrage laid the foundation for the positive conception of freedom. As the 'minimal' state of free market society was a concrete model for a society organised with respect to negative freedoms, the welfare state was the concrete social embodiment of positive freedom.

When the negative view is taken out of its historical context and applied to explain the freedoms and unfreedoms in today's world, then it can only explain the freedoms but is mute on the new unfreedoms. Obviously, a theory that is designed to explain the senses in which capitalism enhances freedom with respect to feudalism, cannot adequately explain how capitalism limits freedoms relative to what is possible in a future society.

On the other hand, the positive view is inadequate in so far as it suggests purely political remedies to economic problems. We cannot impose abstract duties on the state (so that it will serve everyone's interest equally) without analysing the specific forms of unfreedom in capitalism and the mechanism that reproduces them. For example, after realising the link between 'flexible production' and mass unemployment that undermines the foundations of the welfare states, it becomes almost impossible to argue that the welfare state is a universal project, applicable in any society. The future alternatives can be envisioned only on the basis of an evaluation of the actual possibilities of the present society, which requires an immanent critical method, as we have explored in chapter 11.

Marx's account of freedom can be taken as a concrete version of the positive conception of freedom; it introduces the historical dimension of freedom that enables us to evaluate the limits of freedom in capitalism. It is only within this historical materialist framework that the following questions can be formulated.

Does the free market imply individual freedom for all? How does capitalism produce new unfreedoms as well as new freedoms? Which freedoms of whom are enhanced, at the price of what other freedoms?

As we answer those questions by unveiling the ideological distortions, the rosy picture of capitalism as a free society fades; what appear as 'market opportunities' are transformed into 'market imperatives' and we discover our 'illusions of freedom'. Not being interfered with by others, the absence of hierarchical relations of dependence, to have equal rights as citizens really enhance individual freedoms with respect to the feudal society. But how far can we be owners of our selves, controlling our destinies when most of us are compelled by the market forces to be wage labourers, without having secure jobs due to the pressures of 'flexible production' and frequent economic crises? The impersonal market forces do not arise out of indeterminate 'unintended consequences' of individual actions, but rather reflect the specific logic of capitalism that enforces competition, profit maximization and accumulation. It is this specific economic logic that is the source of the deterioration of work conditions, and the increasing disempowerment of people in the economic and political spheres. If freedom means having power and control over the conditions of one's life then capitalism is *against* freedom in today's world. This is not the end of the journey; we have yet to devise new ways of how to enhance individual freedoms beyond capitalism.

Bibliography

Acton, H. B. (1961), 'Objectives', *Agenda for a Free Society: Essays on Hayek's The Constitution of Liberty* (ed. Seldon, A.), Hutchinson of London.

Amin, S. (2000), *Capitalism in the Age of Globalization: The Management of Contemporary Society*, Zed Books.

Ancsel, E. (1978), *The Dilemmas of Freedom*, Akademiai Kiadu Budapest.

Arneson, R. (1985), 'Freedom and Desire', *Canadian Journal of Philosophy*, vol.15.

Atiyah, P. S. (1979), *The Rise and Fall of Freedom of Contract*, Clarendon Press.

Baldwin, T. (1984), 'MacCallum and the Two Concepts of Freedom', *Ratio*, vol. 26/2.

Bauman, Z. (2000), *Globalization: The Human Consequences*, Polity Press.

Bell, D. (1993), *Communitarianism and Its Critics*, Clarendon Press.

Bellamy, R. (1992), *Liberalism and Modern Society: A Historical Argument*, The Pennyslvania State University Press.

Benn, S. I. and Weinstein, W. L. (1971), 'Being Free to Act, and Being a Free Man', *Mind*, vol. 80.

Berger, P. (1987), 'On the Obsolescence of the Concept of Honour', *Liberalism and Its Critics* (ed. Sandel, M.), Basil Blackwell.

Berlin, I. (1969), *Four Essays on Liberty*, Oxford University Press.

Bosanquet, B. (1955), *The Philosophical Theory of the State*, Macmillan.

Bradley, F. H. (1972), *Ethical Studies*, Oxford University Press.

Christman, J. (1991), 'Liberalism and Individual Positive Freedom', *Ethics*, vol. 101.

Cohen, G. A. (1974), 'Marx's Dialectic of Labor', *Philosophy and Public Affairs*, vol. 3/3.

Cohen, G. A. (1981), 'Freedom, Justice and Capitalism', *New Left Review*, vol. 126.

Cohen, G. A. (1981a), 'Illusions About Private Property and Freedom', *Issues in Marxist Philosophy* (ed. Mepham, J and Ruben, D.), vol. 4, Harvester Press.

Cohen, G. A. (1985), 'Are Workers Forced to Sell Their Labour Power?', *Philosophy and Public Affairs*, vol. 14.

Cohen, G. A. (1988), 'Are Disadvantaged Workers Who Take Hazardous Jobs Forced to Take Hazardous Jobs?', *History, Labour and Freedom: Themes from Marx*, Clarendon Press.

Cohen, G. A. (1988a), 'The Structure of Proletarian Unfreedom', *History, Labour and Freedom: Themes from Marx*, Clarendon Press.

Cohen, G. A. (1991), 'Capitalism, Freedom and the Proletariat', *Liberty* (ed. Miller, D.), Oxford University Press.

Dobb, M. (1960), *Political Economy and Capitalism*, Routledge and Kegan Paul.

Dworkin, G. (1988), *The Theory and Practice of Autonomy*, Cambridge University Press.

Elster, J. (1990), 'Self-realization in Work and Politics: The Marxist Conception of the Good Life', *Alternatives to Capitalism*, Cambridge University Press.

Elster, J. (1998), *Making Sense of Marx*, Cambridge University Press.

Feinberg, J. (1973), *Social Philosophy*, Prentice-Hall Inc.

Feinberg, J. (1998), 'Freedom and Liberty', *Routledge Encyclopaedia of Philosophy* (ed. Craig, E.), vol. 3, Routledge.

Frankfurt, H. (1971), 'Freedom of the Will and the Concept of a Person', *The Journal of Philosophy*, vol. 68.

Friedman, M. (1974), *Capitalism and Freedom*, The University of Chicago Press.

Friedman, M. (1980), *Free to Choose: A Personal Statement*, Secker & Warburg.

Galbraith, J. K. (1969), *The Affluent Society*, Houghton Mifflin Company.

Galeano, E. (1997), *Open Veins of Latin America: Five Centuries of the Pillage of a Continent*, Monthly Review Press.

Geuss, R. and Hollis, M. (1995), 'Freedom as an Ideal', *Aristotelian Society*, supp. vol. 69.

Gould, C. (1978), *Marx's Social Ontology: Individuality and Community in Marx's Theory of Social Reality*, MIT Press.

Gould, C (1988), *Rethinking Democracy: Freedom and Social Cooperation in Politics, Economy and Society*, Cambridge University Press.

Goldsmith, E. (1995), 'Development Fallacies', *The Future of Progress: Reflections on Environment and Development*, Green Books.

Gray, J. (1981), 'Hayek on Liberty, Rights and Justice', *Ethics*, vol. 92.

Gray, J. (1988), 'Against Cohen on Proletarian Unfreedom', *Social Philosophy and Policy*, vol. 6.

Gray, J. (1989), 'Liberalism and the Choice of Liberties', *Liberalisms: Essays in Political Philosophy*, Routledge.

Gray, J. (1998), *Hayek on Liberty*, Routledge.

Green, T. H. (1921), 'On the Different Senses of Freedom as Applied to the Will and to the Moral Progress of Man', *Lectures on the Principles of Political Obligation*, Longmans, Green & Co.

Green, T. H. (1991), 'Liberal Legislation and Freedom of Contract', *Liberty* (ed. Miller, D.), Oxford University Press.

Green, T. H. (1999), 'Prolegomena to Ethics: Selections', *Lectures on the Principle of Political Obligation and Other Writings* (ed. Harris, P. and Morrow, J.), Cambridge University Press.

Green, T. H. (1999a), 'Lectures on the Principles of Political Obligation', *Lectures on the Principle of Political Obligation and Other Writings* (ed. Harris, P. and Morrow, J.), Cambridge University Press.

Green, T. H. (1999b), 'Fragments on Moral and Political Philosophy', *Lectures on the Principle of Political Obligation and Other Writings* (ed. Harris, P. and Morrow, J.), Cambridge University Press.

Gutman, A. (1994), 'Communitarian Critics of Liberalism', *Communitarianism: A New Public Ethics* (ed. Daly, M.), Wadsworth Publishing Company.

Hayek, F. A. (1976), *The Constitution of Liberty*, Routledge & Kegan Paul.

Hayek, F. A. (1979), *Law, Legislation and Liberty*, vol.1, Routledge & Kegan Paul.

Hayek, F. A. (1991), 'Freedom and Coercion', *Liberty* (ed. Miller, D.), Oxford University Press.

Hegel, G. W. F. (1975), *Aesthetics: Lectures on Fine Art*, vol. 1, Oxford University Press.

Hegel, G. W. F. (1977), *Phenomenology of Spirit*, Oxford University Press.

Hegel, G. W. F. (1988), *Introduction to the Philosophy of History*, Hackett Publishing Company.

Hegel, G. W. F. (1995), *Elements of the Philosophy of Right*, Cambridge University Press.

Hobbes, T. (1996), 'Leviathan', *Modern Political Thought: Readings from Machiavelli to Nietzsche* (ed. Wootton, D.), Hackett Publishing Company.

Hume, D. (1985), *A Treatise of Human Nature*, Penguin Books.

Kant, I. (1949), *Fundamental Principles of the Metaphysics of Morals*, The Liberal Arts Press.

Kant, I. (1960), *Religion Within the Limits of Reason Alone*, Harper & Row.

Kant, I. (1996), 'Metaphysics of Morals', *Practical Philosophy*, Cambridge University Press.

Kant, I. (1997), *Groundwork of the Metaphysics of Morals,* Cambridge University Press.

Kant, I. (2001), *Critique of Practical Reason*, Cambridge University Press.

Klein, N. (2000), *No Logo*, Flamingo.

Kley, R. (1994), *Hayek's Social and Political Thought*, Clarendon Press.

Kristjansson, K. (1992), 'Social Freedom and the Test of Moral Responsibility', *Ethics*, vol. 103.

Kymlicka, W. (1997), *Contemporary Political Philosophy: An Introduction*, Oxford University Press.

Locke, J. (1996), 'Second Treatise of Government', *Modern Political Thought: Readings from Machiavelli to Nietzsche* (ed. Wootton, D.), Hackett Publishing Company.

MacCallum, G. (1991), 'Negative and Positive Freedom', *Liberty* (ed. Miller, D.), Oxford University Press.

Machlup, F. (1969), 'Liberalism and the Choice of Freedoms', *Roads to Freedom: Essays in Honour of F. A. von Hayek* (ed. Streissler, E.), Routledge & Kegan Paul.

Macpherson, C. B. (1962), *The Political Theory of Possessive Individualism: Hobbes to Locke*, Oxford University Press.

Macpherson, C. B. (1972), *The Real World of Democracy*, Oxford University Press.

Macpherson, C. B. (1973), 'Berlin's Division of Liberty', *Democratic Theory: Essays in Retrieval*, Oxford University Press.

Macpherson, C. B. (1973a), 'Problems of a Non-Market Society', *Democratic Theory: Essays in Retrieval*, Oxford University Press.

Mandel, E. (1976), *An Introduction to Marxist Economic Theory*, Pathfinder Press.

Marx, K. (1947), *Capital*, vol. 1, International Publishers.

Marx, K. (1962), 'Manifesto of the Communist Party', *Karl Marx and Frederick Engels Selected Works*, Foreign Languages Publishing House, vol. 1.

Marx, K. (1967), *Economic and Philosophic Manuscripts of 1844*, Progress Publishers.

Marx, K. (1971), *The Grundrisse* (ed. McLellan, D.), Harper & Row Publishers.

Marx, K. (1975), 'Excerpts from James Mill's *Elements of Political Economy*', *Early Writings*, Vintage Books.

Marx, K. (1976), 'The German Ideology', Marx, K. and Engels, F., *Collected Works*, vol. 5, Progress Publishers.

Marx, K. (1996), 'On the Jewish Question', *Modern Political Thought: Readings from Machiavelli to Nietzsche* (ed. Wootton, D.), Hackett Publishing Company.

Mason, A. (1996), 'Workers' Unfreedom and Women's Unfreedom: Is There a Significant Analogy?', *Political Studies*, vol. 44.

Meszaros, I. (1986), *Marx's Theory of Alienation*, Merlin Press.

McGregor, J. (1989), 'Bargaining Advantages and Coercion in the Market', *Philosophy Research Archives*, vol. 14.

Mill, J. S. (1985), *On Liberty*, Penguin Books.

Miller, D. (1983), 'Constraints on Freedom', *Ethics*, vol. 94.

Miller, D. (1984), 'Reply to Oppenheim', *Ethics*, vol. 95.

Miller, J. (1984), *Rousseau: Dreamer of Democracy*, Yale University Press.

Miller, W. (1999), 'Social Change and Human Nature', *Monthly Review*, vol. 50.

Mills, C. (1990), 'Choice and Circumstance', *Ethics*, vol. 109.

Mulhall, S. and Swift, A. (1997), *Liberals and Communitarians*, Blackwell.

Neely, W. (1974), 'Freedom and Desire', *The Philosophical Review*, vol. 83.

Nietzsche, F. (1990), *Twilight of the Idols/ The Anti-Christ*, Penguin Books.

Norberg-Hodge, H. (1995), 'The Pressure to Modernize', *The Future of Progress: Reflections on Environment and Development*, Green Books.

Norman, R. (1982), 'Does Equality Destroy Liberty?', *Contemporary Political Philosophy* (ed. Graham, K.), Cambridge University Press.

Norman, R. (1987), *Free and Equal: A Philosophical Examination of Political Values*, Oxford University Press.

Norman, R. (1989), 'Book Review of Gould's *Rethinking Democracy*', *Journal of Applied Philosophy*, vol. 6, no. 2.

Norman, R. (1995), *Studies in Equality*, Avebury Series in Philosophy.

Norman, R. (1998), *The Moral Philosophers: An Introduction to Ethics*, Oxford University Press.

O'Neill, O. (2000), *Bounds of Justice*, Cambridge University Press.

Oppenheim, F. (1961), *Dimensions of Freedom: An Analysis*, St. Martin's Press.

Oppenheim, F. (1984), ' 'Constraints on Freedom' as a Descriptive Concept', *Ethics*, vol. 95.

Oppenheim, F. (1995), 'Social Freedom and its Parameters', *Journal of Theoretical Politics*, vol. 7.

Plamenatz, J. (1980), *Man and Society*, vol. 2, Longman.

Polanyi, K. (1957), *The Great Transformation*, Beacon Press.

Rawls, J. (2000), *Lectures on the History of Moral Philosophy*, Harvard University Press.

Raz, J. (1988), *The Morality of Freedom*, Clarendon Press.

Reiman, J. (1987), 'Exploitation, Force and the Moral Assessment of Capitalism', *Philosophy and Public Affairs*, vol. 16

Rose, N. (2000), *Powers of Freedom: Reframing Political Thought*, Cambridge University Press.

Rousseau, J. J. (1988), 'On Social Contract', *Rousseau's Political Writings* (ed. Ritter, A.), Norton & Company.

Bibliography

Sandel, M. (1987), 'Justice and the Good', *Liberalism and Its Critics* (ed. Sandel, M.), Basil Blackwell.

Sandel, M. (1987a), 'Introduction', *Liberalism and Its Critics* (ed. Sandel, M.), Basil Blackwell.

Sandel, M. (1998), *Democracy's Discontent: America in Search of a Public Philosophy*, The Belknap Press of Harvard University Press.

Sartre, J.P. (1957), *Being and Nothingness*, Methuen.

Sayers, S. (1989), 'Work, Leisure and Human Needs', *The Philosophy of Leisure* (ed. Winnifrith, T. and Barret, C.), MacMillan Press.

Sayers, S. (1992), 'The Human Impact of the Market', *The Values of the Enterprise Culture* (ed. Heelas, P. and Morris, P.), Routledge.

Sayers, S. (1995), 'The Value of Community', *Radical Philosophy*, no. 69.

Sayers, S. (1998), *Marxism and Human Nature*, Routledge.

Sayers, S. (1999), *Plato's Republic: An Introduction*, Edinburgh University Press.

Sayers, S. (1999a), 'Identity and Community', *Journal of Social Philosophy*, vol. 30.

Schweickart, D. (1993), *Against Capitalism*, Cambridge University Press.

Schweinitz, K. (1979), 'The Question of Freedom in Economics and Economic Organization', *Ethics*, vol. 89.

Simhony, A. (1991), 'On Forcing Individuals to be Free: T. H. Green's Theory of Positive Freedom', *Political Studies*, vol. 39.

Simhony, A. (1993), 'Beyond Negative and Positive Freedom: T. H. Green's View of Freedom', *Political Theory*, vol. 21.

Singer, P. (1983), *Hegel*, Oxford University Press.

Slater, D. (1997), *Consumer Culture and Modernity*, Polity Press.

Smith, A. (1981), *The Wealth of Nations*, Liberty Classics.

Solomon, R. (1988), *Continental Philosophy Since 1750: The Rise and Fall of the Self*, Oxford University Press.

Steiner, H. (1991), 'Individual Liberty', *Liberty* (ed. Miller, D.), Oxford University Press.

Steiner, H. (1994), *An Essay on Rights*, Blackwell.

Stern, P. (1986), 'Translator's Introduction', Tugendhat, E., *Self-Consciousness and Self-Determination*, MIT Press.

Taylor, C. (1977), 'What is Human Agency?' *The Self: Philosophical and Psychological Issues* (ed. Mischel, T.), Basil Blackwell.

Taylor, C. (1984), 'Hegel: History and Politics', *Liberalism and Its Critics* (ed. Sandel, M.), Blackwell.

Taylor, C. (1985), 'Kant's Theory of Freedom', *Philosophy and the Human Sciences: Philosophical Papers*, vol. 2, Cambridge University Press.

Taylor, C. (1985a), 'Atomism', *Philosophy and the Human Sciences*, vol. 2, Cambridge University Press.

Taylor, C. (1986), 'Self-Interpreting Animals', *Human Agency and Language: Philosophical Papers*, vol. 1, Cambridge University Press.

Taylor, C. (1986a), 'The Concept of a Person', *Human Agency and Language: Philosophical Papers*, vol. 1, Cambridge University Press.

Taylor, C. (1986b), 'Hegel's Philosophy of Mind', *Philosophical Papers: Human Agency and Language*, vol. 1, Cambridge University Press.

Taylor, C. (1991), 'What's Wrong With Negative Liberty?', *Liberty* (ed. Miller, D.), Oxford University Press.

Taylor, C. (1996), *Hegel and Modern Society*, Cambridge University Press.

Watson, G. (1975), 'Free Agency', *The Journal of Philosophy*, vol. 72.

Wood, A. (1990), *Hegel's Ethical Thought*, Cambridge University Press.

Wood, E. M. (1999), 'An Interview with E. M. Wood', *Monthly Review*, vol. 51, no. 1.

Wood, E. M. (1999a), 'The Politics of Capitalism', *Monthly Review*, vol. 51, no. 4

Wood, E. M. (2000), *Democracy Against Capitalism: Renewing Historical Materialism*, Cambridge University Press.

Index

For Product Safety Concerns and Information please contact our EU
representative GPSR@taylorandfrancis.com
Taylor & Francis Verlag GmbH, Kaufingerstraße 24, 80331 München, Germany

www.ingramcontent.com/pod-product-compliance
Lightning Source LLC
Chambersburg PA
CBHW070428270326
41926CB00014B/2990

* 9 7 8 1 1 3 8 7 0 3 6 4 3 *